VOLUME EDITOR

DAN O'BRIEN is a Research Fellow at Oxford Brookes University, an Honorary Research Fellow at Birmingham University, and an Associate Lecturer with the Open University. He is the author of *An Introduction to the Theory of Knowledge* (2006) and *Hume's "Enquiry Concerning Human Understanding": A Reader's Guide* (with Alan Bailey, 2006). In addition, he has recently edited a special volume of *Philosophica* on the epistemology of testimony.

SERIES EDITOR

FRITZ ALLHOFF is an Assistant Professor in the Philosophy Department at Western Michigan University, as well as a Senior Research Fellow at the Australian National University's Centre for Applied Philosophy and Public Ethics. In addition to editing the *Philosophy for Everyone* series, Allhoff is the volume editor or co-editor for several titles, including *Wine & Philosophy* (Wiley-Blackwell, 2007), *Whiskey & Philosophy* (with Marcus P. Adams, Wiley, 2009), and *Food & Philosophy* (with Dave Monroe, Wiley-Blackwell, 2007).

PHILOSOPHY FOR EVERYONE

Series editor: Fritz Allhoff

Not so much a subject matter, philosophy is a way of thinking. Thinking not just about the Big Questions, but about little ones too. This series invites everyone to ponder things they care about, big or small, significant, serious ... or just curious.

Running & Philosophy:
A Marathon for the Mind
Edited by Michael W. Austin

Wine & Philosophy:
A Symposium on Thinking and Drinking
Edited by Fritz Allhoff

Food & Philosophy:
Eat, Think and Be Merry
Edited by Fritz Allhoff and Dave Monroe

Beer & Philosophy:
The Unexamined Beer Isn't Worth Drinking
Edited by Steven D. Hales

Whiskey & Philosophy:
A Small Batch of Spirited Ideas
Edited by Fritz Allhoff and Marcus P. Adams

College Sex – Philosophy for Everyone: Philosophers With Benefits
Edited by Michael Bruce
and Robert M. Stewart

Cycling – Philosophy for Everyone:
A Philosophical Tour de Force
Edited by Jesús Ilundáin-Agurruza
and Michael W. Austin

Climbing – Philosophy for Everyone:
Because It's There
Edited by Stephen E. Schmid

Hunting – Philosophy for Everyone:
In Search of the Wild Life
Edited by Nathan Kowalsky

Christmas – Philosophy for Everyone:
Better Than a Lump of Coal
Edited by Scott C. Lowe

Cannabis – Philosophy for Everyone:
What Were We Just Talking About?
Edited by Dale Jacquette

Porn – Philosophy for Everyone:
How to Think With Kink
Edited by Dave Monroe

Serial Killers – Philosophy for Everyone: Being and Killing
Edited by S. Waller

Dating – Philosophy for Everyone:
Flirting With Big Ideas
Edited by Kristie Miller and Marlene Clark

Gardening – Philosophy for Everyone:
Cultivating Wisdom
Edited by Dan O'Brien

Motherhood – Philosophy for Everyone: The Birth of Wisdom
Edited by Sheila Lintott

Fatherhood – Philosophy for Everyone: The Dao of Daddy
Edited by Lon S. Nease
and Michael W. Austin

Forthcoming books in the series:

Fashion – Philosophy for Everyone
Edited by Jessica Wolfendale
and Jeanette Kennett

Coffee – Philosophy for Everyone
Edited by Scott Parker
and Michael W. Austin

Blues – Philosophy for Everyone
Edited by Abrol Fairweather
and Jesse Steinberg

Edited by Dan O'Brien

GARDENING
PHILOSOPHY FOR EVERYONE

Cultivating Wisdom

Foreword by David E. Cooper

WILEY-BLACKWELL
A John Wiley & Sons, Ltd., Publication

This edition first published 2010

© 2010 Blackwell Publishing Ltd except for editorial material and organization
© 2010 Dan O'Brien

Blackwell Publishing was acquired by John Wiley & Sons in February 2007.
Blackwell's publishing program has been merged with Wiley's global Scientific,
Technical, and Medical business to form Wiley-Blackwell.

Registered Office
John Wiley & Sons Ltd, The Atrium, Southern Gate, Chichester, West Sussex, PO19
8SQ, United Kingdom

Editorial Offices
350 Main Street, Malden, MA 02148-5020, USA
9600 Garsington Road, Oxford, OX4 2DQ, UK
The Atrium, Southern Gate, Chichester, West Sussex, PO19 8SQ, UK

For details of our global editorial offices, for customer services, and for information about how to apply for permission to reuse the copyright material in this book
please see our website at www.wiley.com/wiley-blackwell.

The right of Dan O'Brien to be identified as the author of the editorial material
in this work has been asserted in accordance with the UK Copyright, Designs and
Patents Act 1988.

Library of Congress Cataloging-in-Publication Data

Gardening – philosophy for everyone: cultivating wisdom / edited by Dan O'Brien.
    p.   cm. – (Philosophy for everyone)
    Includes bibliographical references.
    ISBN   978-1-4443-3021-2   (pbk.:   alk.   paper)   1. Gardening–Philosophy.
2. Gardens–Philosophy.   I. O'Brien, Dan, 1968–   II. Title: Gardening – philosophy
for everyone.
    SB454.3.P45G36 2010
    635.01–dc22
                                                                    2010004722

A catalogue record for this book is available from the British Library.

Set in Plantin 10/12.5pt by SPi Publisher Services, Pondicherry, India
Printed in Singapore

1   2010

CONTENTS

Foreword   viii
David E. Cooper

Acknowledgments   xi
Dan O'Brien

Planting the Seed: *An Introduction to*
Gardening – Philosophy for Everyone   1
Dan O'Brien

PART I   THE GOOD LIFE   11

1   The Virtues of Gardening   13
   Isis Brook

2   Cultivating the Soul: *The Ethics of Gardening*
    in Ancient Greece and Rome   26
   Meghan T. Ray

3   Escaping Eden: *Plant Ethics in a Gardener's World*   38
   Matthew Hall

4   Food Glorious Food   48
   Helene Gammack

PART II FLOWER POWER 63

5 Plants, Prayers, and Power: *The Story of the
First Mediterranean Gardens* 65
Jo Day

6 Brussels Sprouts and Empire: *Putting Down Roots* 79
Michael Moss

7 Transplanting Liberty: *Lafayette's American Garden* 93
Laura Aurrichio

8 Cockney Plots: *Allotments and Grassroots
Political Activism* 106
Elizabeth A. Scott

PART III THE FLOWER SHOW 119

9 *Hortus Incantans: Gardening as an Art of Enchantment* 121
Eric MacDonald

10 Gardens, Music, and Time 135
Ismay Barwell and John Powell

11 The Pragmatic Picturesque: *The Philosophy
of Central Park* 148
Gary Shapiro

PART IV THE COSMIC GARDEN 161

12 Illusions of Grandeur: *A Harmonious Garden
for the Sun King* 163
Robert Neuman

13 Time and Temporality in the Garden 178
Mara Miller

14 Cultivating Our Garden: *David Hume
and Gardening as Therapy* 192
Dan O'Brien

PART V PHILOSOPHERS' GARDENS 205

15 The Garden of the Aztec Philosopher-King 207
Susan Toby Evans

16 Epicurus, the Garden, and the Golden Age   220
    Gordon Campbell

17 Gardener of Souls: *Philosophical Education*
    in Plato's Phaedrus   232
    Anne Cotton

Notes on Contributors   245

FOREWORD

"From my point of view, as a gardener, I consider the garden fundamentally as a spiritual and cognitive experience."[1] So writes the distinguished Spanish garden designer – and philosophy graduate of Madrid University – Fernando Caruncho. Appreciation of the garden, he explains, requires a maturity of emotion and understanding alike. The implied contrast is with the experience of the garden simply as a hobby, as a smallholding, or as a source of pleasing sights, sounds, and smells. The contributors to *Gardening – Philosophy for Everyone* write from a viewpoint similar to Caruncho's and, like him, they are as much concerned with garden*ing*, an activity, as with the products of this activity, gardens. Of the many aspects of the "spiritual and cognitive experience" of gardening and gardens discussed in their contributions, three are especially salient: the moral, symbolic, and temporal.

The idea of the garden as a theatre for the cultivation of moral sensibility goes back at least to Pliny the Younger, whose own gardens afforded him the promise of "a good life and a serious one," of "cultivating himself" through cultivating them.[2] As several essays in this book demonstrate, it is an idea that, albeit with many permutations, has persisted. It is attested to, for example, in General Lafayette's estate near Paris, with its celebration of liberty and republican virtues, and in the humbler kitchen gardens or allotments that express an ideal of self-sufficiency. This ethical tradition, for several contributors, is one that, moreover, deserves to persist, for the garden – as a place that invites the exercise of care and humility, a regard for the good of plants and creatures, and an appreciation of nature's workings – is indeed a source of moral education.

There are gardens – like Lafayette's, Stowe, or those in the Sacro Monte tradition – which deliberately aim at moral effects through what they symbolize. But the symbolic roles of gardens extend well beyond that of moral edification, and those historians have a point who encourage us to examine the gardens of past cultures in order to identify how they envisaged their world, themselves, and the connections between nature and culture. Among the many diverse messages or meanings of gardening and gardens – whether self-consciously intended or not – to which contributors draw our attention are the political ones of power and prestige and the sense of home that people living very far from home seek to protect through their gardens. At their most ambitious, gardens or parks like Shanglin in ancient China, Versailles in Enlightenment Europe, or Charles Jencks's in southwest Scotland even attempt to symbolize the order of the cosmos.

This, and other symbolic ambitions, would not be intelligible to the French painter Henri Cueco's gardener who, in reply to the rhetorical question "You must look at other things apart from your lettuces!?" replied, "Maybe, but I don't really notice them."[3] But even he must have taken full notice of the changes and rhythms of season, weather, animal behavior, and much more with which the fate of his lettuces, like everything else in the garden, are intimately bound up. It is, however, to the aesthetics of garden experience that several contributors to *Gardening – Philosophy for Everyone* relate the temporal, even ephemeral aspect of gardens, their ingredients and contexts. For it is in this relationship, one surmises, that the distinctiveness of garden aesthetics lies – in the manner, say, that a garden "presents," or makes mindful of, time, or perhaps in an "enchantment" that unexpected changes in the process of experiencing a garden may trigger. If this is right, then the familiar image of the garden as "mediating" between human creativity and the natural order needs to make proper room for nature's fourth dimension, and not just its spatial aspects. An interesting garden may "borrow" the weather's impending change as much as the distant mountain scenery.

The range of themes addressed in this book, and the variety in the ways they are addressed (philosophical, historical, anthropological, and so on), demonstrate that the topic of gardening is as fecund as many gardens themselves are. Readers will especially benefit from a concreteness of discussion that they might not have expected from a book with "philosophy" in the title. Some of the essays are focused on specific gardens or particular figures in garden history, and the discussion in nearly all of them either draws on or is applied to actual gardens, from Versailles to Dumbarton Oaks, from Cyrus the Great's to Vita Sackville-West's. The book as a whole confirms that, during the last couple of decades, serious (which isn't to say solemn) writing on gardens has come of age, and furthers the aim – as the editors of an earlier volume of garden writing put it – of "bringing gardens and horticulture into the realm of intelligent public discourse … over our relationship with our environment."[4] Better, perhaps, the book illustrates and contributes to a *renaissance* of serious garden writing. The failure, for the most part, of twentieth-century philosophers, cultural historians, and social scientists seriously to attend to the garden was a caesura, a lapse. In earlier centuries, in the traditions of both East and West, the garden occupied an honorable and important place in "the realm of intelligent public discourse" – a discourse engaged in, of course, by philosophers, who had yet to fall victim to the professionalization and specialization that philosophy was to undergo during the last century. One will, admittedly, still hear occasional voices greeting a book on philosophy and gardens with cries of "Get real! What next? Philosophy and safety-pins?" But these are voices of ignorance – ignorance of a long tradition of philosophical dialogue on gardens – and voices in a very narrow register, unable to encompass a broader, richer, more civilized range of philosophical discourse. I would be very surprised if readers of this enterprising and imaginatively devised book were able, at the end of it, to listen to such voices with any sympathy.

NOTES

1 Fernando Caruncho, "The Spirit of the Geometrician," in T. Richardson and N. Kingsbury (eds.) *Vista: The Culture and Politics of Gardens* (London: Frances Lincoln, 2005), p. 111.
2 *The Letters of Pliny the Younger*, ed. B. Radice (London: Penguin, 1963), pp. 43, 112.
3 Henri Cueco, *Conversations With My Gardener*, trans. G. Miller (London: Granta, 2005), p. 3.
4 T. Richardson and N. Kingsbury (eds.) *Vista: The Culture and Politics of Gardens* (London: Frances Lincoln, 2005), p. 2.

ACKNOWLEDGMENTS

First and foremost I must thank all the contributors for their enthusiasm for this project, for their helpful suggestions, and for their patience with my editorial interventions. We haven't met but from their essays I have a picture of them in my mind, tending their vegetables, walking in Central Park, watching the fireflies, and digging up the remains of ancient civilizations. It should be noted that they come from a wide range of professions: contributors work in philosophy, art history, classics, archeology, anthropology, design, archival studies, and history; and in various botanical gardens and the National Trust. This has been an ambitious interdisciplinary project and I must thank all who had faith in it, particularly the series editor, Fritz Allhoff, whose enthusiasm for this book and for the series as a whole is infectious. Thanks also to Jeff Dean and Tiffany Mok from Wiley-Blackwell.

It's true, gardening is the new rock 'n' roll, and I must thank those who have initiated me into the heady world of shed construction, composting, seed catalogues, pruning, mulching, and potting on. Here I think back to gardens past. To my grandmother, her giant Yukka and gooseberry patch; to Mont's regimental roses at Burnside, and to mum's heathers and the various cuttings she gave me that started my gardening off in earnest in the backyard of Armadillo – I hope the fritillaries and day lilies are still thriving there. Since then, raised beds have replaced scavenged chimney pots and greenhouses have taken the place of windowsills. For helping me and Lucy keep (almost) on top of our patch I must thank Paul and Betty for the passing of advice and tools over the garden fence, and especially Tom and Barbara for their unstinting dedication to watering our greenhouse when we are away, garden center trips, and the supply of homemade cakes. (Actually, another Tom and Barbara have probably also been influential, those of 1970s sitcom fame: I think I wanted to be like them when I grew up, and I'm getting there!) Thanks also to Henry and Jones for keeping the rat population at bay, and to Dyl for putting up with the intrusion on his football pitch.

The editor and publisher gratefully acknowledge the permission granted to reproduce the copyright material in this book:

"This is the garden: colours come and go," Copyright 1925, 1953 © 1991 by the Trustees for the E. E. Cummings Trust. Copyright © 1976 by George James Firmage, from Complete Poems: 1904–1962 by E. E. Cummings, edited by George J. Firmage. Used by permission of Liveright Publishing Corporation.

Dan O'Brien

ACKNOWLEDGMENTS

PLANTING THE SEED

An Introduction to *Gardening – Philosophy for Everyone*

This is the garden: colours come and go
Frail azure fluttering from night's outer wing
Strong silent greens serenely lingering,
Absolute lights like baths of golden snow.
This is the garden: pursed lips do blow
Upon cool flutes within wide glooms, and sing
(of harps celestial to the quivering string)
invisible faces hauntingly and slow.
This is the garden. Time shall surely reap
And on Death's blade lie many a flower curled,
In other lands where songs be sung;
Yet stand They were enraptured, as among
The slow deep trees perpetual of sleep
Some silver-fingered fountain steals the world.
("This is the garden," E. E. Cummings)

Gardening is not just a pleasant thing to do on a Saturday afternoon, or a way to reduce one's supermarket bill – gardening is a human activity that engages with core philosophical questions concerning, among other things, human wellbeing, wisdom, the nature of time, political power and ideals, home, aesthetic experience, metaphysics, and religion. That is what the contributors to this volume aim to show, and we hope that the gardener will find rumination on these questions rewarding and illuminating, either at the end of a hard day's digging or as something to think about while deadheading the sweet peas.

The book is also an invitation for philosophers to look down from their ivory tower to the gardens around its base. There they will find this characteristically human practice of cultivating plants for their beauty, arranging them in varying degrees of formality, and accompanying the show with similarly ordered or not so ordered herbs, fruit, and vegetables. Perhaps the first thing to notice about this activity is that a terrific amount of hard work seemed to go into growing, say, those basil plants. There was the disinfecting of the greenhouse, the transportation of compost, and the purchase, planting, and watering of seed. The potting on followed … all looked good, but then the seedlings started to wilt. Thinning them out and pinching the stems back did not lead, as the book said it would, to luscious, bushy Mediterranean plants. Nevertheless the gardener – well, this was me earlier this summer – seemed pleased with the handful of leaves he clutched on the way back to the kitchen. The spaghetti in pesto was delicious. But, the philosopher wonders, why on earth all the effort? A jar of pesto would have cost very little and taken ten minutes to buy. Why do people go through all this effort? In short, why do they garden? The reader will find various answers to this question in these pages.

A first, hedonistic, thought is that gardening makes us happy, and that is why we do it; for the same reason that we lie in the sun or eat ice cream. At odds with such a view, however, are the all-too-common frustrations and physical trials of gardening. Double digging the vegetable plot is not fun, nor is keeping the viciously spined blackberry bush under control, nor are one's battles with bindweed. There are of course great pleasures – the clematis in bloom, the taste of a fresh ripe tomato, and the fragrance of the rosemary bush as you brush past it – but given their generally fleeting nature it is not entirely obvious whether one is happier through gardening than through alternative weekend activities such as watching movies or going to the gym. Here, though, we are thinking of happiness purely in terms of pleasurable feelings, in terms of the sensual pleasure of ice cream as opposed to the pain of digging, and we are attempting to explain our urge to garden in terms of such feelings. There is, though, an older notion of living *a good life* – as opposed to a pleasurable one – and philosophical issues relating to this notion have been discussed since Ancient Greek and Roman times. Living a good life amounts to living a virtuous life and doing so brings with it, not hedonistic pleasures, but a kind of tranquility – the kind of state of mind that philosophers from Epicurus to Hume have seen as the goal of life. What we see as virtuous may to some extent have changed over the centuries – the actions of a chivalrous

DAN O'BRIEN

knight may not be as commendable as they once were – but many of our ideas concerning virtue have remained constant: it is good, for example, to persevere in a task rather than give up at the first obstacle, and it is good to be patient. The good life, then, is one that promotes such traits in an individual, and it is very plausible that gardening does just that. In learning to garden one must, for example, learn to cope with defeat by cabbage fly and slug. One must acquire a certain level of stoicism, a trait that is plausibly a virtue. Gardening, then, can be seen as contributing to a good life, one interspersed with moments of tranquility that have their source in virtuous activity.

Gardening, however, is more than just a means to acquire virtue and the associated tranquility that comes from its exercise; a dogged, ever-patient digger, hoer, and pruner would not be gardening well unless there was a further aspect to her activity. Gardening would seem to require an artistic element; some sense of the aesthetic appreciation of one's work is required, whatever the garden – from the arranging of a few pots in a back yard to the creation of a great estate. It's not clear that a piece of land would be a garden if no thought went into how it looked (even though it might function as one's vegetable plot, yard, or place to play football). Works of art naturally fall into certain categories and, following the philosopher Immanuel Kant, there is a temptation to see gardening as a visual art and gardeners as artists working with a pallet of terracotta pots, plants, and trees. This is certainly something that a gardener some-times sees herself as doing. The pot there is wrong; it takes one's eye away from the bed of hostas; it should be moved instead next to the low wall, and the garish hanging basket display needs to be toned down. Looking through seed catalogues and browsing at the garden center one can be seen as shopping for artistic materials. We have, then, a picture of the gardener, living the good life, a life that is further enriched by the artistic nature of their activity.

Further, even though the activity of the suburban basil grower may, to some – those silly people who buy ready made pesto! – appear to be a rather idiosyncratic route to a tasty supper, gardens fill the Earth and have done so since the first civilizations. And, looking at gardening through time and across cultures, there are patterns there to be seen, and sociological, political, and philosophical conclusions to be drawn from what we find. On a local scale we can see this at home, at the allotment show and in neighborly competition. Plants or cuttings are taken with us when we move house, providing a link with homes past or family past. I can look out at the creeping geraniums, originally taken as cuttings from where I grew up, and at the myrtle bush that was bought from a street market as a seedling to place proudly in my first proper (backyard) garden. Flower and vegetable competitions across the country can be more than temporary diversions. They are taken very seriously and the size of a gardener's leeks confers a certain elevated status on the grower. If one has not been to an allotment show, one should! The prize-winning produce has an unearthly, almost magical, air about it. These growers are not like us; we are not worthy! And, as we shall see later in the volume, these psychological and sociological aspects of gardening are also played out on a global, political scale.

Various garden writers have also noted how great gardens reflect the philosophical predilections of an era. Digging up clods of earth, raking up leaves, and ripping out bindweed are not, one might think, activities that promote meditation on the big metaphysical questions. Much of gardening does not involve looking to the stars; one looks down into the mud. In various traditions, though, gardens are seen as reflecting the cosmic perspective, with some garden designers explicitly setting out with this aim of reflecting the divine order in their earthly creations. Islamic royal gardens and the gardens of Christian monasteries symbolize Eden, with the four rivers of this biblical garden represented by four garden paths or watercourses. The gardens of the French Renaissance, in their formal structure, reflected Descartes' geometric conception of space. And, more recently, the Garden of Cosmic Speculation in Scotland reflects scientific cosmology: plantings and architectural features representing the findings of quantum mechanics, superstring theory, and complexity theory. There is therefore a long history of gardens being used for symbolic effect, and, in these cases, to help us see our place in the grand, metaphysical, scheme of things.

Various philosophers throughout history have noted these aspects of gardening – and more – but one gets the sense that the garden, as a locus of the philosophical issues sketched, is just starting to be taken seriously once again as a subject of intellectual inquiry. It's an exciting time to be a gardening philosopher or a philosophizing gardener. Often, it takes a groundbreaking or daringly against-the-current, synoptic book or essay to make us see the distinctive and important nature of a new field of inquiry, and this I think is certainly the case with respect to gardening and philosophy. Professor David Cooper's *A Philosophy of Gardens* is such a book. It is one of a handful of books on the subject and one that I'm sure was met with intellectual excitement and gratitude by many of the contributors to this volume. This collection of essays was inspired by

DAN O'BRIEN

Professor's Cooper's contribution to this area of philosophy and I was therefore delighted when David agreed to write the foreword to this volume.

Let me now, then, say a little more about the content of the book – prepare the ground, as it were. It is divided into five themed parts, the first focusing on broadly ethical considerations concerning "The Good Life." Isis Brook argues that gardening improves both the land and the gardener. Gardening is an activity that enriches the moral character of those engaged in it, promoting patience, humility, and open-heartedness. Here, Isis sees morality as essentially concerned with virtuous character traits rather than with classifying actions as right or wrong. This is the kind of moral theory pursued by various ancient philosophers, one particularly associated with Aristotle, and one that, in the form of virtue ethics, is having a contemporary revival.

Meghan Ray looks to classical authors to illuminate the connection between gardening, wisdom, and the moral life. Cato the Elder, Varro, Virgil, and Pliny the Elder all argued that horticulture and the cultivation of the soil are central to the life and wellbeing of the individual and of the state. This is true at a practical level – the development of horticultural and agricultural skills was necessary for the survival of the growing population of the ancient world – but also at other, more philosophically interesting levels. Working the land is honorable, pious, and righteous, and thus it is fundamental to the civil, moral, and religious dimensions of society.

Matthew Hall – in danger, as he himself says, of appearing a "crazy" plant-hugger – asks us to consider the ethical dimension of our behavior towards plants. Plants are not usually considered in moral or ethical terms and Matthew finds the root of such an attitude in the Christian conception of the Garden of Eden. God provides plants solely for our benefit, to use how we see fit. Alternative cultural conceptions of the garden, from Greek mythology and from contemporary indigenous cultures, are considered in which plants are shown more ethical respect. Plants are taken to be kin, and the care and attention paid to them by gardeners should be seen as a reflection of this relationship.

Lastly, in this opening section, Helene Gammack looks at the good life in a broader sense and at the history of self-sufficiency in the garden. Her focus is on the seventeenth century, when garden design was driven, for the first time in such a developed way, by both aesthetic and practical considerations. Today's ornamental fishponds and dovecotes were, in the seventeenth century, no mere ornaments; they were features of the kitchen garden prized for their high productivity. After a dinner of trout and pigeon one could stroll by the babbling stream and pond, and under the dovecote, from where one's dinner ingredients had recently been taken. Such a fusion of practical and aesthetic concerns is seen to have had a revival in modern times – the small kitchen garden a not uncommon feature of suburban gardens – but, Helene surmises, the good life is unlikely to be lived again to the level it was in those great seventeenth-century estates.

Part two of the book turns to politics – to "Flower Power." Jo Day discusses the varying ideologies behind the gardens of the different societies of the ancient Eastern Mediterranean, from Mesopotamia to the gardens of ancient Greece, and from the Roman Empire to the Hanging Gardens of Babylon. We are transported back in time to their royal palaces, their scented orchards and to what we would call today their water features. She identifies three main themes that the gardens of these various cultures share. The garden functions as a display of power: a king's conquests symbolized by the plants and trees he brings back from his foreign expeditions. Such non-indigenous booty not only serves as a display of a ruler's power and military prowess, but also adds an air of mystique to his rule, the king living in a rarified world of fragrant trees and unfamiliar, exotic fruit. Lastly, the gardens of this region have complex religious roles: certain plants are linked to particular deities and gardens themselves were often places of rites and worship.

Michael Moss charts a curious episode in the history of the Brussels sprout. During the days of the British Empire, Brussels sprouts and other emblems of Britishness were grown in such inhospitable climes as the Indian plains in order to recreate a sense of home for families who might be away for years at a time. One pictures the Major and his wife sat on the veranda with their gin and tonics, fanned by a servant; their gardeners hard at work struggling to find enough water to grow the essential sprouts and cabbages, and their cooks learning how to boil these unusual vegetables in the English style. Michael's investigation into the kitchen gardens of the British abroad is thus an investigation into the mindset of Empire.

Next, Laura Auricchio takes us to La Grange, the estate of General Lafayette, the French hero of the American Revolution. He devoted vast amounts of time and money to renovating the gardens, farm, and buildings of his "American" estate located 30 miles southeast of Paris. During visits to America to see his former commanding officer, George Washington, Lafayette shipped seeds and plants back to France. But his

DAN O'BRIEN

exports were more than just horticultural. Lafayette aimed, in his estate, to give visual and material form to progressive political and philosophical ideals, that is, to the liberal values of self-sufficiency and beneficent stewardship of the land.

Lastly, Elizabeth Scott takes us over the English Channel and forward 150 years to the wartime allotment gardens of the East End of London. She argues that these gardens and the community work that went into maintaining them were an integral part of working-class culture. In a time of war and food shortages there were practical and moral responsibilities associated with them, with respect to the local community and to the country as a whole; but there were also lasting political benefits to "allotmenteering." Allotment associations fostered a sense of community and autonomy, and they encouraged allotment holders to become politically engaged and empowered.

Part three turns to questions of aesthetics – to "The Flower Show." Eric MacDonald considers the garden as a setting that calls forth moments of enchantment, and thus gardening as involving strategies that cultivate a sense of wonder. After considering the importance of "garden-magic" to the Italian Renaissance garden, his essay focuses on Dumbarton Oaks in Washington, DC. This garden, and gardens in general, should not be seen purely as artistic achievements or as embodiments of the good life; they are also essentially places where we can become enchanted by the fusion of man and nature. Valuable garden moments include the magic of discovering the unplanned nasturtiums flowing over the discarded zinc watering can as one rediscovers the old path to the compost bin, the seeds unknowingly scattered on a previous composting trip.

Ismay Barwell and John Powell suggest that gardens should not primarily be seen as places; gardens, they argue, are at least as much concerned with processes and time as they are with place. Gardens, then, should not be seen as artistic creations akin to painting, that is, as static arrangements of colors and forms. Gardens use the passage of real time as a fundamental artistic material. Gardens are four-dimensional symphonies, ones through which we can stroll, but also ones which develop over time: the visual show developing through the spring, reaching a crescendo during the summer and, in the autumn and winter, dying down to a simple line, a background rhythm – the cyclamen and kale keeping the piece alive – until the "orchestra" returns once again the following spring.

Gary Shapiro explains and explores the aesthetics and design principles of Central Park, New York. He places the park within the history of landscape gardening, concentrating on the distinction between the classical French garden, with its emphasis on order and symmetry, and the picturesque English garden. Central Park inverts the English model: the park is not designed to give the impression of flowing seamlessly into the surrounding countryside, as was the case in classic English estates and gardens; rather, the surrounding metropolis is artfully allowed to flow into the park along paths and roadways, enabling the park to become a place for citizens to experience time and space more fully, and to commune with their fellows.

The fourth part of the book concerns metaphysics – "The Cosmic Garden" – and it begins with Robert Neuman's essay on the close alliance between design and philosophical ideas in the French formal garden. Robert argues that the Bosquet de la Collonade in Louis XIV's garden at Versailles stands as a visible manifestion of universal harmony as a divine creation. The design of the garden incorporates features borrowed from ancient temples to Apollo, the creator of cosmic order, and this theme is reinforced by various other references to music, of which Apollo is also the god. The mathematical proportions of the garden are also no accident. The Greek philosopher Pythagoras found that harmonious notes could be played if the lengths of strings in musical instruments were in certain ratios to each other. These ratios could also be used architecturally, as they were at Versailles, creating buildings and gardens that were harmonious to the eye. Importantly, Versailles should not be seen as merely a display of the king's knowledge of classical themes, or as a meditation on such themes; the allusion is that the king – Louis XIV, the Sun King – is himself the Apollo of his day, the god-like bringer of harmony to Europe.

Metaphysicians are not only concerned with such grand visions of divine creation and control, but also with the fundamental nature of reality, with, for example, the nature of space and time. Mara Miller observes that nothing is more obvious in a garden than change over time. Gardens thus make evident the passage of time and reveal the multi-layered structure of time itself. There is scientific, objective time upon which other schemes of time are layered: the relentlessly flowing time of years, months, days, hours, minutes and seconds. Gardeners, though, do not work to a strict clock – to the metronome of scientific time or to the first day of spring according to the calendar. Gardeners must have a sense of when the time is *right* – to move, for example, the cabbage seedlings from the greenhouse to the beds, to lift the potatoes, and to prune the wisteria. One's experience of gardens is also to some extent free from the steady

DAN O'BRIEN

pulse of scientific time. A garden can stretch subjective time. Immersed in the garden, a few seconds watching a dragonfly hovering over the pond can seem like the most significant part of the afternoon, more than the hours that one has spent doing the housework or sorting out one's papers.

Lastly, in this section, my own contribution starts from an interpretation of Voltaire's enigmatic closing words of *Candide* – "we must cultivate our garden" – and develops a therapeutic conception of gardening influenced by the philosophy of David Hume. Voltaire and Hume reject the metaphysical reasoning of theologians and philosophers and argue that we should focus instead on the concerns of everyday life; the "garden" here being seen as a metaphor for such "common life" reasoning. And gardening itself is an activity that can protect us from the psychological stress that Hume sees as endangering the mental stability of metaphysicians and theologians. It does so by promoting tranquility, a psychological state emphasized by ancient philosophers such as Epicurus and explored today in contemporary accounts of emotional wellbeing.

In the fifth part of the book we turn to the garden philosophies of three diverse philosophers and consider how they conceived of gardening in relation to aspects of our human nature and our social and political relations with others. Susan Toby Evans introduces us to the most ambitious monumental garden in Mexico, Texcotzingo, the creation of King Nezahualcoyotl, the great fifteenth-century Aztec poet and philosopher. The retreat he designed, though now in ruins, still impresses the visitor with the splendor of its setting and design, and stands as a monument to this great philosopher-king's unique concept of beauty and meaning. His "magic mountain" was bathed in the sacred substance of water; aqueducts and pools adding beauty to the garden, but also pulsing with the life force of his dynasty and his people.

Gordon Campbell focuses on Epicurus, whose presence is felt throughout the volume. Epicurus taught his philosophy in his "Garden School," the garden having an important ethical function as the source of the pleasures that heal both mind and body. These are not the indulgent pleasures and luxuries mistakenly associated with the Epicurean, but simple pleasures such as breaking bread with friends and sharing fresh water. Protected within the walls of the garden the philosopher can preserve the peace of mind essential for true happiness. Further, Epicurus' garden is a recreation of a lost golden age of simplicity and life lived in accordance with nature, that it may be possible to regain if we embrace and cultivate Epicurean wisdom. Call your friends, take some freshly baked bread out into the garden along with a jug of iced water, pick a plum or two from the tree, and the Epicurean revolution starts now!

We end with Anne Cotton's discussion of Plato's striking dialogue concerning philosophical education in *Phaedrus*. He compares the nurturing of a soul to the tending of plants in a garden. Education, like gardening, is what enables an organism to attain its natural and most perfect flowering. Plato's dialogues – his seeds – provide fertile ideas and in forcing us to think for ourselves, they ensure we, in our turn, become live seeds, who are growing towards the flowering of philosophical understanding.

Thus, in the spirit of Plato, this book will have succeeded if from time to time a gardener's thoughts turn to enchantment, the passage of time, Epicurus, morality, or political ideals, when weeding or mulching – as it will also have done if it entices the bookish philosopher to get his hands dirty.

Hope you dig it!

DAN O'BRIEN

PART I

THE GOOD LIFE

CHAPTER I

THE VIRTUES OF GARDENING

The central argument of this essay is that the activity of gardening improves both people and land. The claim about improving land is modest because I recognize the critique of our attitudes of domination towards nature – of seeing nature as just a resource to be shaped and used by humans – that has been developed in the field of environmental philosophy. However, I argue that in regard to the specific context of the garden we nevertheless can and, indeed, should endorse gardening activities like increasing the fertility of the soil by good husbandry, assisting the flourishing of plant life, and designing with an awareness of wider environmental contexts. I also argue that something that is for the good of the garden (as opposed to good only for human enjoyment) is required to support the stronger claim that gardening is an activity that improves the moral character of those who engage appropriately in it. To develop this argument I look at those gardening practices that, as an incidental side effect of their purpose, increase our patience, humility, respect for reality, caring for others, and open-heartedness. Although these virtues can be learnt through practice and engagement with nature in general, I argue that they are brought together in a unique way in the relationship between garden and gardener – and that they can proceed from small things such as the micro-practice of noticing a bud open.

What Counts as a Garden

The definition of a garden I will be using is an enclosed or demarcated out-side space with living plants. Definitions are hard to frame precisely and often examples better serve the purpose of getting clear what is meant. Typical examples I would include in the term "garden" are: a small urban front or back garden, larger suburban gardens surrounding a house on all sides, extensive cultivated grounds of a large house that can merge into park-land, a domestic vegetable plot or allotment, and even a patio or yard if it has plants.[1] The proviso that it is outside would seem to exclude bottle gardens and even conservatories, which seems a shame, though not balconies, guer-rilla gardens on vacant plots, or the transitory gardens created by homeless people.[2] My insistence on the inclusion of living plants could exclude some Japanese gardens and artworks such as Martha Schwartz's "Splice Garden." Excluding Japanese gardens of rocks and raked gravel seems controversial and certainly the qualities of care and attention that they can exhibit might suggest their inclusion on those grounds alone. Martha Schwartz would, I imagine, be pleased to have the "Splice Garden" excluded for the very reason that we might think the rock and gravel garden should be included. The "Splice Garden" (which contains Astroturf and plastic plants) is on the roof of the Whitehead Institute for Biomedical Research, which, as Schwartz discovered, had no water and no means of sustaining life. Thus the "garden" is a polemic about society's wanting everything and quickly, but without wanting to invest either money or care. As she says:

> This piece is all about the idea of the garden, and about what one expects from a garden – this mantra that it should be quick, cheap and green. We all want to see green but we don't want to spend any money on it – yet we really love nature, right? This garden was an angry response to that. It was: If you want green and you don't want to pay for it, here it is.[3]

Inherent in the idea of a garden is some kind of care or attention beyond the initial design. The actions by a person to nurture plants, to shape and develop, or just to encourage what grows, we call "gardening."

How Gardening Improves the Land

The claim that gardening improves the land has been criticized from a perspective that sees any interference with nature as detrimental to the

ISIS BROOK

land, and any engagement in such an activity as detrimental to the human character, as it reinforces the notion that nature is there for us to shape as we wish and bend to our will. Thus I need to establish that improvement of land is at least a reasonable supposition before moving on; the claim that we are improved by damaging or degrading something else would seem hard to defend.

When we garden we take a circumscribed area – usually already a garden, allotment, or a plot of thin soil over builder's rubble – and we combine our labor, imagination, ideas, and expression of feeling with what is there. We might introduce new plants or artifacts in an attempt to improve on what was there. The crucial question, though, is *improve* in what sense, or rather whose sense?

If I began by setting out what I think makes a good garden, this would be an unsubstantiated claim or a statement of preference. It would be better, philosophically speaking, to arrive at a notion of a good garden via the examination of what is good about gardening. However, I don't want Claim 1, *that gardening improves land,* to rest on Claim 2, *that gardening improves people.* That would reduce the role of the garden to something akin to an exercise bicycle: entirely there for us as a means to some thing that has nothing to do with the furtherance or wellbeing of the bicycle. It's fine to treat exercise bicycles that way – I don't have a problem with that – but not gardens. There needs to be some sense of improvement that is good for the garden itself, such that after the gardening intervention, it is in a better state than before, or perhaps in a similar state – rather than the impoverished one that would have resulted from our lack of intervention. Of course, I am using the phrase "good for the garden" as a kind of shorthand here for "objectively better regardless of our human preferences." How, though, in a post-environmental philosophy context – where the dominant discourse has been about protecting wild nature from human interference – can we legitimately maintain that activities such as weeding and pruning are for anything other than the exercise of human power and preference?

I am going to suggest three gardening activities that we can say improve the garden objectively. The first is the role of the gardener in the endless toil of improving the fertility of the soil. The garden as a quasi-ecosystem does this itself, but the gardener engages with those processes through mulching and weeding, but mainly through composting. Composting is the major player here because it improves the structure of the soil (allowing the plants to develop healthy supporting roots), it improves water retention (necessary for plant survival), it increases the number of micro-organisms that break down vegetative matter into plant nutrients, and it supplies the raw material of those chemicals and trace elements the plant needs. Thus by improved soil I mean soil that is more fertile or supportive of a rich and varied range of plant life. It is sometimes said of keen aquarium keepers that "they don't keep fish, they keep water." A focus on water quality brings in its train the ability to keep healthy fish specimens. Likewise the gardener is a soil keeper who attends to this background element as much as to the showy plants that attract the attention of the non-gardener. When ardent gardeners visit gardens open to the public they can sometimes be seen feeling the texture of, and smelling, the soil while their less obsessed brethren merely photograph attractive floral arrangements or, if already some way down that road, read the plant labels. As Karel Čapek puts it in his 1931 classic, *The Gardener's Year*:

> A rose in flower, is, so to speak, only for the dilettanti; the gardener's pleasure is deeper rooted, right in the womb of the soil. After his death the gardener does not become a butterfly, intoxicated by the perfumes of flowers, but a garden worm tasting all the dark, nitrogenous, and spicy delights of the soil.[4]

The second related activity that improves the garden is nurturing specific plants. Here the actions of gardening are activities that allow specific plants to flourish, things like staking tall perennials so they don't blow over, watering tender seedlings, appropriately addressing any disease conditions, and preventing overcrowding by thinning and weeding. In this way the action of gardening allows plants to flourish in a way that, left entirely alone, they might not. There are, of course, exceptions that arise when we put together the first and second point, such as the soil nutritive demands of a wild meadow style of garden requiring it to be left on the hungry side rather than provided with compost. But these are exceptions that speak to the next point about knowing one's land and what is possible and fitting there, and finding the best accommodation between what one is given and what is possible.

The third aspect of objective improvement of the garden that I want to lay out is how it relates to its context. The activity of gardening can, and indeed good gardening activity should, develop the land in such a way that is contextually appropriate. We could talk in terms of it harmonizing in some way with the house and the surrounding land. However, harmonizing should not be taken to mean in accord with dominant stylistic

ISIS BROOK

preferences or indeed with just anything that happens to be around. For example, a neighbor's garden that has perhaps taken on a "vehicle breaker's yard" motif should not direct our plans.

To maintain a garden in a way that is not just a personal preference but is informed by a more grounded form of contextualization I would need to employ something like Warwick Fox's theory of responsive cohesion, which includes a conception of nested contexts with priority rules that obtain between them.[5] Put briefly, Fox identifies three basic ways in which "things" – anything at all – can be organized or "hold together" (i.e., cohere): they can hold together in highly regimented ways (e.g., a dogmatic view, a dictatorship, or a formulaic novel); they can hold together by virtue of the mutual responsiveness of the elements that constitute them (e.g., a healthy organism, a democracy, or an exciting tennis match between equally talented players); or they can simply fail to hold together (e.g., a severed limb, the lawless, non-mutual aid version of anarchy, or an alleged art work that simply "fails to hang together"). Fox refers to these basic forms of organization as fixed cohesion, responsive cohesion, and discohesion. Though devised as the basis of an ethical theory, he provides examples across many fields – science, psychology, personal relationships, conversations, economics, organizational management, and architecture – in order to argue that our considered judgments about any field will always prefer those examples that most exemplify responsive cohesion as opposed to fixed cohesion or discohesion. For Fox, then, responsive cohesion represents the most fundamental value there is since we find it underpinning all other values. Whether in ethical systems and judgments or ice-skating partnerships we can see that it is not only common to the best examples of their kind, but it also picks out a feature that exists at their most basic level of organization. Thus, Fox refers to responsive cohesion as the *foundational value* and argues that we should seek to preserve and generate this value both in terms of the *internal* responsive cohesion that any item has and in terms of its *contextual* responsive cohesion. Just as this theory is already being applied in the architectural world,[6] it is easy to see how we might apply it in the gardening world. In terms of gardens we can easily see that the overly rigid management of a space would not allow for the maximum dynamic, mutually enhancing flourishing of living things, and that it would be a kind of fixed cohesion where the parts might work together but in a constrained way. A monoculture supported by artificial fertilizers, or figurative topiary, would be examples.[7] Or in terms of actions I need only call to mind the local park management where formal bedding schemes are still used in some areas to good effect, but the plants are sometimes pulled out when they are just approaching full bloom because it is "time," i.e., the specific day on the work plan, to change the display. A garden exhibiting discohesion would be one where nothing was supporting anything else and no healthy nutrient exchanges were taking place, or perhaps where alpines have been planted in deep shade and cyclamen in all day sun.

However, even a garden that itself exhibits a great deal of responsive cohesion needs to do so within its wider context, including the widest context of all – the biosphere. Taking these considerations into account would not mean that the biophysical realm or "raw nature" always trumps any development, but that in the action of gardening the biophysical realm needs primary consideration. For example, the extensive use of peat, from fast disappearing richly biodiverse bogs, to enable the growing of particular ericaceous plants in soil that would normally be inappropriate for them works against the widest contextual responsive cohesion. No matter how well those azaleas seem to increase the internal responsive cohesion of the garden, they should be avoided or, if already there, perhaps given to a friend with naturally more acid soil so both they and the peat bogs can flourish, thus increasing the overall amount of responsive cohesion in the world.

Thus there seem to be enough reasons to put forward as a reasonable supposition the (to a gardener, commonsense) view that gardening can improve the land.

How Gardening Improves Us

Gardens, it can be said, play a fundamental role for many people in living "the good life" and here "good" ties in with the development of the virtues rather than with the increase in real estate values.[8] With the three land improvements – increasing fertility of the soil, aiding the flourishing of plant life, and guiding the development of the land in a contextually informed way – the idea of improvement seems unproblematic. But what does it mean for a human being to be improved – surely not to exhibit bushier growth – and yet many of the terms already used about the land do commonly work as metaphors for what we tend to think of as improvements in human beings. "Cultivated" works in this way. But we also describe with admiration someone having a "fertile" mind. Emotional "growth" has become a watchword for the human potential movement. We even say of someone who "comes into their own" in a situation or through a new challenge that they have "blossomed." The vocabulary associated with flourishing plant life is used again and again, both literally and metaphorically, to describe flourishing human life. Physical health is carried across literally, but where the metaphor operates is in the transition from an expression of flourishing in the plant realm to an expression of flourishing in the mind and soul of the human being. (By mind and soul I do not mean to invoke some kind of mysterious entity unconnected with the body but, rather, aspects of our embodiment that are not a possibility in the plant realm.) The questions remain though – what does it mean for humans to be improved? And how does gardening as an activity bring about such improvements? I need to have an approximate answer to the first question in order to select the activities to discuss and also to be able to identify when such activities fall away from their "improving" form into various detrimental forms.

If we take a virtue ethics approach the terrain is clear. The improved human is one who, in the best way that their situation allows, lives a good life, and an important aspect of this is that they continue to improve and thereby continue to live an even better life. However, replacing "improved" with "good" does not help very much in setting down a marker for what this amounts to or how it would inform our actions or ways of being in the world. The standard criticism of virtue ethics is that this becomes a circular argument. That is, we develop the virtues to lead a good life and a good life is one that exemplifies the virtues. The solution to this criticism offered by David Cooper is to see the criticism as misplaced. It takes virtue ethics to be like other moral philosophies in stating a means to an end; obey this rule and the target situation will follow. But the virtues do not work in this end-gaining manner. The circularity is in fact a necessary part of the approach because it just is the case that, to quote Cooper, "there can be no question of first spelling out the nature of the good life and only then proceeding to identify the virtues, for no substantial account of the good life could be given that does not already invoke the virtues."[9] This would mean that by discussing the human virtues that come about through the activity of gardening we will at the same time be arriving at a picture of a good human being.

Some of these improvements can be brought about by other activities; my claim is just that gardening is a particularly rich source of improving activities and, as we will see, some of these qualities seem to be uniquely connected to engagement with other living things. I am not going to deal with the obvious and very real benefits of physical exercise, fresh air, and having a wider area of activity than the office or sitting room. My focus is more on the inner qualities that physical engagement with the garden brings in its wake.

Let us start with something that is perhaps an obvious quality that is nurtured in the process of gardening – patience. Many gardening activities involve long periods of time between the involvement and the outer fruits of the involvement. Whether we are talking about planting radishes or an avenue of trees, both involve a delay between the action and the result that the action is intended to bring about. There is a sense in which, in the garden, things happen in their own time and a desire to see immediate results will impair our ability to properly engage with the activity of gardening. Impatient actions never seem to bring about the same degree of pleasure in the action, nor such pleasurable results. When a novice asks at a nursery when a Mulberry *Morus nigra* sapling could be expected to reach its label's purported maximum of 20 feet and is told "in the fullness of time," they have to move into a different way of thinking. To combine two adages, one could say that "patience is its own reward" and this is never so clearly seen as in the garden. Whether we call these things gardening virtues or not, what is clear is that, like virtues, they are fecund in the sense that the exercise of them brings with it their internalization and the ability to express them more often, or more deeply, or under more difficult circumstances. The impatient person just has to wait and in the waiting learns how to wait and that waiting is okay – even enjoyable. When little seedlings at last germinate and the seed leaves appear with the seed husk still attached to their tips the gardener can enjoy their sudden appearance all the more. In the nurturing of a garden we are thereby nurturing patience as a personal disposition.

It is in this context that we can see that the contemporary prevalence of gardening television programs and gardening supplies that promulgate an "immediate gratification" picture of gardening are missing the point. Perhaps they serve a purpose in getting the consumption orientated modern person interested in the possibilities of gardening and from that starting point a richer more engaged relationship can take root; but their "this could be yours tomorrow" message is a message that fits the time not the garden as either concept or reality. The agency of the plants and garden as a whole means that even with an appreciation of time we can never totally predict what will happen in the space between the imagining, planning, and implementation of the garden, and the garden as a mature instantiation. An experienced gardener needs something of the reticence of Vita Sackville-West who, with Harold Nicholson, designed and developed one of the most acclaimed gardens in the UK, Sissinghurst Castle, including one of its most innovative and often copied "rooms," the white garden. In her garden diary at the time of its laying out she wrote:

> For my part, I am trying to make a grey, green, and white garden. This is an experiment which I ardently hope may be successful, though I doubt it. One's best ideas seldom play up in practice to one's expectations, especially in gardening, where everything looks so well on paper and in the catalogues, but fails so lamentably in fulfilment after you have tucked your plants into the soil. Still one hopes.[10]

In her reticence Sackville-West introduces another way in which humans can be improved by gardening, that is, with the introduction of some humility. As with patience, humility can be overdone. For example, in the face of oppressive social conditions too much patience with regard to bringing about change or too much humility on the part of those oppressed would be a bad thing. (Although, perhaps, it is correct to say that these attributes would no longer be patience and humility but rather apathy and subservience.) The activity of gardening promotes humility through the process of seeing our human plans and fancies overridden by natural processes in the garden. It is only when we come to see the activity of gardening as a form of collaboration with nature that the garden takes on the form that we now understand was right for us to want it to be all along. This might seem a minor aspect of human improvement, but it is where we can learn important lessons about the dangers of hubris.

Of course, gardening can become an expression of hubris like no other. To manipulate the land, to constrain living things, and to bend everything to our own will with no regard for what these things are or how they would be without our intervention, is exactly the mode of domination to which environmental philosophy has developed its telling critique. But hubris is also to do with not being willing to be helped by, or to lean on, others, or to learn from tradition.[11] In the activity of gardening we quickly learn that working with the grain of nature rather than relying only on our own ideas, and learning from others, is so much more effective and pleasurable. For example, I was so beguiled by the pictures in gardening magazines and seed catalogues of the plant *Cerinthe major purpuascens* that I tried to grow it three years running in my yard, each year with more elaborate preparation such as germinating the seeds in autumn and overwintering them indoors. Even in the best year they were straggly little plants – nothing like the iridescent purple flowers and glaucous blue-green leaves in the pictures. My yard receives nothing like the amount of sun that these particular plants need and eventually I had to recognize that my apparent need for these plants was just a misjudged want, an attempt to bend the situation to my will rather than to read the situation and understand what would really flourish there. Now the yard is filled with many different types of fern: some bought, some given by friends, some just turned up by themselves, that grow larger, greener, and healthier looking every year and the glossy emerald green clumps or delicately waving fronds bring me great pleasure. It is not the case that I have the humility thing sorted for all time and any situation (after all, how could such a statement be made!), but through such experiences, in collaborating with nature in a garden, little shifts are made in one's approach to the world and the shift towards humility for most of us is a good thing.

Gardening as a social activity has many ways of developing social virtues. Despite the stereotypical picture of the cut-throat competition of village flower and produce fêtes, with their Machiavellian characters locked in decades of animosity over who can grow the biggest marrow, in fact, any visit to an allotment site or garden open day will reveal the depth of sharing that takes place even among strangers. People share technical knowledge and tips, they share cuttings, seeds and surplus plants, they share gluts of vegetables and cut flowers, and all with such insistence that it is hard to leave a garden empty-handed or unenlightened about yet another way to avoid carrot root fly. This generosity is partly learned from the fecundity of the plant world. Many gardeners when pruning a bush cannot resist the temptation to pot up a few of the strongest cuttings "just to see" if they might take root. Then, once rooted and growing strongly, the problem emerges of having nowhere to plant them out. The friend, relative, neighbor or, indeed, complete stranger with a rather more sparsely planted garden becomes the obvious recipient. The abundance of seed produced by plants just seems to call out for being saved and shared around. The seemingly magical appearance of even more courgettes on those few plants prompts the gardener to pass on this largesse of nature and even extend the, now internalized, virtue of sharing to what can less easily be spared. (Though I have to say, this never extends to parting with their own compost!)

Another type of social sharing is that of the garden as a space for others. Here the idea of responsive cohesion can be again pressed into service,

ISIS BROOK

this time to find the correct balance for the garden regarding its place within the social realm. One could ask questions such as: Has my control over the neatly manicured garden left nowhere for my children to play? Has my encouragement of robust, wind-dispersed species left my neighbors with a weed control problem in their vegetable beds? Has my nourishing of plants left nowhere for anyone in the house to hang out some washing? For an example of gardens that exhibit a high degree of responsive cohesion in the social realm we could look to the design and maintenance of William Morris's various gardens. His gardening principles include respecting the surrounding landscape and building traditions, being productive and beautiful with an emphasis on native plants, and keeping established trees wherever possible. His gardens always included spaces for sitting, for playing, for walking; social spaces for others to share in the work and the pleasure of the garden.[12]

My next gardening virtue I call, simply, recognizing reality. Gardening brings us face-to-face with the world, and with gardening, unlike say the latest findings in physics or neuroscience, it is with our world *as experienced by us* in the context of the home environment. We need to be able to meet the world as it is, not how we have created it in our imaginations. The significance we create for ourselves in the world has to accommodate how the world is, and engaging in this accommodation is another counter to our hubristic tendencies. This is a means to what Iris Murdoch calls "unselfing" that goes along with the recognition of reality as separate from ourselves.[13]

In gardening this recognition of reality comes about through an embodied engagement rather than, for example, the way we might come to understand some fact about the world through reading a book or watching a documentary. And it is learning through embodied engagement that brings about the change in character that lies at the heart of this notion of improvement. In gardening we carry out actions that are for the good of the garden itself and in doing so we recognize that there is a garden outside of our plans and desires that can express itself rather than be putty in our hands to use for whatever we want to express. In our imaginative, creative work in the garden we do express ourselves, but partly through making space for the expression of the other. It is in this regard that we can see the overly constrained garden or the thoroughly acontextual garden as demonstrating flaws of character in the gardener.

That gesture of making space for the other is at the core of why and how gardening improves humans. By gesture I don't mean the outer expression of, say, letting that *pachysandra* continue to spread under the trees because even though unplanned it just seems right. I mean the inner gesture that makes that possible – possible, that is, to allow and possible to see the rightness of doing so. This inner gesture is one of openness. Generosity of spirit does not quite capture it, as generosity seems to suggest we have something of value to give; what we do is not give, but hold back to let the other be.

We are taught this very easily by the plant realm. Recall if you will the experience of coming across a first flower bud, perhaps the first snow-drop or crocus in spring or any flower that wasn't there ... then suddenly it is, and we smile, don't we? This experience is very special in one's own garden. Not special in the sense of "Great, I planted that and there it is doing exactly what I wanted"; no, in that instance of first encounter, the flower finds that openness in us. Our wonderment at this being opens our hearts and in that openness we receive something and are improved by it. To call this experience pleasure, even a higher pleasure, requires that we take away pleasure's hedonistic overtones, or perhaps we should just leave pleasure behind and call it grace. We receive something from nature and in that instant, in that involuntary smile, we recognize that we have been touched. The experience is uplifting in a way that no self-imposed attempt to cheer up, nor any personal effort to be open-hearted, can ever achieve. These shifts in consciousness and their attendant poten-tial to improve one's character do not work in the same way as exercising one's biceps, and yet there is something of the same process of engaged activity involved. What is distinctively different is that we cannot garden in order to cash in on those benefits. Katie McShane expresses this point in the context of loving nature:

> Ironically no matter how good for us caring for nature can be it cannot be done for only self-serving purposes. Love of nature or respect for nature, if it is really love or respect, has to take us outside of ourselves and our needs. We reap the benefits of such a relationship by not having our eye on the prize of reaping the benefits.[14]

By engaging with gardening practices in order to nurture the plants and improve the soil and respond appropriately to the wider context of nature and the social realm, the lessons and skills of patience, humility, experi-encing reality, caring for the other, and being open-hearted are learnt and deepened. Gardening can therefore be said to improve both the gar-den and the gardener.

NOTES

1 I mean "yard" in the UK sense of a concrete or paved area behind a house with pots of plants rather than the US or Australian sense of what we in the UK would call a garden.

2 M. Morton and D. Balmori, *Transitory Gardens Uprooted Lives* (New Haven: Yale University Press, 1995).

3 M. Schwartz, quoted in T. Richardson (ed.) *The Vanguard Landscapes and Gardens of Martha Schwartz* (London: Thames and Hudson, 2004), p. 95.

4 K. Čapek, *The Gardener's Year*, trans. M. and W. Weatherall (London: George Allen and Unwin, 1946), p. 37.

5 W. Fox, *A Theory of General Ethics: Human Relationships, Nature, and the Built Environment* (Cambridge, MA: MIT Press, 2006).

6 T. Williamson, A. Radford, and H. Bennetts, *Understanding Sustainable Architecture* (New York: Spon Press, 2003).

7 I. Brook and E. Brady, "The Ethics and Aesthetics of Topiary," *Ethics and the Environment* 8, 1 (2003): 127–42.

8 D. Cooper, *A Philosophy of Gardens* (Oxford: Oxford University Press, 2006).

9 Ibid., p. 90.

10 V. Sackville-West, quoted in P. Nicholson (ed.) *V. Sackville-West's Garden Book* (London: Book Club Associates, 1974), p. 16.

11 D. Cooper, *The Measure of Things* (Oxford: Oxford University Press, 2007), p. 163.

12 Jill, Duchess of Hamilton, P. Hart, and J. Simmons, *The Gardens of William Morris* (London: Francis Lincoln, 1998).

13 I. Murdoch, *The Sovereignty of Good* (London: Routledge, 2007), p. 91.

14 K. McShane, "Anthropocentrism vs Nonanthropocentrism: Should We Care?" *Environmental Values* 16, 2 (2007): 169–86; J. O'Neill, "Happiness and the Good Life," *Environmental Values* 17, 2 (2008): 125–44.

CHAPTER 2

CULTIVATING THE SOUL

The Ethics of Gardening in Ancient Greece and Rome

Life in the modern world provides us with ample opportunity to attach moral meaning to professional practice. We need only examine our culturally received ideas about firemen, architects, or used car salesmen to see how many careers stand as metaphors for moral qualities. In the Mediterranean basin during the classical period, professional life was more limited. Soldier, farmer, mariner, and often a combination of all three were the options commonly facing the working population.

Agriculture and farming life have long been important topics in the literature of ancient Greece and Rome. The farm and garden were settings that evoked a rich and complex set of cultural meanings about human nature. Theatrical characters in drama and especially comedy were drawn from agrarian life as often as they were found in the real world. These characters were taken from every level of society, from the Gardener/King described by Xenophon to the poor peasant whose small farm barely supports his family. In comedy we can find the farmer playing a comic yokel; conservative, reactionary, yet gullible. But just as often he was portrayed as the stalwart foundation of society and at times as a heroic figure of endurance and bravery. Rural topics were often treated pragmatically in works that read as instructional manuals, apparently passing on only the most prosaic aspects of rustic life. But it does not require a very close reading of the texts to see that they contain a host of other meanings and address more than routine farming matters. They are telling the reader not just how, but what it means, to cultivate the soil.

Farming and gardening were often described positively in literature either in contrast to less honorable professions or as essential components of a well-ordered society. To tend the garden was pleasing to the gods, pleasing to the state, and was frequently described as the healthiest and pleasantest of occupations. In addition to providing a living, the benefits attributed to this way of life accrued to its practitioners in two primary arenas. First, in civic life, the diligent farmer builds up a surplus so that he can share with his neighbors and with the state. In addition, he improves wastelands to increase produce, develops personal endurance and strength that make him a better soldier and, because his wealth is in the land itself, he has a strong interest in protecting it from invaders. In addition to these civil advantages, cultivating the soil was pious. Most authors agree that farming is agreeable to the gods. Often, it is described as the only profession that pleases them. In contrast to the civil incentives for farming, the rewards of divine approbation are received by the individual himself, since by pleasing the gods he averts divine anger and he has a better chance of keeping his earnings. This juxtaposition of divine will and the life of the soil gave philosophical weight to otherwise pragmatic enthusiasms for farming.

We find these themes were repeated in many contexts: the farmer as the foundation of civic life and farming as the profession that was most gratifying to the gods. In order to explore some of the ways these ideas were expressed in literature, we will consider examples produced by authors in Greece and Rome through different periods, with an emphasis on practical treatises that focused on the farm and garden.

Greece

There are a host of gardening characters in Greek literature. They range from clownish boors, stinking and slurring, to brave and loyal citizens to gentlemen/farmers, courtiers, and kings. There are poetic depictions of famous gardens like the description of the fruitful garden of Alcinous, the fine farm and garden of Laertes in Homer's *Odyssey*, and the evocative agrarian images on the shield of Achilles in the *Iliad*. Comedy boasts farmers of every stripe – from the clever farmer who "overcomes all adversities ... and manages to impose his comic vision on reality" in Aristophanes' comedies *Peace* and *The Acharnians* to the narrow-minded and stubbornly ignorant characters of Middle and Late comedy like Menander's Knemon.[1] There are also texts that offer detailed descriptions of the best practice for farm and garden and illustrate what is needed to run a successful estate. Hesiod and Xenophon produced two extant treatments of rural life, the *Works and Days* and the *Oeconomicus*. These works locate the farmer within a larger cultural context and help us understand some of the meanings attached to an agrarian life.

Works and Days is an 800-line poem about farming, composed in the eighth century BCE. It is addressed to the poet's brother, with whom Hesiod had legal struggles over the division of their family estate. The substance of the poem is a persuasive lecture on the way to a just and successful life. The poetic action moves from city life, with its corrupt judges and gossiping smiths, to the country where the just farmer does his work in good season, does not impose on his neighbors, and assists those in need. Hesiod as a historic figure is a matter of controversy, yet whether there was a single poet or a group of poets collected under that name, the extant *Works and Days* remains as evidence of a set of opinions about the relationship of men to the divine and to the world at large. It is also the clearest extant expression of the mores of rural life in Greece from the pre-classical period. Later writers treated Hesiod not only as a historical figure but, along with Homer, as a founder of Greek classical culture.

Because Hesiod was drawing on an oral tradition, we have no way to evaluate the originality of his contribution to the genre of gardening lore. However, his texts give expression to the little documented values of the rural communities of Greece during a period for which we have scant literary evidence. The community portrayed in *Works and Days* is one that is resentful of urban authority when it interferes with village life (cf. the bribe-devouring judges) and is mindful of the rules that govern its society and the productive year. The way to prestige in this milieu was to be a good grower and to build a surplus that allowed for generosity toward less prosperous neighbors. This goal could only be accomplished by forsaking the temptations of the town, litigation, and gossip and concentrating on the life of the soil, hard work, and sound practice in accordance with the laws of the gods. When we first encounter Hesiod's brother Perses, he is bribing the corrupt judges and running through his inheritance (even though he has wrongly received more than his share), and yet he has nothing to show for his effort. Thus, much of the dramatic force of

MEGHAN T. RAY

the poem is derived from the contrast between the life of the industrious farmer and that of the lazy, litigious, agora-loving city dweller (the agora being the civic and administrative center for the surrounding country-side). The poet has created an "ethical geography"[2] where physical distance from the farm and the work of the soil equals moral distance from the good and the just. It is possible, the *Works* tells us, for Perses to rehabilitate his reputation and regain wealth through the simple remedy of hard work and sound practice.

We have seen that the narrative framework of the poem is driven by the attempt by Hesiod to save his brother from poverty and persuade him to return to country life. He says, "Work, you stupid Perses, at the tasks that the gods have set for men to do."[3] In setting the stage for his argument, Hesiod first details the religious/mythological background behind man's need to labor through the stories of Prometheus, Pandora, and the Ages of Man. This mythological history provides the underlying principle for agricultural pursuits. Not only can "the race of iron never rest from labor" due to the ire of Zeus, but "neither famine nor disaster ever haunt men who do true justice; but light-heartedly they tend the fields which are all their care."[4] The rules of the village, where the details of proper conduct are strictly laid out, are ordained by the will of Zeus. Hard work on the farm is the formula for the just man and the only strategy that will not arouse the anger of the gods. The gods reward the man who builds his wealth honorably and through hard work. He lays low the man who seizes wealth unjustly, through litigation, robbery, and war.

The calendar framework of the productive year used in *Works and Days* emphasizes how the annual cycle reflects the will of Zeus. Actions please the gods in their proper sequence and in due season. Understanding divine will helps the farmer minimize error and avoid the dire consequences of poverty. The theme of divine timeliness is reinforced in the sailing section where, while clearly despising seafaring himself, Hesiod tells us when, by the will of the gods, it is safest to travel on water. *Works and Days* ends with a series of lucky and unlucky days, closing with the idea that the gods determine right and wrong and it is man's lot to discover their will.

Writing in the fourth century, Xenophon (431–350 BCE) addressed a different world to that of Hesiod's rural farmer. Although the majority of men still made their living from farming, society and literature had changed. Cities, trade networks, and literary production were flourishing. Politics affected the countryside as many city-states pursued expansionist policies that were changing agrarian life, drawing off agricultural labor and damaging productive fields during conflicts. Cultural life was also changing as festivals that featured dramatic production spread outward from Athens to other parts of Greece and created a forum for a common culture.

Unlike Hesiod, Xenophon was born near Athens into an upper-class family. He knew the wealthy elite of Athens and was given an education and the advantages of his class. He was a disciple of Socrates and wrote dialogues including an *Apology* and the *Symposium*. While he is the author of many texts, perhaps his most famous work is the *Anabasis*, the story of the Greek mercenary escape through enemy Persian territory in which he took part.

In addition to being a follower of Socrates and a soldier of fortune, Xenophon was also a farmer, running an estate in Scillus, south of Olympia. The *Oeconomicus*, dated after 401 BCE, is organized as a dialogue and features Socrates and successful gentleman/farmer Ischomachus. While the meaning of this dialogue is open to (vastly varied) interpretations, the discussion is putatively intended to illustrate for his friend Kritoboulos the ways and means to profitable estate management. It contains a wealth of detail about domestic economy during the period, as well as thoughts on the qualities necessary to run a successful farming enterprise. The text treats agrarian pursuits in several contexts with reference to famous exemplars and offers the reader practical advice.

It is in the *Oeconomicus* that Xenophon develops the theme of the Gardener/King with respect to both Cyrus the Great and the pretender Cyrus the Younger. Xenophon tells us that the great Persian king valued horticultural pursuits as highly as military matters and considered them essential to the state. He describes how Cyrus rewarded courtiers who brought new land into cultivation. In addition, the king himself spent time in his gardens whenever possible and took credit for being an accomplished gardener. Xenophon goes on to tell how he believes horticultural knowledge is an indication of leadership and ability. As an example, he describes the Spartan General Lysander's visit to Cyrus the Younger's garden paradise in Sardis. When Lysander admired the skill with which the garden was constructed, Cyrus was able to boast of having done the planning and the planting himself.

Xenophon develops several ideas concerning cultivating the soil as part of estate management. Book 5 is a list of all the pleasures and benefits that come to the farmer either through his labor or its fruits. These include health, fitness, gifts for the gods, wealth for men, and lessons in integrity, since "earth teaches justice to those who have the ability to learn from her."[5] Farming also teaches men leadership and corporate action, skills that translate into successful soldiery.

Continuing the theme developed in Hesiod of hard work as a means to wealth, Xenophon insists upon the ability of the hard worker to succeed despite gaps in his knowledge or mistakes in his practice. Diligence is the key to success. At length he describes how, while many things may go awry on the farm, the causes of the farmer's failure are more often from neglect than from ignorance. It is through inattention that all can be lost. For example, he points out that the best way to understand the soil and what will grow best is simply to look at your neighbor's garden and see what he is growing. Even waste ground can be figured out this way, since the weeds will indicate the cultural conditions just as well as garden plants would.

Hesiod and Xenophon, authors from vastly different backgrounds and historical contexts, express how cultivating land was necessary, beneficial, and pious. Both authors emphasize the advantages for the individual and for his community. They also insist on the religious righteousness of the practice and the sanction of the gods. These themes recur in Rome (with some modifications) and were repeated by Roman authors from the days of the Republic to the late Empire.

Rome

But it is from the farmers that the bravest men and the strongest soldiers come, and those who follow this occupation are most highly respected, most stable and least hated.

Cato, *De Agri Cultura*[6]

There is a substantial body of Roman agrarian literature dating from the Republic to the last days of the western Empire. This legacy has been well mined as a source for information about Roman farming practices, agricultural implements, and economic life. While these treatises have been of value to historians of rural life and economy, the texts are also reflections of an extensive literary tradition concerning the qualities of moral, civic, and religious duty. The Romans assigned multiple meanings to the practice of husbandry and the rural landscape. Religion, civic life, and the land were bound up together and the rustic treatises reflect the complexity of this relationship. Even in the city of Rome, about as urban a situation as you could find in the Mediterranean basin, religious festivals and traditional practices preserved the associations with cultivating the soil. For example, the Suovetaurilia, a sacrificial procession of sheep, cows, and bulls used in the city to mark the completion of a census or the purification of the returning army, was originally a rite for the purification of the fields.[7] However, pastoralism for the Romans, as for the Greeks, was not connected to a state of naïve innocence; it was the basis of sturdy bravery, producing a soldier who was inured to hardship. This vision of the hardworking farmer was an ideal of the Roman character and as an ideal it persisted long after it ceased to reflect the condition of much of the Roman citizenry.

The world described in the literature of these rustic treatises was far from paradise. It is not a pristine natural world admired from a distance, but a productive landscape that was the result of disciplined activity. For a Roman citizen, the rigors of life on the farm might have contrasted favorably with urban luxury and decadence, but distaste for city sophistication did not lead to an appreciation of wild nature. Unprofitable wastelands were not places of romance but missed opportunities. Rural and civic life were closely connected so that in Rome the owner of a country estate was considered the state's most valuable citizen. Later, the Roman virtues of the yeoman farmer had to be adapted to reflect the new circumstances of the owners of large estates. However, the orderly nature of the farm and the farmer's control over his gardens and fields remained a first principle.

Famous farmers run through Roman history: from the statesman Cincinnatus who was immortalized laying down his plough, reluctantly leaving the farm to serve his country, to the less famous consuls Gaius Fabricus and Curius Dentatus, who similarly turned away from political power to return to an agrarian living, to the orator and author Cato the Elder quoted above, for whom cultivating the soil and citizenship were connected ideas. Comedy, poetry, and farming manuals all provided fertile ground for the treatment of this concept. Cicero, Virgil, and many of Rome's finest writers contributed to the development of an ethic of yeomen/citizens. This philosophy was drawn from a respect for the ancient ways of Rome's earliest citizens, from religious precedent, and from practical economic realities. Four Roman authors who treated agricultural subjects were published together as *Scriptores Rei Rusticae*. These authors were M. Porcius Cato (234–149 BCE), M. Terentius Varro (116–27 BCE), L. Iunius Moderatus Columella (ca. first century CE), and R. Taurus Aemilianus Palladius (ca. fourth century CE). These agricultural writers

MEGHAN T. RAY

were published in collections during the Renaissance and onward. As the *Scriptores Rei Rustiae* they became the canonical authorities and their texts were used by later scholars and gentlemen/farmers alike.

Cato, Varro, and Columella each served in the military before retiring to country estates that they ran as commercial enterprises. While their texts are often practical in intent and content, they also have a moral component connected with their use. Cato and Columella both explicitly state that farming is the only honorable way for a Roman to make money. However, it is important to note that the moral function of the texts is only available in so far as the reader was willing to put their practical rules into action. The morality achieved through this vision of agronomy came through successful deployment of its principles.

M. Porcius Cato Censorius began his military career serving during the Second Punic War, a conflict which ravaged the Roman countryside for 16 years. Since many of the battles were fought on Roman soil, agricultural practice was disrupted both through the physical destruction of fields and the conscription of farmers to fight as soldiers for lengthy periods. During this period wealthy Romans were buying up tracts of land from peasant farmers. This consolidation of farmland changed the face of Roman agriculture. Resistance to the luxuries bought with the wealth that accompanied this change was the hallmark of Cato's philosophy.

Although he treated a variety of subjects, *De Agri Cultura* is the only complete text extant. Cato was the first Roman to take up the subject of farming, although the earlier Greek writers were known and studied. His work covered the running of an estate, including plants, treatment of slaves, and many lists concerning the proper numbers of tools and equipment, as well as recipes for wine and oil and ingredients for ritual pursuits. He makes his case for farming life succinctly in his preface; farming is the only profession that combines security and profitability with honor and tradition. His text is prescriptive and specific, written in the imperative voice, and his advice does not rely upon foreign scholarship. This focus on Roman experience suited Cato's political agenda, turning attention away from Hellenistic literature toward good, practical Roman prose. This insistence on the here and now distinguished Cato from the writers who came after him for whom authority and past practice were much greater preoccupations.

Writing during the tumultuous last days of the Republic and the first of the new Empire, M. Terentius Varro was a prolific writer and was considered, along with Cicero and Virgil, one of Rome's greatest thinkers. Of his prodigious literary corpus, his extant works include only part of his philological *De Lingua Latina* and the three books of the *Rerum Rusticarum*. Varro's treatise, written in his eightieth year, was constructed as a series of dialogues between famous agronomists. His intent, stated in Book I, was to advise his wife on the cultivation of her recently purchased estate. The text discussed the merits of various methods of agricultural practice and animal husbandry. Varro begins by invoking 12 gods who have a special connection to the farm and garden and then describes some important harvest festivals. The position of this subject reinforces for the reader the strong connection between successful farming and the will of the gods. Next, Varro cites his authorities. It is interesting to note that many of the authors Varro quotes are philosophers and not agricultural writers. It is clear that Varro believed that competence in this subject required familiarity with many disciplines. Yet, after naming his sources, Varro stated that he would treat his subject according to three principles: what he observed by practice, what he had read, and what he heard from experts. This blending of practical experience and inherited wisdom became a major theme that appears in later authors.

Varro identifies farming as an important and necessary art and one that has two goals: profit and pleasure. How to do things in the most profitable way is a dominant theme for Varro, but he also acknowledges the pleasure derived from working with the soil. He discusses the dual ideals of health and strength that result from country life. For while town dwellers are feeble, farmers enjoy health and vigor and do not have to go to the gym like the citified Greeks who are the frequent target of patriotic Roman writers.[8]

Varro included a calendar of labors in ten chapters of Book I. This way of organizing the productive year emphasized the importance of timing and weather for the farmer. It is a fundamental tenet of the agronomical literature that there is a proper time for things to be done and that the ability to control the future in the face of unpredictable nature can be achieved though knowledge and careful planning. Seasonality and timing had long been major ideas in the agronomical books and the calendar of operations became an ideal medium for expressing them. This emphasis on seasonality signifies the connection of farming to astronomical learning, since only by observing the stars and moon can the farmer act in a timely manner. We can still see this preoccupation with timing in the farmer's almanacs and gardener's years that fill the gardening sections of bookstores today.

Columella is often considered the most comprehensive of the Roman agronomists. He was the author of 12 books on different aspects of the productive landscape, plus a short edition of some of his chapters called *On Trees*. He treated the organization of the farmstead, field crops, animal husbandry, and bee keeping. In addition, he included a verse treatment of garden plants inspired by Virgil, a chapter on selecting an overseer, and a calendar of farm operations with a list of duties for the overseer's wife.

Columella lamented the state of agricultural learning in his day and advocated a return to the standard Roman virtues associated with tending the soil. He amplifies Cato's treatment of farming as the only safe and honorable profession, considering and then dismissing soldiering, seafaring, usury, begging, freeloading, and litigation as occupations before returning to farm and garden. Here, he offers a brief nod to Xenophon's theory that diligence and hard work can compensate for lack of experience and knowledge and then paraphrases Varro's contrast between a life of slothful luxury (steaming out our daily indigestions) versus the qualities of energy and bravery that are found in farmers – not so unlike our modern dilemma of working in the garden or going to the gym. He also reiterates Varro's description of early Romans who only came to the city once in a nine day "week" and were more successful farmers with larger yields than his contemporaries who spent their time complaining about depleted soil and climate change.

In Book I he cites 50 authorities beginning with Hesiod, including the famous but now lost works of Mago the Carthaginian. Yet, Columella warned that without practical farming experience it would be impossible to understand the literature. He believed that the virtues achieved through farming were those of an earlier age: toughness, good judgment, and thrift. An extreme example of this economy is found in Columella's warning against the traditional practice of hiring laborers to pre-chew the figs that were used to fatten birds. He felt this should be avoided because the chewers tend to swallow some of the figs instead of spitting them out as they should.

Columella is the only author of the rustic treatises who indulges in a poetic treatment of gardening. His verse chapter on horticulture, inspired by Virgil and Hesiod, has dryads and muses as well as cabbage and beets. But even here amid flights of poetic fancy, we find the emphasis on the importance of timeliness, what to plant and when, and on hard work.

Virgil (70–19 BCE) was Rome's poet, its historian, and favorite agronomist all in one. He was the author of three major poems: the *Eclogues*, a collection of pastoral vignettes; the *Georgics*, four books about farming, bee keeping, and stock raising; and the *Aeneid*, the epic story of the Trojan

Aeneas' flight from Troy to Italy. His works were adopted as canon during the Empire and became the foundation of educational literature. Thus the *Georgics* and *Eclogues* were very widely read and Virgil's authority became an essential part of the vocabulary of farming literature. Virgil was born on a farm in the north of Italy, but was living in Rome when he published the *Georgics* in 29 BCE. Like all great poetry, the *Georgics* are open to interpretation and critics have found many and often conflicting ideas expressed in them. The text has been interpreted sometimes as an optimistic vision of a return to the Golden Age and sometimes as a cynical prediction of the dire future of Rome. That serious scholars find merit in these opposing views speaks to the complexity and layered meanings of the poem itself. Yet most agree that Virgil's vision of farm life came from a real appreciation of the countryside and its pursuits.

The *Georgics* is firmly rooted in the tradition of Hesiod's *Works and Days*, which Virgil acknowledges in the famous line: "I sing the song of Ascra throughout the Roman towns."[9] His view of farming is more complex than that found in *Works and Days* because it reflected a more complex agricultural reality than the rural small farmers of Hesiod's day. The giant slave-run estates of the Empire were a long way from the small family farms of earlier times and land ownership was complicated as returning soldiers were paid off with the deeds to other families' farms.

The moral aspects of the poem are shaded with ambiguity and its mood can change radically from book to book. However, despite all that had changed in rural life and the complexity in the *Georgics* itself, many early Roman values remained intact. The farmer was still strong and brave and still had to hazard his fate against ill fortune and capricious gods. These were beliefs about farming that remained unchanged in Virgil's work despite changing patterns of land ownership and shifting economic and political realities.

Conclusion

The authors we have considered here believed that working the soil fulfilled some of life's most basic values. It provided necessities and met the requirement to work that had been man's lot since the end of the Golden Age. It was honorable in ways that other professions were not. Beginning with Hesiod, all the authors agree that cultivating the soil is the most respectable and praiseworthy profession. Varro and Columella both built

MEGHAN T. RAY

on Cato's description of the working man's professional choices, determining that farming is both honorable and secure unlike any in the catalogue of alternative vocations. In addition, it is pious and satisfies the gods as an old and venerable way for man to live righteously.

The texts of Xenophon, Cato, Virgil, and Columella were written following periods of devastation as part of the effort of rebuilding. After wars, civil or foreign, barbarian invasion or internecine strife, restoring productive land became a major preoccupation. The idea of renewal through cultivation, for the benefit of the individual and the state, is often a main objective of the literature of agronomy.

These authors offered their visions of what it meant to be a farmer in Greece and in Rome from the eighth century BCE to the days of the early Roman Empire. While the texts are widely different in construction and voice, they share an essential belief in the satisfactions and benefits derived from the farm and garden. Although the exact form of this way of life changed over time, there remained many common beliefs and practices and the ideal of cultivating the soil remained fundamental to their understanding of the way to a civic, moral, and religious life.

NOTES

1   I. Konstantakos, "Aspects of the Figure of the *Agroikos* in Ancient Comedy," *Rheinisches Museum* 148 (2005): 5.
2   A. Edwards, *Hesiod's Ascra* (Berkeley: University of California Press, 2004), p. 178.
3   S. A. Nelson, *God and the Land: The Metaphysics of Farming in Hesiod and Virgil, with a Translation of Hesiod's Works and Days by David Grene* (Oxford: Oxford University Press, 1998), p. 19.
4   Hesiod, *The Homeric Hymns and Homerica*, trans. H. G. Evelyn-White (Cambridge, MA: Harvard University Press, 1977), p. 21.
5   S. Pomeroy, *Xenophon, Oeconomicus* (Oxford: Oxford University Press, 1994), 5.12.
6   Cato, *De Agri Cultura* (Totnes: Prospect Books, 1998), my translation.
7   E. Leach, *Vergil's Eclogues: Landscapes of Experience* (Ithaca: Cornell University Press, 1974), p. 58.
8   L. Storr-Best, *Varro, On Farming* (London: G. Bell, 1912), Bk. 2, 1–2: 121.
9   Nelson, *God and the Land*, p. 82.

CHAPTER 3

ESCAPING EDEN

Plant Ethics in a Gardener's World

Plants are thought to be alive, the juice is their blood, and they grow. The same is true of trees. All things die, therefore all things have life. Because all things have life, gifts have to be given to all things.

William Ralganal Benson[1]

The idea of a garden ethics throws up images of hosepipe bans, slugs poisoned by pellets or drowning in (ethical) beer traps, and campaigns against the use of peat and the sustainable sourcing of garden furniture. Curiously (for me at least), however, the plants in the garden are generally excluded from any notion of moral consideration. Within philosophy there are many ways of conceiving of morality, but most theories of morality pertain to matters of right and wrong. In a general sense, morality involves considering the wellbeing of others as well as our own wellbeing; but the question of who should be the subject of moral consideration is an interesting topic with respect to the garden. The gardener may kill hundreds of plants in the course of a growing season, yet there is very little discussion among gardeners and/or philosophers about the morality of such gardening practice.

The aim of this essay is to question the exclusion of plants from gardening ethics and to open up a debate on the garden as a location for human-plant ethics. The essay will be an exploration into the exclusion of plants from the ethical notions of gardening. Its foundation will be an exploration of the archetypal Western garden, Eden, and then, after discussing concepts of gardening which are centered on the human, I will travel out of Eden to consider alternative gardens in which human-plant relationships are quite different from those in our biblical paradise. In doing so I will consider gardens and gardeners (in a broad sense) for whom ethical recognition for plants emerges from an understanding of the connections between plants and human beings. From here I will discuss the introduction of an ethics towards the plants in the domestic Western garden.

Eden and Plants for Human Use

While there are many overlapping historical, philosophical, political, and sociological factors at play in the exclusion of plants from ethical discourse,[2] the most relevant to the practice of gardening are those which help to formulate the basic ideas of the garden – what a garden *is* and what a garden does. In this matter, it is crucial to examine the prototypic garden, the Garden of Eden, the most famous and influential of gardens in Western cultures. The concept and content of the Garden of Eden have acted as a blueprint for gardening ever since the development of enclosed gardens in Europe in the Middle Ages. John Prest argues that the "equation of the enclosed garden with the Garden of Eden, was to have important consequences for the history of gardening."[3] In medieval England gardens were fenced or walled to keep wild animals out, with the resulting garden echoing the peace and tranquility of the original Eden. Thus, "the earthly Paradise came to be identified with the small, contemporary, enclosed garden from which the animals were excluded altogether."[4] In *A History of British Gardening* historian Miles Hadfield also notes the importance of Eden to contemporary gardening and cheerfully laments that "[w]e cannot, alas, claim Eden among our British gardens."[5] Despite this, it is my contention that Eden has acted as the philosophical template for all British gardens.

The story of the Garden of Eden appears in Genesis 2–3. Within this story, God appears as the world's first (rather proud) gardener. It is said that God first planted a garden in the East and in it he placed the man he had made from a mixture of dust and the breath of life. With the man Adam as the Earth's second (first human) gardener, God then determined both the character of Eden and the blueprint for the gardens which Adam's descendants still tend today. In the description of God's green-fingered handiwork around the garden, Genesis 2 makes it clear that the plants of the garden have two functions. Plants are either aesthetically pleasing or they are resources for human needs: "And out of the ground the lord God made to spring up every tree that is pleasant to the sight and good for food."[6] Eden is cultivated for (human appreciation of) beauty and as a place where human beings use plants in order to survive. Therefore, it is relatively safe to assert that the human relationships with plants in the Garden of Eden are wholly instrumental, that is they are entirely based upon the use of plants for human benefit.

The Genesis story makes it clear that God's gardening skills in the Garden of Eden have created a human-oriented domain. The garden is carved out of the wilderness as a home for his newest and most favored creations: human beings. The garden plants within the garden are all directly beneficial to humankind, while the plants outside the garden are wild, and Genesis 3 identifies these generally as "weeds" – "the thorns and thistles it shall bring forth for you."[7] These unwanted plants are to be met by the humans after their fall from grace. Genesis therefore sets up a sharp dualism between wild and cultivated plants, which is maintained in our perception of garden plants to this day. Think of the difference in the general appreciation for roses and for bindweed and you will have quite nicely summarized this dualism.

What is remarkable about the plants both inside and outside Eden is that they are not given the breath of life that makes man a living creature. Therefore, neither the cultivated nor wild plants are deemed to be alive. They can be used at will by humanity without any thought about ethics. Plants can be dug up, chopped down, and cut back with impunity and without any notion of killing because plants are not proper living creatures. Plants are deemed to have no autonomy of their own and no other purpose but to serve the human good.

This position is further confirmed by other biblical passages from both the Old and New Testaments. Perhaps the most striking example is found in Mark's Gospel, where Jesus destroys a fig tree during Passover because it could not provide him with fruit – a somewhat unreasonable request as figs are out of season at that time of year. This view of plants as passive resources lends itself to the claim (still perpetuated today) that the biblical Eden was a paradise where there was no suffering, destruction, or death. These facts of life only arose after the fall from grace, when humans were forced to eat animal flesh, which contained blood, breath, and therefore life.

MATTHEW HALL

Within the story of Eden there can therefore be no code which sets out the boundaries of ethical human behavior towards plants. Effectively, there are no limits on the human use of plants, and so plants are implicitly excluded from the realm of moral consideration. (Humans are banned from eating from the Tree of Knowledge, but as I have yet to encounter one of these plants in a contemporary garden I have to assume that this tree is purely symbolic!) Humans can use plants as they wish because they have been given to humans by God, but also because the plants both inside and outside of the garden are deemed to be lesser beings than the humans and animals which populate the Earth. Man was allegedly made in God's image, whereas the plants do not even get the breath of life given by God.

It is a fact that the literal truth of the biblical story is no longer widely accepted (apologies to any Christian fundamentalist readers). We are taught from an early age that plants are alive and that natural selection has brought them into being, rather than an overbearingly creative gardener. Nevertheless, the cultural importance of Eden still remains. The very word "Eden" is synonymous with gardens. There are literally hundreds of references to Eden in gardening books, gardening blogs, gardening websites, and garden centers, while the most successful new botanic garden of the last decade is itself called Eden (www.edenproject.com). It is my contention that while we may have (rightly) rejected some of the details of the Eden story, its basic concept of the garden remains with us; the garden is a place for humans to do as they wish with plant life. This concept is akin to something like a Platonic idea – an ethereal, changeless entity which is in some way responsible for the structure, character, and functioning of the visible world – which has embedded itself in our collective gardening psyche, and, like the spines of a prickly pear cactus, remains stubbornly difficult to remove.

Gardening with Kin: Alternatives to Eden

Eden, however, is not the only garden. Across the Earth there are many examples of gardens and gardening practice that demonstrate alternatives to our Edenic exclusion of plants from moral consideration. Some of the most interesting examples arise from considerations of indigenous cultures in which plants are included within a "kincentric ecology"[8] in which the recognition of a direct kinship relationship between plants, animals, and humans forms the basis of moral considerations towards these non-human beings.

From a gardening point of view, a good example of this can be found among the Achuar peoples of Amazonia. In the gardens of the Achuar the cultivated manioc plants are created, mothered, and fertilized by Nunkui, the "mistress spirit" or animating force of cultivated plants.[9] The Achuar women gardeners see themselves as sharing with Nunkui the actual motherhood of the plants that they cultivate. Remarkably, they view the plants in their gardens as their children, and nurture them with the same responsibilities that childrearing entails. The plants in these manioc gardens are therefore powerfully animated and dynamic, as well as being well within the realm of moral consideration through the recognition and responsibility of direct kinship.

Importantly, in indigenous cultures, there is not a sharp distinction between notions of cultivated and wild, which in our gardens emerges to a large extent through the influence of Eden. To the Raramuri peoples of North America, all the things of the natural world, whether "cultivated" or "wild," are related by descent. This relationship is also expressed in notions of the interpenetration of human and plant existence and an emphasis on the similarities in our lives, rather than on the strikingly obvious differences. For the Raramuri, before the origin of this world, "people were part plant ... [and when] the Raramuri emerged into this world, many of those plants followed. They live today as humans of a different form."[10] Enrique Salmon explains that Raramuri *feel* directly related to these plants. As kin, the plants on Raramuri lands (whether garden, forest, or plains) are *humans in plant form*, that is, these plants are recognized as fully alive – autonomous, dynamic, and aware in the same way as human beings. This recognition brings the plants in Raramuri gardens into the moral sphere. Most interestingly, the recognition of plants as autonomous, active, and dynamic, and their inclusion in a web of kinship ethics is not restricted to non-Western cultures. It also occurs in another important garden for Western culture, the Ancient Greek garden of the Hesperides.

In Greek mythology the Hesperides were nymphs who traditionally have been described as the guardians of a tree (or trees) bearing golden apples. The Hesperides feature in many of the sources of Ancient Greek mythology and major classical works, including Apollodorus, Euripides, Virgil, and Seneca, but they first appear in Hesiod's *Theogony*: "The Hesperides who guard the rich, golden apples and the trees bearing fruit beyond glorious Okeanos."[11] The site at which these trees grew is known as the garden of the Hesperides, which is identified as beyond the river Oceanos by Hesiod and by Pliny the Elder as in the city of Benghazi, the largest city in the region of Cyrenaica on the Mediterranean coast of modern-day Libya.[12] The most commonly accepted story of the origin of these apple trees is that they are a gift from Gaia (Earth) on the occasion of the wedding of Hera and Zeus. In order to prevent theft from the apple tree it is said that the Hesperides were posted outside the apple trees to keep watch over them.

However, an older fragment of the Hesperides myth perhaps lends a slightly different perspective on this ancient garden, enabling us to provide an alternative to the mute plants in the utilitarian Eden: "The beautiful island of the gods, where the Hesperides have their homes of solid gold."[13] In this fragment, the nymphs appear to live *within* the apple trees; they are at home in the apples of gold. Traditionally, the nymphs, who have a semi-divine origin and possess human form and characteristics, are thought to be separate entities from the plants with which they are associated. However, as in other ancient Greek myths, here they appear to share the same body as the plants themselves. As beings emergent from Gaia (Earth), the apple trees and the Hesperides share a divine origin, for as Hesiod's *Theogony* relates, the holy Earth gave birth to all creatures, including gods, animals, humans, nymphs, and plants.[14]

Therefore, unlike in Eden where the plants are mute, inferior, passive, and open to arbitrary human use, the presence of the Hesperides imparts a strong, dynamic presence to the apple trees in this garden. The nymphs are alive, active, and have their own purposes. Their presence signifies that these trees are not simply for humans to use as they wish. As subjects in their own right and as the Earthborn kin of human beings, the apple trees of the Hesperides demand a certain respect and ethical consideration.

Plants, Exclusion, Ethics

While many modern gardeners have dismissed much of the detail of the biblical creation stories, we have for the most part maintained the blueprint of the garden as a human domain where silent plants serve human purposes, and human beings are able to treat plants as they wish. The exclusion of plants from ethics is so deep-seated that even the notion of ethical behavior towards plants is commonly regarded as nonsensical.

Even among keen gardeners there is often an implicit, ingrained, somewhat carefree acceptance of the maltreatment of plants and the killing of them through experimentation and simple lack of care. Deep exclusion ensures that plant ethics is regarded as something for the crazy people that believe in plant feelings and plant suffering.

In Eden, plants are denied life and denied any purpose of their own; these denials are the basis of exclusion. The maintenance of this exclusion in the face of knowledge that plants are indeed alive and (according to the latest evolutionary theory) have not been placed on Earth for human beings (they were around quite a while before we got here) suggests a necessary revision of our perception of plants and our behavior towards them. Moreover, in their idealist pursuit of a human-centered Eden, domestic gardens can quite easily become a "part of the war on nature" and an extension of human superiority and priority over the natural world.[15] Looking at our garden plants with an ethical eye may well be the first step towards ending this war, for the good of the natural world and the good of humankind.

In this important ethical quest the question of vitality is very important. While the plants are seen as non-living in Eden, in the gardens of the Achuar, Raramuri, and the Ancient Greek myths the plants are recognized as being fully alive. Plants are closely related to humans through descent and their behavior as living, aware, active, autonomous beings requires human awareness, respect, and consideration. The question is: How do we bring plants within the realm of moral consideration?

For Albert Schweitzer, the most famous ethical theorist to deal with non-human living beings, moral consideration begins with a reverence towards other lives, in the same way that we value our own lives. This leads towards a morality in which "evil is what annihilates, hampers, or hinders life.... Goodness, by the same token, is the saving or helping of life, the enabling of whatever life I can to attain its highest development."[16] For Schweitzer, in the context of their conduct towards non-human life, the moral person therefore "goes out of his way to avoid injuring anything living ... tears no leaf from its tree, breaks off no flower, and is careful not to crush any insect as he walks."[17]

For Schweitzer, plants have a will to live (that is they want to go on living) and have their own purpose on this Earth. Therefore, Schweitzer's first ethical suggestion is that plant life should not be harmed. While this is a commendable ideal, in the garden and in everyday life this is simply not possible. For human beings to live and grow, plants must be killed. In the garden, vegetables must be dug, cut, and pulled. Wood must

MATTHEW HALL

be cut, weedy species must be removed. In Eden, as plants are not deemed to be alive, such actions are allowed to proceed unchecked. However, in kincentric cultures such as the native cultures of North America, plants are alive. Weeding, cutting, and eating involves killing and there are moral limits to this human use of plants. This is expressed powerfully in the words of William Ralganal Benson, a Pomo tribesman from northern California: "Plants are thought to be alive, the juice is their blood, and they grow. The same is true of trees. All things die, therefore all things have life. Because all things have life, gifts have to be given to all things."[18] For Benson, giving gifts means offering something in exchange (and thanks) for the life that humans must take to sustain themselves. However, to reverse the exclusion of plants from ethical discussions, offerings towards plants must occur in life as well as in death. In life, the first offering is an acknowledgment of plant autonomy; recognition that plants have their own purposes and cannot simply be used as human beings wish.[19] As plants are closely related to humans and require our care and responsibility, the second gift is the provision of care, attention, and nurturing. The garden is an ideal site for such behavior, and in our Western culture the gardener is *the* expert at plant care. Gardening involves regular practices such as watering, potting on, sowing, and pruning, which require intimate attention to, engagement with, and the treasuring of plant life. Such care helps to build significant relationships between humans and plants: relationships of care which can form the basis of ethical behavior towards the cultivated plants in the garden.

However, where plant care is directed solely towards useful and/or aesthetically pleasing plants, we are still in the realm of Eden where "the wild plant, the unplanned, the unplanted is invariably rejected as a weed."[20] In order to overcome exclusion and human mastery of the plant kingdom and the natural world, care, attention, and responsibility need to be extended outwards from our "cultivated" plants towards those plants that keep on coming back into our Edens from the wild lands outside. Thus, the third offering is the gift of space. Countering Eden requires giving over space to those plant lives that make their way into our gardens of their own accord: the wildflowers, grasses, climbers, and ruderals. It requires giving space and being open to the spontaneous arrivals and actions of plants that are not completely under human control. Setting aside space for plants to grow unchecked can help transform Eden from a human orientated space into one that is at the forefront of ethical reparations to the natural world.

If extending space to "weed" species goes against the natural inclinations of gardeners, a request to extend them care and respect might very well just tip most gardeners over the edge! However, treating plants ethically must involve respecting all plant lives as significant. Giving plant life the gift of respect means not destroying plant life arbitrarily or unnecessarily. Necessity, of course, is open to interpretation, but respectful actions towards the plant life that supports human life should include questioning the destruction of plant life and minimizing harm to plant life in the garden wherever possible. As Schweitzer argues, wasting, or taking life unnecessarily, is unethical. This does not mean that we should abandon our gardens, but that we need to think about our garden practices with this in mind. For example, many of the techniques found in permaculture reduce the disturbance of the soil and the need for weeding. Practices such as not tilling the soil and simple mulching not only reduce human labor but also reduce the amount of plant life that we destroy (as well as saving huge amounts of water). Using the past experience of others to grow the right plants for the conditions also prevents the unnecessary loss of plant life. For example, if you have a garden that has moist to damp soils, you would be better (both morally and financially) to follow the advice of my neighbors to plant azaleas (which will thrive) rather than geraniums (which will not).

As we begin to give plants the gift of love and respect, we would do well to remember that plants are constantly giving gifts to sustain human life. Each plant life that nourishes us, each life that we take in our gardens and fields is a present to human life which (politeness dictates) requires a gift of thanks in return. In kincentric plant cultures, gifts of thanks often take the form of offerings – either material offerings of valued goods, or more commonly of words or actions, such as stories, songs, and dance. While it would be pleasing to see gardeners dancing and singing their thanks to the basil, bindweed, peas, marrows, and rose, perhaps we can begin with simple words of thanks; thanks for our gardens, and thanks to the plants whose lives make gardening (and living) both possible and enjoyable.

NOTES

1 M. K. Anderson, *Tending the Wild: Native American Knowledge and the Management of California's Natural Resources* (Berkeley: University of California Press, 2005), p. viii.

2   M. Hall, *Plants as Persons: A Philosophical Botany* (New York: State University of New York Press, 2010).

3   J. Prest, *The Garden of Eden: The Botanic Garden and the Re-Creation of Paradise* (New Haven: Yale University Press, 1981), p. 21.

4   Ibid., p. 23.

5   M. Hadfield, *A History of British Gardening* (London: John Murray, 1979), p. 1.

6   Genesis 2: 5–9. All Bible quotes are taken from the English Standard Version.

7   Genesis 3: 18.

8   E. Salmon, "Kincentric Ecology: Indigenous Perceptions of the Human-Nature Relationship," *Ecological Applications* 10 (2000): 1327–32.

9   L. M. Rival, "Seed and Clone: The Symbolic and Social Significance of Bitter Manioc Cultivation," in L. M. Rival and N. L. Whitehead (eds.) *Beyond the Visible and the Material: The Amerindianization of Society in the Work of Peter Rivière* (Oxford: Oxford University Press, 2001), p. 58.

10 Salmon, "Kincentric Ecology," p. 1328.

11 Hesiod, *Theogony*, trans. H. G. Evelyn-White, in *Hesiod, the Homeric Hymns, and Homerica* (London: Heinemann, 1914), pp. 215 ff.

12 Pliny the Elder, *Natural History* (London: Heinemann, 1945), 5.30.

13 Stesichorus, Geryoneis Frag. S8 (Oxyrhynchus Papyrus 2617), trans. D. Campbell, in *Greek Lyric*, Vol. 3 (London: Loeb, 1991).

14 Hesiod, *Theogony* 2.116–38.

15 V. Plumwood, "Decolonizing Australian Gardens: Gardening and the Ethics of Place," *Australian Humanities Review* 36 (2005). Available online at www.australianhumanitiesreview.org/archive/Issue-July-2005/09Plumwood.html (accessed July 10, 2009).

16 P. Cicovacki, *Albert Schweitzer's Ethical Vision: A Sourcebook* (Oxford: Oxford University Press, 2009), p. 158.

17 Ibid., p. 143.

18 Anderson, *Tending the Wild*, p. viii.

19 M. Hall, "Plant Autonomy and Human-Plant Ethics," *Environmental Ethics* 31 (2009): 169–81.

20 Plumwood, "Decolonizing Australian Gardens."

CHAPTER 4

FOOD GLORIOUS FOOD

"Grow your own" and "food glorious food" are the rallying cries in the world of gardens at the moment, spurred on by the current pressures of sustainability and predicted food shortages. The plea for growing food is being eagerly taken up by the gardening public, with allotments enjoying a resurgence in popularity and countless books on fruit and vegetable gardening, along with hen and bee keeping, dominating the shelves of bookshops everywhere. This trend has come about for a variety of reasons, not least as an almost inevitable reaction to the domination of aesthetic considerations in our gardens during the latter part of the twentieth century, where the ornamental qualities of flower and form, color and texture, determined how we gardened. The visual beauty of the best of these gardens cannot be denied, but where are the sensuous pleasures of plucking a ripe plum, still warm from the rays of the sun and eating it fresh from the tree, or the temptation of eating sweet freshly picked peas before they reach the kitchen?

The balance between use and ornament culminated in the seventeenth-century garden, which was designed to appeal to all the senses, evident from Sir William Temple's descriptions of the fruit in his garden, and Roger North's obvious delight in fish ponds. What follows is a look back to the various features of these proudly self-sufficient estates, from the cultivation of a wide variety of fruit and vegetables to the keeping of livestock, all of which not only fed the household but contributed to the ornamental appeal of the park and garden.

In 1661 the Dutch artist William Schellinks visited Bridge Place in Kent, the home of his friend Sir Arnold Braems. The entry in his journal describes a harmonious coexistence of pleasure and productivity in the quintessential seventeenth-century estate:

> There is ... a large deer park with many deer and does, woods, a rabbit warren in the hills, and very beautiful, well kept pleasure grounds with fruit trees, well watered by a fast flowing, fresh sparkling stream of wonderfully clear, sweet water. This splits up into several branches and rivulets, also some fishponds, in which a certain kind of fish called trout is bred, which is very similar to a large carp, and, prepared in the English manner, tastes very delicious. There are also some vineyards round the house and gardens, producing yearly two to three hogsheads of wine. There is a dovecote like a chapel, in which are at all times so many young pigeons that throughout the whole summer and longer 12 to 14 dozen can be taken out every week and put into pies or prepared otherwise. His people go out hunting everyday and catch a lot of partridges and pheasants, which we had everyday on the table, besides a choice of other delicate food, all with the most delicious English sauces; there is an ample supply of drinks, different kinds of wine and perry, which is made from pears. He also has his own brewery, bakery, wine press, hop garden, barns, stables, oxen, cows, sheep, pigs, geese, ducks, corn and fruit, everything that one can desire in such an establishment.[1]

Braems made his fortune developing the Dover sea front and spent it building one of the largest houses in east Kent. The cost of maintaining such an establishment would have been prohibitive to all but the very wealthiest families. Schellinks, on a leg of his Grand Tour of Europe, arrived in England only a year after the Restoration, but his journal reveals that he was conscious of the destruction of many buildings and parks by the ravages of the Civil War seven years earlier. Luckily, Bridge Place had escaped unscathed; however, it would only be a matter of time before the parks and gardens of Britain were under threat again, this time not by war but by the fashion that swept across England in the second half of the eighteenth century: the landscape park. Schellinks' description of the deer park, the fruit trees, vineyards, dovecote, along with all the domestic offices such as the brewery and bakery, represent the pinnacle of the ideologies of the self-sufficient estate that had prevailed since the Middle Ages, where gardens were unified in their purpose of pleasure and profit.

Self-sufficiency was an essential way of life, rather than a lifestyle choice, for landowning classes up until the agricultural and industrial revolutions of the eighteenth and nineteenth centuries. From the Middle Ages, early manorial and monastic establishments would have a dovecote, fish ponds, a deer park and rabbit warrens, orchards with bees, a brew house, vineyards, herbs, and a wide variety of fruit and vegetables growing in the gardens, all contributing to a varied diet. Land would have been let to tenant farmers responsible for cultivating grain crops. Peasants and cottagers grew vegetables on small parcels of land adjoining their houses and may have kept a pig for meat, and hens, valued mainly for their eggs. There would have been little distinction between the idea of an ornamental garden and the productive garden; at Ightham Moat in Kent during the fourteenth century six long terraced beds were arranged for growing vegetables, herbs, and flowers. Where vegetables were grown in great quantity sections of the garden may have been given over to single varieties, for example in the "kale yards" or "leek gardens" which would have been around two acres or more in size and would have fed the manorial household.

Already, the cultivation of vegetables was a well understood craft, and by the end of the sixteenth century many manuals were being produced on the subject. William Lawson, in *A New Orchard and Garden with The Country Housewifes Garden* (1618), includes instruction about the "Rules for Hearbes of common use"; the term "Hearbe" referred to not only the culinary and medicinal plants commonly known as herbs today, but also to "potteherbes," which implied any vegetable used to make pottage, a soup or stew-like dish, the staple diet of peasants and gentry alike. "Sallets," or salad vegetables, were also popular and eaten with a dressing of oil, vinegar, and salt. Onions, leek, garlic, and kale were the staples of the early medieval vegetable diet; root vegetables such as carrots and skirrets became available in the fourteenth century, and by the end of the seventeenth century a wide range of vegetables were cultivated. At Ryston Hall in Norfolk, for example, the list included artichokes, asparagus, skirret, scorsa, lettuce, radishes, spinach, nasturtiums, celery, french beans, sugar peas, carrots, turnips, shallots, onions, parsnip, and cabbage, together with fruit such as strawberries, raspberries, currants, and gooseberries.

In the Middle Ages raw fruit was regarded with suspicion and believed to be the cause of many ailments. However, fresh plums, damsons, cherries, and grapes, and later peaches, were consumed by the wealthy at the beginning of a meal, as an appetiser, and small wild strawberries would

HELENE GAMMACK

have been enjoyed with cream from the dairy in country households. Many varieties of apples and pears had been introduced from the Continent as a result of the Norman invasion, and were cultivated alongside damsons, bullaces, mulberries, quinces, and medlars.

A wide variety of fruit trees, admired by the Elizabethans for their ornamental qualities, were grown in the formal gardens of the gentry and aristocracy. John Parkinson's *Paradisi in Sole* (1629) lists 57 varieties of apple, 62 of pears, 61 varieties of plum, 35 of cherries, and 22 of peaches. The fashion for manipulating the growth of trees by pruning, training, and grafting had spread from Europe. Horticultural manuals were filled with all manner of experiments for changing the shape, taste, and scent of flowers and fruit. Many of these experiments, or "secrets," were derived from Italian and German books which extolled the power of man over nature. In *Natural Magick*, translated in 1658 from the sixteenth-century Italian version, Della Porta explains how to manipulate trees into fruiting at all times of the year, how to alter the size and shape of fruit, and how to produce fruit and flowers of "diverse colours, such as are not naturally incident to their kind," or to see that "fruits that are in their growing, may be made to receive and resemble all figures and impressions whatever."[2] The principle behind many of these experiments is grafting: "and not only every tree can be grafted onto every tree, but one tree may be adulterated with them all." Similar treatises were written in English, such as Leonard Mascall's *A Book of the Arte and Manner, Howe to Plant and Graffe All Sorts of Trees, How to Set Stones, and Sow Pepines to Make Wylde Trees to Graffe On* (1572) and Thomas Hill's *A Brief and Pleasant Treatise on Natural and Artificial Conclusions* (1581).

Conflicting ideologies during this period resulted in a backlash against such artificial methods of cultivation, as expressed in 'The Mower Against Gardens' by Andrew Marvell (1621–78):

> Had he not dealt between the bark and tree,
> Forbidden mixtures there to see.
> No plant now knew the stock from which it came;
> He grafts upon the wild the tame:
> That uncertain and adulterous fruit
> Might put the palate in dispute.[3]

Marvel was a Puritan and as such advocated an appreciation of nature and the idea of an earthly paradise. Orchards in particular came to represent Puritan ideologies, due in part to religious connotations and also to the benefits of producing fruit. Since at least the medieval period orchards had been a valuable component of the estate, comprising grassy walks studded with flowers such as violets, daisies, and periwinkles, which, together with the blossom and fruit of the apple trees, evoked the idealized notion of the Garden of Eden. In 1618 the clergyman William Lawson had defined paradise as "a Garden and Orchard of trees and hearbs, full of pleasure,"[4] and he valued the sensual qualities of the orchard as highly as the profitable: "What can your eye desire to see, your eares to heare, your mouth to taste, or your nose to smell, that is not to be had in an Orchard, with abundance of variety?"[5] Ralph Austin, a fervent Puritan, nurseryman, and author of a *Treatise of Fruit-trees* (1653), likewise espoused the spiritual and economic benefits of the orchard, where pleasure and profit go hand in hand. This is illustrated quite literally in the title page of his treatise by two arms clasping hands as they emerge from clouds labeled "Profits" and "Pleasures" (figure 4.1).

Austin was especially interested in cider, which had until then been little known outside the West Country, but was adopted by the Puritans who promoted its benefits on various levels: cider, they believed, soothed the mind (unlike beer, which provoked subversive behavior), had powerful medicinal properties, and tasted delicious enough to supplant the expensive French wines that were being imported, thereby benefiting the struggling economic situation in the country. A fellow Puritan, Samuel Hartlib, proposed a new law to make the planting of fruit trees compulsory among the landowning classes. His treatise *Design for Plentie By a Universal Planting of Fruit Trees* (1653) expressed his conviction that fruit trees were "for the benefit and public relief of this whole Nation ... for the relief of the poor, the benefit of the rich, and the delight of all."[6] His proposal was never taken up, but his cause epitomized the Puritan ideologies that prevailed at the time.

Ironically, Hartlib was to strike up a friendship with the royalist and devout Anglican John Evelyn through their mutual love of fruit trees and as exponents of good husbandry. Evelyn was a member of the recently established Royal Society and was therefore interested in scientific improvements. He had been exiled to the Continent during the Civil War and was influenced by the gardens he saw in France and Italy. On his return he wrote prolifically on many aspects of horticulture, most famously on trees in his *Sylva, a Discourse of Forest Trees and the Propagation of Timber* (1664). He also offered practical instruction as documented in his *Kalendarium Hortense* (1664), which gives a month-by-month guide

HELENE GAMMACK

Profits — Pleasures.

A Treatise of
FRVIT=TREES

Shewing the manner of Grafting, Setting, Pruning, and Ordering of them
in all respects : According to divers new and easy Rules of experience;
gathered in y space of Twenty yeares.
Whereby the value of Lands may be much improued, in a shorttime, by
small cost, and little labour
Also discovering some dangerous Errors, both in y Theory and Practise
of y Art of Planting Fruit=trees
With. the Almentall and Physicall vse of fruits.
Togeather with
The Spirituall vse of an Orchard: Heldforth in divers Similitudes be=
tweene Naturall & Spirituall Fruit=trees: according to Scripture & Experiece.

By RA: AUSTEN.
Practiser in y Art of Planting

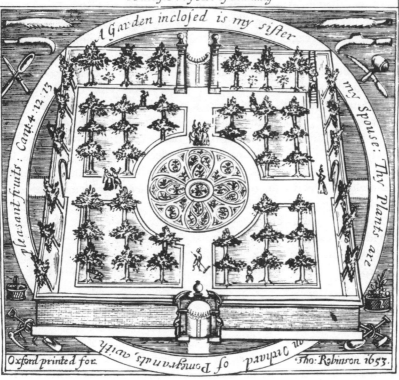

A Garden inclosed is my sister my Spouse: Thy Plants are an Orchard of Pomgranats, with pleasant fruits: Cant: 4:12:13

Oxford printed for Tho: Robinson 1653.

FIGURE 4.1   Title page of Ralph Austin, *Treatise of Fruit-trees* (1653).

to the cultivation of fruit and vegetables. His travels qualified him to influence the country on a cultural level; he would have been familiar with the literature of ancient Greece and Rome, which had in turn inspired the Italian Renaissance. Pliny, for example, describes the ideal country estate, the noble acts of cultivating fruit, herbs, vegetables, and livestock, and bee keeping, all of which were recurrent themes in the seventeenth-century estate.

Sir William Temple, ambassador at the Hague, was also familiar with the classics and appreciated the spiritual nature of the productive garden. In his essay *Upon the Gardens of Epicurus* (1685), Temple's interest in moral philosophy led him to look back to the classical world in search of health and tranquility, which he finds in the cultivation of fruit, both as food and for its aesthetic qualities that appeal to all the senses. Temple planted his own garden at Moor Park with a wide variety of fruit. He believed that no country "equals us in the Variety of Fruits which may be justly called good; and from the earliest Cherry and Strawberry to the last Apples and Pears, may furnish every day of the circling year."[7]

Fashionable estates during the second half of the seventeenth century embraced the formal styles of the European gardens, consisting of allées and avenues, open plats and parterres and walled enclosures, as represented in the many illustrations of the late seventeenth-century estates, most notably the bird's-eye views by Kip and Knyff published in *Britannia Illustrata* (1707), in which it is possible to make out dwarf and wall-trained trees and probable vegetable beds within the formal gardens (figure 4.2). The enclosures provided an ideal micro-climate in which to grow a variety of fruit, including cherries, apricots, peaches, figs, vines, and melons. This display of fruit in the ornamental garden is frequently noted in the journals of Celia Fiennes, who traveled throughout Britain on horseback from the 1680s visiting many great estates. Her journal provides an invaluable insight into the use of plants in the formal gardens, with the latest advances in cultivation perhaps contributing to the "improved" nature of what she found. Of Coleshill in Wiltshire, she wrote:

> By Farington is a fine house of sir George Pratts called Coalsell; all the avenues to the house are fine walks of rows of trees, the garden lyes in a great descent below the house, of many steppes and tarresses and gravel walkes with all sorts of dwarf trees, fruit trees with standing apricock and flower trees, abundance of garden roome and filled with all sorts of things improved for pleasure and use.[8]

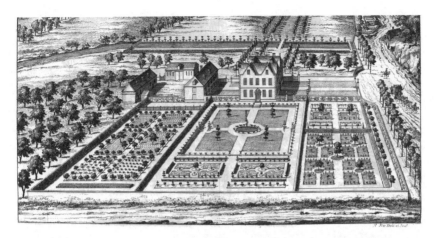

FIGURE 4.2   Detail of a view of Sevenhampton showing climbers, possibly fruit, and vegetables in the formal gardens (J. Kip and L. Knyff, *Britannia Illustrata*, 1707).

A significant improvement was in the development of glasshouses to provide winter protection to the recently introduced exotics. Fiennes comments on the pots of "fine orange citron and lemon trees in the square by the dining roome window." Citrus fruit was much coveted at this time and had long been imported from Portugal, but the British climate prevented citrus trees from being grown outside all year round, leading to the creation of glasshouses. John Evelyn was an innovator in this field, creating structures that were the forerunners of the ornamental orangeries and glasshouses of the eighteenth and nineteenth centuries. He has also been attributed with introducing the term "greenhouse" (greens being the newly introduced evergreen plants). Citrus fruit became a status symbol and orange and lemon trees could now be grown in pots and placed in formal areas of the garden during the summer. Evelyn, ever the pragmatist, enjoyed citrus seedlings as a salad, declaring that "[o]range seedlings impart an aromatic exceedingly grateful to the stomach."[9]

Women played an important role in creating and managing their estates. Mary, first Duchess of Beaufort, was one of the leading collectors of exotics during the late seventeenth century and took particular pride in her orangery where she produced "custard apples, bananas, aloes, cotton trees, cape figs, guavas and cacti."[10] Her collection was considered second only to that of Queen Mary at Hampton Court, such rivalries suggesting the heights of fashion that the new exotic introductions had reached, culminating in the elusive pineapple, the ultimate status symbol of the seventeenth- and eighteenth-century glasshouse. Mary was influential in designing the gardens at Badminton, having turned to the natural world as a relief from the melancholy she suffered during her life. Apart from her passion for exotics, she also ornamented the estate with a variety of animals such as rabbits, guinea pigs, and pheasants. The poultry yard was historically the domain of the lady of the house, as was the dairy, both valued not only as provision for the kitchen but also for their ornamental contribution to the aesthetics of the garden.

Other components of the self-sufficient estate were mentioned by Fiennes on her travels, the most significant perhaps being the deer park. At Woburn in Bedfordshire she noted:

> a fine park full of deer and wood ... there are very good stables and offices, laundry yard, etc; the Gardens are fine ... there is a seat up in a high tree that ascends from the green 50 steps, that commands the whole park round to see the deer hunted.[11]

Deer parks were the living larders of the great estates. Since medieval times a royal warrant was required to impark land and keep deer, and a deer park therefore became the ultimate status symbol of the landed classes, later to be adopted by the landscape gardeners of the eighteenth century for its aesthetic qualities. The original function of the park was to provide meat, in particular venison, although rabbits would have been harvested from the warrens especially constructed to protect them from predators and the cold British climate. The deer park also provided sport in the form of the hunt, which, as Fiennes points out, was enjoyed not only by the participants but also by the spectators who viewed the sport from a strategically placed platform or grandstand. Hunting involved many rituals, some seemingly bloody, as witnessed by Schellinks and recorded in his journal:

> On the 10th we saw a hart shot with a crossbow in the deer park of Sir Arnold Braems; everybody, especially the ladies, washed their hands in the warm blood, to get white hands. The hart was immediately gutted and cut up into quarters. On the 11th a venison pie and other dishes of the hart were on the menu.[12]

Washing hands in the blood of the quarry, as with most of the rituals, had its origins in the medieval period. Hunting evolved from training for warfare, exercising fundamental military skills such as horsemanship and the use of weapons. Concurrent with this it was associated with chivalry since hunting required the combination of qualities expected from a knight, such as courage, honor, and courtesy. This echoed the writings of the Greek soldier Xenophon who declared that hunting provided people with "health for their bodies, better sight and hearing and keeps them from growing old; it also educates, especially in things useful for war."[13] Traditionally, hunting occurred in royal forests, or chases, but also in the parks where deer coursing took place by the seventeenth century, primarily as a spectator sport. However, the principal purpose of the park was to contain the deer, a valuable and highly revered animal. Parks ranged in size from about one mile in circumference to ten miles for the royal parks. The pale, one of the major expenses of the park, usually consisted of a ditch and bank construction topped with an oak fence, designed to allow deer to jump in over the deer leaps, but not out. Parks also provided timber for building and wood for the fires. The trees were usually pollarded or coppiced, and those that have survived are now appreciated for their iconic status in the landscape.

As with other components of the self-sufficient estate, the deer park was appreciated for its aesthetic qualities. The word "paradise" has its origins in the Greek word *paradeisos*, meaning "royal (enclosed) park," which, as with the orchard, had connotations of earthly paradise and the Garden of Eden. One of the earliest parks in Britain was Henry I's park at Woodstock in Oxfordshire; it was a "pleasance" or park created for pleasure as well as utility, which by 1110 was enclosed by a stone wall and contained a menagerie of wild and exotic animals. Therefore, the concept of the park as a pleasure garden appears to have developed alongside its purpose as a living larder and as an arena for sport.

However, hunting contributed to the social divide in the country: the majority of the population were precluded from participating in the hunt and many suffered the penalties of flouting the Forest Laws that dictated who could hunt. Therefore, deer parks, the supreme status symbol of the aristocracy, were a target for the discontented anti-royalists during the Civil War, resulting in the destruction of many herds of deer.

Apart from royal parks and those of the wealthiest landowners, many smaller estates in the seventeen century had relinquished their deer parks due to the prohibitive cost of maintaining the park pale alone. Several were turned over to the more profitable rearing of sheep and cattle, as Robert Carew noted in his survey of Cornwall in 1602: "Deere leap over the pale to give the bullockes place."[14] Sir John Oglander ran a small estate at Nunwell on the Isle of Wight during the first half of the seventeenth century, and recorded his "Good Rules of Husbandry" in great detail, advising that one should:

> Have a small warren for some rabbits when thy friends come. Build a pigeon-house and fit up a fishpond or two that at all times thou mayst have provisions at hand. Pale in a place to breed or keep pheasants and partridges in.[15]

Even without large-scale herds it was possible to supply the household with meat and game throughout most of the year.

From these descriptions it is possible to build a picture of the self-supporting estate integrating pleasure and use, and it was this holistic approach to self-sufficiency that impressed Roger North, a Norfolk landowner, during a visit to the Duke of Beaufort's estate at Badminton in the 1680s. It was the inspiration behind his own, more modest, self-supporting estate at Rougham in Norfolk, which is well documented since North was a prolific writer on many subjects, including architecture and estate management. Having acquired the estate in 1691, he proceeded to remodel the house and equip the estate with the necessary offices such as a laundry house, dovecote, barns, stables, a brew house, and fish ponds, in which he showed a particular interest. In his *Discourse of Fish and Fishponds* (1713) he describes the ideal siting of a stew pond for practical and ornamental purposes:

> The peculiar use of these is to maintain fish for the daily use of your House and Friends, whereby you may with little Trouble, and at any Time, take out all or any Fish they contain; therefore it is good to place them in the same inclos'd Grounds near the chief Mansion House. Some Recess in a garden is very proper, because the Fish are fenc'd from Robbers, and your journey to them is short and easy, and your Eye will often be upon them, which will conduce to their being well kept, and they will be an ornament to the Walks.[16]

By the second half of the eighteenth century the most fashionable estates had abandoned the old-fashioned series of ponds in favor of naturalistic lakes to fit in with their newly landscaped parks. However, as North suggests, the fish ponds, as with all aspects of the self-sufficient estate, were required to contribute to the aesthetic appeal of the park. The dovecote was no exception, generally positioned close to the house to protect the pigeons from predatory hawks, as North recommends: "Woodlands harbour Hawkes, the desperate enimys of these poor birds that inhabite with us. And it is for that reason not to pitch houses too far from company."[17] This also reinforces the dovecote as a status symbol, the right to build one having traditionally been a manorial privilege. Pigeons provided feathers for pillows and dung as a fertilizer for the garden, their eggs would also have been eaten, and they had been prized since medieval times primarily for their flesh during the winter months when fresh meat would have been unavailable. By the eighteenth century improved winter fodder made it possible to stagger the slaughter of cattle and sheep, resulting in the decline of large-scale pigeon keeping. Despite this, dovecotes continued to be built as decorative features in the landscape, evoking the status they once conferred on the country estate.

Towards the end of the seventeenth century the expense of maintaining the formal garden contributed to its demise in favor of the landscape park, where aesthetics prevailed, inspired by scenes from classical antiquity. Apart from sporting pleasures such as shooting and fishing, food production was in the main contained within vast, walled kitchen gardens and the home farm, both ornamental in design and retaining their role as status symbols, certainly featuring on the visitors' tour of the park, yet generally concealed from view and divorced from the aesthetic aspects of the garden.

The Victorians continued to grow food for their households in these elaborate kitchen gardens with an increasing emphasis on the challenges of producing ever more exotic varieties, and encouraging crops to fruit out of season, now possible with the heating and irrigation systems that would have been installed in the glasshouses: strawberries in winter, for example. The industrial and technological revolution benefited not only the wealthy with their new glasshouses, but also the growing urban population, as food production became increasingly centralized. The railways were able to transport food greater distances than had previously been possible, and storage methods such as refrigeration and canning enabled food to be kept for a longer period of time. It was now possible to produce food on a more commercial scale, with many provisions being imported from abroad. Consequently, a greater variety of food became available. However, as a result the tradition of growing food at home began to decline.

This pattern continued into the twentieth century, interrupted only by the two world wars when "dig for victory" was the rallying cry to overcome the shortages of food supplies from abroad. Pleasure and aesthetics were not a priority during this period of self-sufficiency, the motivation being to feed the nation in order to win the war. However, the impact of this wartime push seemed to have a negative effect on the perception of "growing your own." In the postwar years people wanted to escape the toils from which they had so recently been liberated and enjoy their free time in more leisurely pursuits. Newly introduced intensive farming methods once again resulted in cheaper food, minimizing the need to work in the vegetable garden and freeing up a considerable amount of the household income to spend on non-essentials.

Despite these economic "improvements," the cultivation of fruit and vegetables has remained an obsession with many sections of society, and there has prevailed among a growing number of the population a desire to cultivate the land and "grow your own." The reasons for this are as varied as the people who practice it: for country dwellers, especially before the widespread availability of cars, the distance from shops has been a practical motivation, as have the economic benefits, while for many the quality in terms of freshness and flavor justifies the effort. Ethical and health issues such as food miles and chemical use have also led to a revival of interest in local food, and provenance is now an important consideration. Keeping livestock, in particular hens, is enjoying a resurgence in popularity, mostly for supplying eggs to the household, although the sight of attractively feathered birds animating the garden, together with the range of ornamental poultry houses available, echoes the aesthetic qualities of the historic poultry yards. A compelling motivation for many is a backlash against the overwhelming waste and consumerism of the late twentieth and early twenty-first centuries. For many, the notion of getting out of life what you put in can be translated quite literally into the garden. There have been a growing number of exponents of self-sufficiency, such as John Seymour who, in his *Complete Book of Self-Sufficiency* (1976), instructs the reader how to achieve their goal. These books reflect the same deeply ingrained urge to cultivate the land and "grow your own" as extolled by Roger North and his contemporaries 300 years earlier.

Self-sufficiency in the early twenty-first century has become a lifestyle choice although, with climate change predictions and a growing population, people may be increasingly encouraged to grow a proportion of their own food where possible. The pigeons, now bred purely for sport, may once again inhabit the dovecotes, flavor may dominate the choices of fruit and vegetables, rather than size and conformity, and a resurgence in orchard cultivation is already under way for "the benefit of all." However, it is unlikely that the utopian picture of self-sufficiency as epitomized by Schellinks in his account of Bridge Place will be seen again, since the financial demands for maintaining such an establishment eventually led to its demise. Nevertheless, the value of such estates to future generations is surely in their portrayal of the harmonious relationship between beauty and use.

NOTES

1   M. Exwood and H. L. Lehmann (eds.) *The Journal of William Schellinks' Travels in England 1661–1663* (London: Royal Historical Society, 1993), p. 43.
2   Cited in R. Bushnell, *Green Desire: Imagining Early Modern English Gardens* (Ithaca: Cornell University Press, 2003), p. 142.
3   Andrew Marvell, *The Poems of Andrew Marvell*, ed. G. A. Aitken (London: Lawrence and Bullen, 1892), pp. 83–4.
4   W. Lawson, *A New Orchard and Garden*, ed. M. Thick (Totnes: Prospect Books, 2003), p. 87.
5   Ibid., p. 87.
6   Cited in C. Quest-Ritson, *The English Garden: A Social History* (London: Penguin, 2001), p. 67.
7   Sir William Temple, *Upon the Gardens of Epicurus* (London: Pallas Athene, 2004), p. 38.
8   C. Morris (ed.) *The Illustrated Journeys of Celia Fiennes* (Exeter: Webb and Bower, 1982), p. 47.
9   Cited in J. Grigson, *Food with the Famous* (London: Grub Street, 1991), p. 17.
10 T. Mowl, *Historic Gardens of Gloucestershire* (Stroud: Tempus Publishing, 2002), p. 50.
11 Morris, *The Illustrated Journeys of Celia Fiennes*, p. 117.
12 Exwood and Lehmann, *The Journal of William Schellinks' Travels*, p. 43.
13 Rupert Isaacson, *The Wild Host* (London: Cassell, 2001), p. 42.
14 Cited in S. Lasdun, *The English Park* (London: André Deutsch, 1991), p. 40.
15 F. Bamford (ed.) *A Royalist's Notebook: The Commonplace Book of Sir John Oglander* (London: Constable, 1936), p. 203.
16 R. North, *A Discourse of Fish and Fishponds* (London, 1713), p. 21.
17 H. Colvin and J. Newman (eds.) *Of Building: Roger North's Writings on Architecture* (Oxford: Clarendon Press, 1981), p. 100.

PART II

FLOWER POWER

JO DAY[1]

CHAPTER 5

PLANTS, PRAYERS, AND POWER
The Story of the First Mediterranean Gardens

The shape of the garden is a square, and each side of it measures four plethra. It consists of vaulted terraces, raised one above another, and resting upon cube-shaped pillars. These are hollow and filled with earth to allow trees of the largest size to be planted. The pillars, the vaults, and the terraces are constructed of baked brick and asphalt. The ascent to the highest storey is by stairs, and at their side are water engines, by means of which persons, appointed expressly for the purpose, are continually employed in raising water from the Euphrates into the garden.

Strabo, *Geographica*[2]

This description is of the Hanging Gardens of Babylon, one of the seven wonders of the ancient world, and perhaps the most celebrated of all ancient gardens. However, they were following a long tradition of Near Eastern royal gardens, where well-watered parks filled with exotic plants and animals were created and used by powerful kings. Nor was the Near East the only place where gardens were important: Egyptian pharaohs incorporated them into their palaces, temples, and tombs from the Old Kingdom onwards, and there may even have been gardens in the palaces of Minoan Crete. In later times, the Roman peristyle gardens of Pompeii and the temple gardens and public parks (*gymnasia*) of Classical Greece were integral to society.

Such gardens were not simply pleasant places to spend time, they had other more symbolic roles in society. These deeper meanings, embedded in the soil and plants, and in the very act of garden creation, are the subject of this chapter. Our knowledge of these ancient gardens is based on a combination of archeological and textual evidence, with the earliest reference to gardens found in the third millennium BCE Sumerian epic of Gilgamesh. This chapter will use these complementary sources to explore the earliest gardens of Mesopotamia, Egypt, and Crete. The roles of plants and gardens in creating and maintaining status, and their links to ritual practices and mythological beliefs, emerge as key underlying themes in all three regions. It is important to bear in mind, however, that the gardens considered here are those of the elite, of kings and high ranking officials, and even of gods. This is not to say that those at the opposite end of the social spectrum did not have gardens; indeed, tending plants as a source of food and pleasure is an ancient and worldwide practice. However, it is the gardens of the elite which have been the focus of most archeological work, as well as the subject of inscriptions and literature, hence there is currently a far greater body of knowledge to draw upon.

Finding out about ancient gardens is a challenge; after all, the very material out of which gardens are constructed (soil) is that which archeologists dig through in the search for less ephemeral remains of the past. Indeed, the definition of a garden is problematic in itself and culturally determined. For this essay, a garden is understood as a bounded area filled with plants which are deliberately brought there or selected by humans, and which require human supervision to ensure their ongoing survival. Despite these material and semantic difficulties, it is still possible to find traces of gardens through careful excavation. Planting patterns can be discovered by identifing soil changes or root cavities, most famously illustrated by the work of Jashemski at Pompeii.[3] Boundaries, water courses, pavilions, and flower pots also all help to indicate the presence of a garden. Paleobotanical studies can be of assistance in recreating the flora which once lived in these gardens, but it is not always possible to conclude with any certainty that the identified species were actually planted in the garden. Problems include the fact that pollen is carried on the wind from miles around, seeds are eaten by wildlife and excreted in other places, and many plant parts are simply too soft to survive centuries in the ground. Fortunately, in literate societies such as Egypt and the Near East, as well as the Classical world, texts can tell us about the plants grown in gardens as well as the reasons for this choice of species. Iconographical studies also help: Egyptian paintings often illustrate

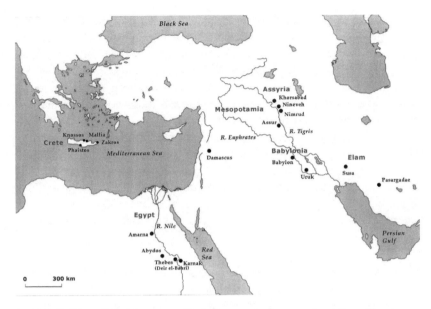

FIGURE 5.1   Map of the eastern Mediterranean in the second and first millennia BCE.

gardens, while in the Near East the king's garden or park was a suitable subject for sculptural programs.

The region of Mesopotamia, lying between the Tigris and Euphrates Rivers, was home to some of the earliest complex civilizations of the world (figure 5.1). Here the Sumerians, in the south, and the Akkadians further north, gradually developed into the Babylonian and Assyrian empires which would dominate the Near East for much of the second and first millennia BCE. Ambitious rulers carried out great building projects at cities whose names still seize the imagination – Nineveh, Nimrud, and Babylon – and left us annals explaining their deeds. The most famous gardens of the ancient Near East are, of course, the Hanging Gardens of Babylon. Known primarily through later classical texts, physical traces have yet to be discovered despite extensive excavations at Babylon. Ancient descriptions include details of the engineering feats required to create a terraced garden on an artificial hill and then provide it with a water supply. Recent research, however, has suggested that in fact it was not made by King Nebuchadnezzar II in Babylon, as tradition records, but rather by Sennacherib (ruled 704–681 BCE) at his "Palace without Rival" at Nineveh.[4] Certainly, Sennacherib boasted of his invention of an ingenious water-screw device which brought water from the river to his new gardens. Wherever they were located, these gardens were supposedly a gesture of love by the king for his Persian wife/concubine, who was longing for the mountaineous meadows of her homeland. Such a project speaks volumes of the king's power, both over his subjects, who constructed and maintained the gardens, and also over the natural world, which he was seen to be controlling.

These semi-mythical gardens are part of a long tradition of garden and park creation by Eastern rulers. Both courtyard gardens within palaces, as well as large parks on the outskirts of cities, were popular projects for rulers. An inscription from the reign of the Middle Assyrian King Tiglath-Pileser I (1114–1076 BCE) records that he brought back foreign trees and plants from military campaigns and established a garden at his capital city:

> I took cedar, box tree, Kanish oak from the lands over which I had gained dominion – such trees which none among previous kings, my forefathers, had ever planted – and I planted [them] in the orchards of my land. I took rare orchard fruit which is not found in my land [and therewith] filled the orchards of Assyria.[5]

Neo-Assyrian rulers followed this lead, and creating new gardens became a feature of their rule. Indeed, collecting exotic materials, including plants, has been shown to be a consistent motif in the construction of royal identity in Mesopotamia. Ashurnasirpal II (883–859 BCE) established a new capital at Kalhu (modern Nimrud) and built a great garden on the banks of the Tigris: "From lands I travelled and hills I traversed the trees and seeds I noticed [and collected]... The canal water came flowing down from above the gardens: the paths [are full] of scent; the waterfalls [glisten] like the stars of heaven in the garden of pleasure."[6] Sennacherib, too, established a new capital, at Nineveh, with a variety of gardens, including "fruit-bearing trees of the hills and all lands, all the aromatics of Syria," a game park, and an artificial swamp.[7] Relief sculptures from Nineveh support his claims, showing various animals amid reeds. Reliefs from the time of Sennacherib's father, Sargon II, at Dur-Sharrukin (Khorsabad), also depict royal gardens with exotic trees, lakes, and little kiosks, showing how the king "had all the spices of the land of the Hittites and all the vegetation from their mountains planted close to each other."[8] A particularly well-known sculpture from Nineveh from the seventh century BCE, now in the British Museum, shows King

Ashurbanipal and his queen apparently relaxing in a garden, surrounded by grape vines, date palms, and conifers, while servants play music and gently fan the royal couple.

All of this inscriptional and iconographic evidence demonstrates that creating and using gardens and parks were essential elements in Near Eastern kingship from the second millennium BCE onwards. Certainly, they would have been pleasant places to pass the time, enjoying the fragrant and beautiful plants, pausing in the shade below the tall trees, resting in the kiosks to admire the views, and even hunting animals in the larger parks. Indeed, the later Persian word *pairidaeza*, which referred to Eastern royal hunting parks such as that of Cyrus the Great at Pasargadae, remains in use today as "paradise," via the Greek *paradeisos*, and is now synonymous with gardens of great abundance and beauty. However, these early Eastern gardens were more than locations for recreation, and should be understood as tangible representations of royal power. On one level, simply having access to the resources to create and maintain such gardens sends clear messages. Land is removed from potential food production or housing, irrigation must be provided, and trained staff are required to ensure the garden thrives. Professional gardeners did in fact exist in ancient Mesopotamia, as attested by records of payments and work done. Pollinating the date palms which grew on the outskirts of many cities was one of their key responsibilities. These gardeners were highly skilled and valued accordingly, as their job of ensuring the health of the precious plants in their care reflected the power of the king himself to sustain prosperity in the land. It should also be remembered that access to such royal gardens was restricted, a practice mirrored in more recent times at such places as Versailles, where pleasure grounds were reserved for the royal family and invited guests only. The great unwashed beyond the boundaries can only wonder at what lies within, and thus the belief in the garden as a place of marvels is intensified.

The carved stone relief of Ashurbanipal and his queen in the garden underlines such statements of power when considered more carefully. On the table next to the king lie a bow, quiver, and sword, all of which can be stylistically identified as Babylonian or Elamite, while hanging in the tree further left is the severed head of the defeated Elamite king. Whether a depiction of a real garden, or a sculptural creation, it is replete with signs of "the might of kingship,"[9] and importantly the garden is perceived as a suitable locus for such display. The practice of receiving visitors in the garden meant that it was a prime location for presenting a carefully orchestrated impression of authority. The plants themselves are also key elements in this semiotic barrage. Frequently they are listed in the annals as tribute or among the spoils of war, equally as important as the more traditional booty of metals and precious stones, slaves, grain, and exotic animals. Captured plants can be seen as a metaphor for military victory, uprooted from their homeland and then forced to grow in distant lands. The king's power extends not just over the defeated peoples, but over the very fruits of their homeland. Indeed, the destruction of an enemy's gardens was often recorded by Assyrian kings, such as that by Shalmaneser III at Damascus and Ashurbanipal at Susa. Other inscriptions carefully itemize the species of plants brought home by the triumphant king. Ashurnasirpal II's garden at Nimrud included cedar, cypress, pine, juniper, myrtle, almond, date palm, ebony, rosewood, olive, oak, tamarisk, terebinth, willow, ash, fir, pomegranate, pear, quince, fig, and grapevine. Sennacherib planted "fruit-bearing trees of the hills and all lands, all the aromatics of Hatti … every type of wild vine and exotic fruit tree, aromatics, olive trees," as well as "trees bearing wool," now thought to be cotton.[10] Following Helms's ideas, such lists function to show the king's knowledge of and control over distant domains, thus legitimizing and enhancing his social status.[11] A royal garden could even become a microcosm of the world brought under Assyrian control, as in the case of Sennacherib who recreated the specific environments of the places he had conquered.

Two points should be noted here. Firstly, there is a preponderance of trees mentioned in all the inscriptions as well as carved in reliefs. Few species of tree are native to central and southern Iraq, so importing them, as saplings or seed, was the only way actually to grow a variety of trees in a garden or park. Many trees which grew in the king's garden simply could not have survived anywhere else in Mesopotamia and would be seen as novelties or wonders. Secondly, many of these trees and plants were not only beautiful to view but useful too, providing fruits, nuts, wood, or fragrant materials. The smell of the blossoms on trees, as well as furniture made from fragrant woods like cedar and pine, and also plants which provided incense, all played a part in the somatic experience of these royal gardens. Although scents of the past are intangible today, we know that this was another important aspect of ancient gardens. Indeed, one of the tasks of the king was to please the senses of the gods by collecting exotic new materials which could then be offered to them. This concept of general utility of plants was key in the garden of the Babylonian ruler Marduk-apla-iddina II, which was planted with beds of culinary and medicinal herbs. The idea of a royal garden which was both functional and beautiful recurs in Book 7 of Homer's *Odyssey*, where the magical gardens of Alcinous are described, filled with pears, pomegranates, apples, figs, olives, grapes, and herbs or vegetables. Interestingly, it has recently been suggested that this description was influenced by Near Eastern practices and royal ideology, or at least by Archaic Greek stereotypes of Assyrian palaces.[12]

Gardens in the ancient Near East were also associated with religious practices and myths, although the evidence for this is less abundant. Offerings for deities seem to have been produced in at least some of them, such as for the god Marduk from Nebuchadnezzar's garden. Sennacherib constructed a grove or orchard at the main temple of Assur; this has been identified by the archeological remains of planting holes for trees which surround the temple precinct and also occur within the inner courtyard. It is likely that such temple gardens were the source of the essential aromatic substances which often accompanied Assyrian and Babylonian rituals; myrrh, herbs, and aromatic woods like juniper, cedar, and cypress could all be grown there. Indeed, the concept of "feeding" or communicating with the gods via sweet scents is common to many societies, including contemporary use in Orthodox and Catholic churches. Iconography suggesting pollination of date palms by *apkallus* (protective deities) may be indicative of actual rituals which incorporated such a hands-on element, perhaps performed by the king symbolically to ensure the prosperity of his realm. The luxuriant floral iconography of the reliefs of the king's gardens emphasizes this trope of fertility. Yet we know little for certain about the staging of rituals in, or associated with, gardens in Mesopotamia. However, with many ceremonies concerned with the prosperity and abundance of the land, and plants such as the date palm linked to fertility and the goddess Ishtar, it is likely that the gardens of these powerful kings were the location for the performance of ceremonies both relating to and involving the plant world.

Ritual use of gardens was however essential in Egyptian religion. Whether the garden was associated with a temple, tomb, or royal palace, it was often a location for performance and always replete with symbolism. Egypt (figure 5.1) had been under the control of kings (pharaohs) since the third millennium BCE, the Old Kingdom ushering in the first in a long line of dynastic rulers. As in the Near East, these rulers were responsible for the prosperity of their kingdom, at the heart of which was the annual flooding of the Nile river. It was this river which made possible the variety of Egyptian gardens, often linked to the life-giving water by canals and irrigation channels, or watered with a lever and bucket

FIGURE 5.2   Egyptian tomb painting of Nebamun's garden and pool. © Trustees of the British Museum.

device known as a *shaduf*. The types of plants grown in these gardens were deliberately selected for their links with deities or mythological incidents. Sycamore figs were synonymous with the goddess Hathor and supposedly had shaded the tomb of Osiris, while their wood was used for royal coffins. Water lilies were also common, due to the prominence of this plant in the various Egyptian cosmogonies (stories about the origins of the gods and the world), and many other trees and flowers held similar mythic meanings. We know which species of plants were grown in Egyptian gardens thanks to both texts and tomb paintings, where depictions of gardens had to survive, alongside their owner, for eternity (figure 5.2). For example, Ineni, an official in the reign of Thutmose I (1504–1492 BCE), not only had his garden painted in his tomb, but the number of each species he planted was listed there: 73 sycamores, 31 persea, 170 date palm, 120 doum palm, 5 fig, 2 moringa, 5 pomegranate, 16 carob,

5 garland thorn, 1 argun palm, 8 willow, 10 tamarisk, 2 myrtle, 5 acacia, 12 vines, and 5 other unidentified types.[13]

These painted tomb gardens were for the soul of the dead, a place for them to find rest, shade, and refreshment, while the actual real garden surrounding the tomb was for the living relatives and priests to perform funerary ceremonies and rites of remembrance. Maintaining the link with myth, royal tombs were modeled upon that of Osiris (a mound with tamarisks growing on it), and so a garden or grove of trees became a key element in royal burial sites. Seti I, for example, stressed this link with Osiris and buried his tomb at Abydos under a huge mound surrounded by conifers and tamarisks. A grove can also be recreated at the funerary complex of Mentuhotep II at Deir el-Bahri, where planting pits and wood fragments indicate that sycamore, fig, and tamarisk formed an avenue. This whole area on both the east and west banks of the Nile at Thebes was the location of numerous funerary temples and royal tombs and a focal point of Egyptian religion for centuries. By the time of the New Kingdom, ceremonial pathways leading from the temples down to the river, and passing through gardens en route, were standard. At important festivals the statues of the gods or pharaohs were carried down these paths onto boats to be rowed between the city of the dead on the west bank and the Karnak temples on the east. Quays linked the gardens to the Nile, and navigable lakes could also be constructed as part of the royal funerary complexes and were used in rituals. On the other hand, private tomb gardens might simply include a small pool which could provide flowers for offerings.

Gardens also belonged to temples, and their plants were grown specifically as offerings for the deity of that temple: lettuces were cultivated to offer to Min, god of fertility, their milky sap reminiscent of semen. Thutmose III (1479–1425 BCE) created a new garden for the god Amun at Karnak "in order to present to him vegetables and all beautiful flowers" and Rameses III (1184–1153 BCE) offered 3,410 bouquets of water lily at the temple of Amun.[14] Some ceremonies were based around picking the flowers or fruits for the deities. As with Near Eastern gardens, fragrance was very important and certain plants were selected for the perfumed oils or incense they could provide. Hatshepsut, the New Kingdom female pharaoh (1473–1458 BCE), sent an expedition south to the land of Punt, charged with bringing back to Egypt precious 'ntyw incense trees. This expedition, prominently depicted on the walls of her funerary temple at Deir el-Bahri, can be seen as another example of the botanical imperialism practiced by ancient rulers. Egypt would no longer have to rely on trade with Punt for incense, and Hatshepsut's authority is reflected in this reordering of nature. These saplings were apparently planted beside a temple to Amun on arrival in Egypt. However, they may not have thrived; during the reigns of Thutmose III and Amenhotep II (1427–1400 BCE) expeditions also returned with living *'ntyw* trees. One possible reason for their failure to flourish in Egypt is that the Puntites deliberately gave Egyptians inferior trees and/or inadequate care instructions in order to preserve their hold on this lucrative trade. Thutmose III, a pharaoh who embarked on numerous military campaigns, had depictions of exotic and fantastical plants carved onto the walls of the Sun Rooms in the Festival Temple at Karnak, giving rise to its modern name of the "Botanical Garden." An accompanying inscription notes that they were "plants that His Majesty has found in the land of Retenu" (Syria). In this instance, rather than living plants, these stone-carved ones will serve as a permanent tribute to the god Amun: "My majesty hath done this from a desire to put them before my father Amun, in this great temple of Amun, as a memorial forever and ever."[15] However, they are not just offerings to a god but eternal reminders of a pharaoh's prowess and military conquests, as well as a physical expression of his knowledge of lands overseas.

Moving across the Mediterranean to the Aegean, the second millennium BCE Bronze Age civilization of Crete is also considered to have created elite gardens. The Minoans, named by the British archeologist Sir Arthur Evans after the mythical King Minos, nowadays are well known for their so-called "palaces." These large architectural complexes, initially believed to be the homes of royal families (such as Minos at Knossos), are now thought to have been multifunctional. Based on the archeological evidence, they supported a range of activities including large-scale food storage, ritual or ceremonial activity, manufacturing of pottery and other crafts, trade, administration, and feasting, and perhaps served as residences also. That they were closely linked to elites in society is also suggested, both by their scale in comparison to other Minoan settlements and buildings, and by the richness of the material found in them. Polychrome frescoes, elaborate ceramics, ivory, precious stones, metals, and Linear A (the untranslated writing system of Minoan Crete) all indicate that the people using these complexes were at the upper end of a social hierarchy. Of particular relevance here is that in each of the palaces, as well as a number of other elite buildings, locations have been identified by scholars as gardens.

At Knossos, the largest of the palaces, a garden terrace was suggested to the east of the Hall of the Double Axes, while two garden areas were identified at Phaistos, in southern Crete, one in the north of the palace and the other to the east. Mallia, a palace on the north coast, features a potential garden stretching beyond a portico towards the north, and the palace in the far east of the island, Zakros, was adjacent to gardens spreading across terraces on the hills north of the entrance. Further locations across the island have been proposed for other Minoan gardens.[16] Interestingly, a rocky outcrop which was incorporated into the palace at Phaistos has been interpreted by one scholar as a rock garden, the small cavities in the rock identified as holes for bulbous plants.[17] In iconography, too, there are hints that gardens may have played a role in Minoan social and religious identity. Frescoes such as that at Amnisos have been interpreted by some as depicting a sacred garden, while wall paintings like the Birds and Monkeys scene from the House of the Frescoes at Knossos or the Adorant from Ayia Triadha have also been suggested to show tamed nature or gardens. Moreover, Minoan art displays a very real interest in the natural world, with many representations of flowers and trees on frescoes, ceramics, and other media.

It seems therefore that the Minoans, like the Egyptians and the Near Eastern civilizations, may have incorporated gardens into their monumental elite architecture. However, the role of gardens in Minoan life is more difficult to assess than for the other societies because our understanding of their beliefs has been hampered by the lack of texts, in contrast to Egypt and the Near East. The language of Linear A has not been deciphered, leaving us without the actual words and thoughts of the Minoans themselves. Physical remains of mountain shrines (peak sanctuaries), sacred caves, potential areas for ritual within palaces (such as the sunken lustral basins, dark pillar crypts, theatral areas, and courtyards), frescoes of offerings and processions, and vessels with libation functions, suggest that ritual practice was deeply embedded in Minoan society. Gardens may well have been the setting for rituals, as they were so often in Egypt. Exotic or foreign species of plant could also have played a role in defining status; iconography demonstrates a knowledge of non-indigenous plants such as papyrus, date palms, and lotus. If this imagery reflects actual plants rather than iconographic transfer, we should imagine a late Bronze Age Aegean where exotic plants were exchanged or traded in a similar way to other luxury goods, and valued for their roles in creating and maintaining hierarchy. However, undisputed evidence for Minoan gardens remains elusive, and while they do fit in rather well with academic traditions of a nature-loving (or even nature-worshipping) and ritually oriented society, not all scholars would accept their existence.

Pulling together the main themes emerging from this discussion about gardens in three ancient Mediterranean civilizations, some key points emerge. It is indisputable that the earliest gardens of the elite were intimately associated with status. At the most basic level, like other large-scale building projects, the gardens of rulers required skilled manpower to create and to maintain. Trained workers were needed to ensure that the relatively fragile plants survived, and while we do not know of Minoan gardeners, in both Egypt and Mesopotamia such a job did exist from a very early date. Ensuring that a garden thrived in the relatively dry lands of Egypt, Assyria, and Crete also required advanced hydraulic engineering. In fact, all three civilizations were adept at providing water, whether through managing the rivers, creating mechanical aids, or maximizing the benefits of rainfall. A successful garden was both a reflection of the authority of the ruler over the natural world and a justification of their right to rule.

Gardens can also be seen as opportunities to showcase military prowess, places to plant the captured spoils. We should not be surprised that plants were deemed worthy booty; one only need think of the espionage and smuggling which surrounded cinchona bark, famed for its antimalarial properties, or the tulipomania of the seventeenth-century Netherlands. This botanical imperialism was especially a feature of Assyrian monarchs, who liked to project an image of global conqueror. But who were the audience for these plants? Apart from the gods, the gardens were not just for the use of the ruler; they were also a place to receive foreign ambassadors and conduct other business. So while there were gardens for the king and his family like those of Akhenaten at Amarna, or at Babylon, they were not private spaces. In fact, they were part of an elaborate presentation of ideal kingship, of a leader and a warrior who has traveled to distant lands, overthrown all foes, and returned home safely, with souvenirs. This ties in with the "marvel effect" of exotic species. At a time when the majority of people's experience of plants was limited to those found locally, exotic species would have aroused interest. If these plants provided fruits, scented resins, or other useful products, this element of wonder was increased. By creating and using such gardens, the elite could be seen as controlling wondrous things and thus placing themselves on a different social plane to the wider community. Plants therefore should be seen as another form of prestige artifact, enhancing status within the community and contributing to the formation of hierarchies.

The garden as a setting for ritual and performance is the other major theme emerging from this discussion. Plants and their products were used for offerings to deities; indeed, it has been suggested that such rituals may have contributed to the initial domestication of many species of plant.[18] But the garden was also a setting for ritual, a place to encounter deities and for interaction between worlds. Surrounded by lush plant life, some of which had mythic importance, and maybe foreign species too, the magical element of rituals was enhanced. If real plants did not grow, they could always be painted or carved, as in the decoration of the Maru-Aten at Amarna, the "Botanical Garden" at Karnak, or Minoan frescoes. This had the advantage of being permanent, allowing fantasy to flourish, as is the case with some of the invented hybrid plants in the "Botanical Garden."

A final few words must be added on the potential interconnections between these three regions. There is no doubt that throughout the second and first millennia BCE the societies of the Aegean and Levant were in contact with one another. Trade, military exploits, diplomatic ventures, artists and craftsmen, and even adventurers contributed to the spreading of goods and ideas. While it would be injudicious to suggest that the concept of "garden" as a political and religious tool emerged in one of these places before spreading further afield, it would be equally shortsighted to imagine that there was absolutely no transfer of garden ideology or practices. Indeed, at a basic level, a common philosophy about the roles of a garden in society does seem to have been shared by elites across the eastern Mediterranean, and multiple levels of social power were displayed and enacted within the ancient garden walls.

NOTES

1 Thanks are due to Donncha O'Rourke, Heather Graybehl, and Dan O'Brien for their support and encouragement during the writing of this essay, and to my colleagues at NUI Galway.

2 *The Geography of Strabo*, trans. H. Hamilton and W. Falconer (London: Henry G. Bohn, 1857), 16.1.5.

3 W. Jashemski, *The Gardens of Pompeii, Herculaneum and the Villas Destroyed by Vesuvius* (New Rochelle: Caratzas, 1979).

4 S. Dalley, "Nineveh, Babylon and the Hanging Gardens: Cuneiform and the Classical Sources Reconciled," *Iraq* 56 (1994): 45–58; "Ancient Mesopotamian Gardens and the Identification of the Hanging Gardens of Babylon Resolved," *Garden History* 21, 1 (1993): 1–13.

5 A. Kuhrt, *The Ancient Near East c. 3000–330 BC* (London: Routledge, 1995), p. 310.

6   D. Wiseman, "Mesopotamian gardens," *Anatolian Studies* 33 (1983): 137–44.

7   Ibid., p. 138.

8   M. Carroll, *Earthly Paradises: Ancient Gardens in History and Archaeology* (London: British Museum Press, 2003), p. 44.

9   P. Albenda, "Landscape Reliefs in the Bit-Hilani of Ashurbanipal (Part II)," *Bulletin of the American Schools of Oriental Research* 225 (1977): 29–48; see also P. Albenda, "Grapevines in Ashurbanipal's Garden," *Bulletin of the American Schools of Oriental Research* 215 (1974): 5–17.

10 Wiseman, "Mesopotamian Gardens," p. 138.

11 M. Helms, *Ulysses' Sail: An Ethnographic Odyssey of Power, Knowledge, and Geographical Distance* (Princeton: Princeton University Press, 1988).

12 E. Cook, "Near Eastern Sources for the Palace of Alkinoos," *American Journal of Archaeology* 108 (2004): 43–77.

13 L. Manniche, *An Ancient Egyptian Herbal* (London: British Museum Press, 1989), p. 10.

14 A. Wilkinson, *The Garden in Ancient Egypt* (London: Rubicon Press, 1998), p. 140; Manniche, *An Ancient Egyptian Herbal*, p. 127.

15 R. Schwaller de Lubicz, *The Temples of Karnak* (London: Thames and Hudson, 1999), pp. 636–8.

16 For detailed references to all these gardens, see J. Day, "Flower-Lovers? Reconsidering the Gardens of Minoan Crete," in J.-P. Morel, J. Juan, and J. Matamala (eds.) *The Archeology of Crop Fields and Gardens* (Bari: Edipuglia, 2006), pp. 189–95.

17 M. Shaw, "The Aegean Garden," *American Journal of Archaeology* 97 (1993): 661–85.

18 J. Goody, *The Culture of Flowers* (Cambridge: Cambridge University Press, 1993), p. 28.

MICHAEL MOSS[1]

CHAPTER 6

BRUSSELS SPROUTS AND EMPIRE

Putting Down Roots

Growing and eating vegetables have long antecedents in the United Kingdom that stretch back at least to medieval times, and by the middle of the nineteenth century there was a well-recognized list of what might be thought of as British vegetables. By then the Brussels sprout had become an essential ingredient of the winter diet, especially the Victorian Christmas dinner, accompanying roast beef, Yorkshire pudding, roast potatoes, and horseradish sauce; symbols, as it were, of being British. Christmas dinner, even in the heat of the tropics, would be unthinkable without Brussels sprouts. It was therefore perhaps only to be expected that the British should have carried such culinary reminders of their home and identity with them to the countries of the Empire, which by the end of the nineteenth century spanned the globe. Brussels sprouts, like other brassicas, are vegetables of temperate climes and are challenging, if not impossible, to grow in the tropics. However A. J. Jex-Blake in *Gardening in East Africa*, which was compiled by members of the Kenya Horticultural Society and of the Kenya, Uganda and Tanganyika Civil Services (1934), praised Brussels sprouts as "[m]ost useful, as it is the longest standing of all vegetable crops here, and with constant picking and attention can be induced to last at the higher altitude up to a year."[2] W. Gollan in his *The Indian Vegetable Garden* (1892) described the Brussels sprout as "a popular and much esteemed vegetable and worthy of a place in the garden";[3] while Milsum and Grist in their *Vegetable Gardening in Malaya* (1941) noted ruefully: "Brussels sprouts and savoys are not ordinarily grown and little is known regarding their possibility."[4] From our contemporary perspective, where we have come to eat vegetables from around the world, such preoccupation with Brussels sprouts seems strange; but that is to fail to understand the mentality of Empire.

Arthur Crosby has argued that European plants and animals were critical to the success of the colonial project, creating what he calls "new Europes."[5] As anyone who has visited New Zealand knows, there is an immediate impression of going all that way from here to here. Charles and Caroline Carlton in their study of *The Significance of Gardens in British India* state boldly that "gardens emerged as a critical symbol of British control. Gardens were a symbol of home, places where the British would surround themselves with a natural world that was distinctly British."[6] It may seem odd that flowers and vegetables should be tropes of Empire rather than the Union Jack or the Queen, but the historian John Mackenzie reminds us that from the late eighteenth century "possession of Empire was significant in a fuzzy sense of Britishness."[7] In contrast to the metropolitan culture of much of the United Kingdom, the Empire was dominated by "home and hearth," imbued with the sort of imagined rural idyll to be found the length and breadth of Britain and Ireland. The philosopher David Cooper translates this into gardening as an "epiphany" or manifestation prompted by its apparent simplicity and familiarity.[8] This helps us to think of the imperial garden not only as a metaphor for home but a literal way of putting down roots. Sir George Birdwood, at the time an official in the India Office, in his foreword to Donald McDonald's *English Vegetables & Flowers in India & Ceylon* (1890), makes this explicit when he observes that the settlers "render the surrounds of their bungalows or other dwellings with English flowers and plants."[9] It is possible to conceive how this might play out in the flower garden where individual plants could be carefully cosseted in the conservatory or on the veranda; it is much more difficult to visualize how the common vegetables of the British garden might prosper in the cold of central Canada or on the hot plains of India.

There is a wealth of literature about gardening in the colonies and the Empire designed to inform the would-be horticulturalist in a foreign land. The most striking impression of all this literature irrespective of the region of the world or even date is the overwhelming predominance of vegetables that were familiar at home. Beetroot, broad beans, Brussels sprouts, peas, and runner beans abound. W. J. Tutcher's advice in

Gardening for Hong Kong, first published in 1906 and republished as late as 1964, opens with the report that "[w]atercress found on the banks and streams in England and Scotland survives our tropical summer."[10] Edith Cuthell in her book *My Garden City in the City of Gardens* published in 1895 describes sitting down to Christmas dinners to "sup of tomatoes from our own garden from English seed, also French beans and new peas, *not* the tinned article which pervade Indian dinner parties."[11] The irony that the beans were French seems lost on her, but there could be no better expression of the feast of an epiphany of Britishness. Andrew Thomas Jaffrey's *Hints to the Amateur Gardeners of South India* of 1858 includes a section entitled "English Kitchen Garden Vegetables, Their Cultivation, Uses, etc.,"[12] while McDonald's book of 1890 opens: "to make our great Eastern possessions their home for a period extending, more or less, over a number of years, and are desirous, so far as is possible, to cultivate vegetables, flowers, bulbs, roses and fruits, as had been their custom in England."[13]

Except in the most temperate parts of the world, such as New Zealand, the western seaboard of Canada, and the highlands of India, Malaya, and east Africa, such ambitions to cultivate European vegetables were not without their challenges and frustrations. Andrew Thomas Jaffrey confessed that "cultivation of vegetables on the plains is a work beset with many difficulties," and added unhelpfully: "I have little to boast of which could be called into action successfully to combat such an *anti-horticultural climate* if I may so call it as the Carnatic."[14] Robert Riddell in the section on "Directions for Cultivating European Vegetables etc." in his very popular *Indian Domestic Economy* of 1860 lamented that parsnips were very difficult to grow "as it does not often happen that the seeds come up." G. T. F. B. Speede in his *New Indian Gardener* of 1848 suggested that if hotbeds were "more extensively used, not only should we not hear of so many failures of seed, but we might, even in the plains of Bengal, Coromundel etc., succeed in raising seeds from plants, thus acclimated, of most European vegetables and flowers."[15] Mrs. E. D. Butler in her *Gardening for Amateurs in Malaya* of 1934 regretted that "[u]nfortunately no kind of lettuce will grow to its proper size and produce good 'heart' in the lowlands in Malaya," which, given the heat, seems hardly surprising.[16] Likewise David Tannock in his *Manual of Gardening in New Zealand* of 1916, writing of Brussels sprouts, warned: "It is a rather difficult matter to get them in a dry, hot season, as the dryness of the atmosphere tends to make them sprout open."[17] Lieutenant W. H. Lowther, writing from Feerozpore (now Firozpur) in the Punjab in 1851, commented: "This is the worst station of all India for the culture of strawberries, whole beds often perish at once without any perceptible cause." Although he could report that "peas never were so successful, everyone is vigorous and grows strong" and that capsicums were "very fruitful," he noted that Cape gooseberry was "a failure," lettuce and endive were "backward," tomatoes were "dried up," runner beans weakened by "hot winds," and Brussels sprouts did well "last year only."[18]

The explanation advanced for this preoccupation with vegetables that were familiar at home was not simply to recreate a home from home, but because they were thought to be better and more nutritious than their Indian counterparts, for example, carrots, peas, and onions. The section "Our Garden" in *Curry & Rice* by George Atkinson of 1858 includes: "Then there are the melons and the cucumbers, and there are strawberry-beds and the celery, and the spinach and the cabbage and lettuces and potatoes. Then there are fifty different native vegetables."[19] India was unusual in that there was a long tradition not just of gardening but of growing a wide range of vegetables, many of which were unknown to British gardeners and whose method of cultivation was very different from the ordered regimented rows of the British vegetable plot. Speede criticized the Hindu mali or gardener for growing "with a pride an immense drumhead," when "you would prefer a small close York, or the delicate Savoy" cabbage. He grudgingly admitted that the native pea, *Pisum arvense desee* or *Huraoo mutur*, "may be sown if desired, which is questionable for they are tough skinned and deficient in flavour."[20] The Reverend Thomas Firminger's popular *Gardening Manual for Bengal and Upper India* of 1864 included some native vegetables with the qualification: "It is only on rare occasions that these prove acceptable where European vegetables can be obtained, though welcome as a substitute where they cannot." He condemned sag (red spinach) as "to my taste a most insipid vegetable, half acceptable even when nothing else in way of green vegetables is to be had." He praised the Mukum-seem (smo), *Canavalia gladiator*, as "about the nicest of all native vegetables, little if anything inferior to French beans."[21] Lieutenant Frederick Pogson in the section on vegetables in his *Indian Gardening* of 1872 was adamant that "the vegetables of Europe and America were favoured for their superiority, succulence, flavour, nutrition and restorative power."[22] Major J. Clarke, deputy commissioner at Shaikhoopoora in the Punjab, reported that when he arrived at the station the only vegetables to be had were onions, garlic, pumpkins, and two kinds of local cucumbers.[23]

There may be some truth in the claim that vegetables from home were better than their Indian counterparts. By the mid-nineteenth century European vegetables had been bred selectively for over a hundred years and distinct varieties for different seasons, palates, and purposes were well established. Such developments were an outcome of improvements in European agriculture which were described as "scientific" and in the United Kingdom were bound up with Whig and Enlightenment ideas of progress. In the colonies progress and improvement reinforced the widely held belief in British superiority. This was often interpreted as the transformation of the local population into what the politician and historian Thomas Babington Macaulay quaintly dubbed in his minute on education in India of 1835 "Brown Englishmen." Backwardness in vegetable production was largely a matter of poor cultivation rather than unreliable seed, just as it was at home. W. G. Hay castigated the people in his district of Kooloo in the Himalayas as "particularly indolent and lazy" when they would not "take the trouble" to plant the potatoes he had introduced.[24] Speede wrote of "the simple Hindoo mallee" and thought it not surprising that in the bazaars "we have, what we have."[25] While Lieutenant Pogson admitted that the British onion came from India, he considered its "cultivation poorly understood" and complained that the mali harvested the large varieties well before they had matured.[26] Education was a means of raising standards or as Sir George Birdwood, echoing Macaulay, put it in his introduction to McDonald's book: "they too are becoming people trained by ourselves to follow acts and adopt that new national life that we ourselves have called into being." In his view, learning to garden would exercise a "refining influence over their lives."[27]

Such moral virtue with no concern for any practical outcome is shared by John Updike, who reflects in his poem "Hoeing": "there is no knowing how many souls have been formed by this simple exercise ... Ignorant the wise boy who has never rendered thus the world fecunder."[28] The philosopher David Cooper, drawing on the ideas of "dynamic" engagement of both Heidegger and Merleau-Ponty, explains this higher purpose when he argues that "certain garden practices necessarily induce virtues."[29] This may well have been what Birdwood, who after all was a skilled gardener, was driving at; but he probably had a more utilitarian purpose in mind as he went on to state that the 23 "great" botanical gardens established by the British in India disseminated "useful information respecting vegetable production."[30] Nevertheless Speede had no doubt that if gardening were to be regarded as a "mere mechanical art that may be efficiently practiced by the most ignorant labour, manuals or books of instruction will be useless."[31] William Speck in his *A Guide on Gardening in Jamaica* published in 1891 declared:

> If there is one thing of which a man is insufficiently proud, it is a "good garden." The vegetable garden especially needs not to be confined but should receive far greater attention by every working man ..., not only would it be a healthy recreation for his children, he would obtain from it a large portion of his necessary daily food, tomatoes, chow-chow, skellion and a bed of sweet herbs.[32]

E. C. Thompstone, deputy director of agriculture in Burma, in his *An Introduction to Practical School Gardening in Burma* (1913), was convinced of such higher purpose. Writing of the Macdonald School Gardens of Calcutta, he opined that they "have proved to be some of the most successful in existence" and were "designed to encourage the cultivation of the soil as an ideal life-work, and are intended to promote above all things else, symmetrical education of the individual." This included powers of observation and deduction, but also as C. Drieberg, superintendent of the School Gardens in Ceylon, declared: "To make a schoolboy take an honest pride in manual 'labour'." It goes without saying that the vegetables boys in India and Burma were to be taught to grow were almost universally European, even though there was an injunction to cultivate "seeds suitable to your particular soil and climate." Boys were also to be taught how to grow some economic crops, such as sugar cane, and even instructed how to cure and ferment tobacco; but they were not taught the arts of Indian or Burmese horticulture.[33]

The virtue of gardening was not just a matter for the Indian population on their journey to becoming "Brown Englishmen," but also for the soldiers of the Raj. Just as at home where allotment and cottage gardening were inextricably linked to the temperance movement, so in India gardening was seen as a way of keeping men out of trouble. According to H. E. Houghton, the author of *The Amateur's Guide to Gardening in Southern India* (1917): "Gardening has the power of drawing away men's attention from gloomy and even wicked pursuits, and inculcating cheerfulness."[34] It was apparently also useful in prisons, even after men had fallen from grace. Barracks were provided with garden ground and seeds were distributed to encourage horticulture. G. Marshall Woodrow's *Hints on Gardening in India*, probably first published in 1867 specifically for the use of British soldiers, summed up such thinking: "A beneficent Government not only offers the use of land, but yearly presents a supply

MICHAEL MOSS

of flower and vegetable seeds and prizes for the successful treatment, with a view to providing for the men a pleasant and useful employment for their leisure hours."[35] Such competitions were divided into two classes for European and native vegetables, but competition was open to both British and Indian horticulturalists, with natives sometimes carrying away prizes in the European section. Why those who extolled the moral virtues of gardening imagined it to be a wholesome occupation that would deter practitioners from drink and sex was never explained.

The British garden, though, was in some senses part of the female sphere, particularly as the nineteenth century progressed. This was not only because women such as Miss Ellen Wilmott and her ghosts (she scattered seeds of *Eryngium giganteum* wherever she went) and Gertrude Jekyll with her "decrees on garden beds" challenged the male horticulturalists, but because domestic economy was firmly within the female realm. Women played a significant role in the movements for social reform and improvement, often linked to popular evangelicalism that was as much a feature of imperial life as it was at home. In the colonies, particularly the tropics, female concern was dominated by health and hygiene. R. E. Holtrum, writing about vegetables in Mrs. E. D. Butler's *Gardening for Amateurs in Malaya*, warned: "It is unsafe to eat raw salad vegetables bought in the market, as it is possible that they may carry infection of various kinds owing to the prevalent method of cultivation and such infection cannot be removed by cooking. In order to ensure salad vegetables are safe, it is necessary to grow them oneself."[36] Speck had similar advice for his readers in Jamaica: "Surely it is well worthwhile for every household to grow a sufficiency for his own table, instead of purchasing and injuring the health of his family, by using stale, unripe and overgrown vegetables."[37] Manuals on domestic life and households in all but the most temperate climates repeated such warnings about the danger of buying local produce without pausing to consider how the local population survived on such fare.

Houghton associated gardening directly with the female sphere: "Whatever the excuse man may have for neglecting gardening, the ladies have no excuse, for flowers are intimately associated with the distinctive qualities of the female mind, the first sympathies of whose character are linked with flowers, which have been the delights of their childhood, the cherished ornaments of their girlish beauty, and the sunshine of their old age."[38] Such associations scarcely suggest the sweat of the brow, but rather the sort of aestheticism that is summed up in Gertrude Jekyll's flower pictures, which are to be admired and looked at, not to be worked.

The Victorians drew little distinction between the aesthetic pleasures of the flower garden and vegetable plot. George Eliot, reflecting on her childhood in "Janet's Repentance," remembered a world decked with both flowers and vegetables. There was

> no finical separation between flower and kitchen-garden there, no monotony of enjoyment for one sense to the exclusion of another, but a charming paradisiacal mingling of all that was pleasant to the eye and good for food ... you gathered a moss-rose one moment and a bunch of currants the next; you were in a delicious fluctuation between the scent of jasmine and the juice of gooseberries.[39]

The aesthetic appreciation of the vegetable garden, at least to the European mind, depended on order and discipline, the neat rows of perfectly formed produce. As Edith Cuthell reminded her readers, in India, at least, this was achieved by the labor of others:

> In the garden I have been very busy sowing fresh seeds in the hotbed. There has been a great deal to do pricking out annuals in little beds on the veranda wall. Be it well understood that I speak of doing a thing in the garden myself, it merely means I sit, or stand, and see it done. In this land no one does any gardening personally, but the supervision of the ignorant untrustworthy and uninterested *mallee* is far more trouble.[40]

This statement, which hardly speaks of the virtues of dynamic engagement, was not untypical of those colonies and imperial possessions where labor was plentiful, and contrasted with experience at home where in better-off households the garden was the Head Gardener's domain. It does not, however, negate the notion of putting down roots that in itself could result in an exchange. In her delightful autobiographical essay *The River* that has much to say about the Indian garden of her childhood, Rummer Godden described the connectedness of her self and her three sisters with the country through their cork tree that was somehow immutable: "Under Harriet's feet, where she stood among the red lilies, its roots went deep into the earth, down into the pit of the earth."[41]

In some ways the colonial vegetable garden represents the ultimate expression of man's struggle with nature. If Michael Pollan is right in describing his gigantic ugly Sibley squash as a "gift,"[42] it is a gift hard won by order and disciplined attention to detail. Authors of manuals on gardening in the Empire repeatedly stressed the need for order and the calendar. S. Percy Lancaster, the author of *An Amateur in an Indian*

Garden (1929), was emphatic that "there is no 'closed' season in a garden. If you think that you can allow your beds and shrubs to be unattended for 3 months and then rush in a gang of labour, dig in manure and plant up in a week or two and obtain a first class garden, you are mistaken."[43] Almost every gardening volume included a calendar in much the same way as they still do. William Gowrie's *Gardening in South Africa* (1912) warned that the calendar "calls for exercise of judgement on the part of the reader," and "if blindly Followed ... may prove as often wrong as right." However, this did not prevent him giving specific directions for particular times of the year:

> March — To secure a supply of vegetable for winter and early spring all arrangements not already completed should be made without delay, the growth of those already planted should be encouraged by hoeing and stirring the earth about the roots.[44]

This seems a little odd, as March is the autumn in the southern hemisphere and it makes one wonder if he had ever been there. Similarly, the anonymous author of the *Amateur Gardener in the Hills* had no doubt there was little use "laying down hard and fast rules"; but was not above telling his readers that with vegetables "make it a golden rule to set in all crops as early as possible."[45] One of the few honest commentators was the Honourable Mrs. J. C. Grant who, from her experience of vegetable gardening in East Africa, advised:

> Owing to the tremendous variations in altitude, season and climatic condition, it is impossible to draw up any 'time-table' or programme of work applicable to the whole country, but if (i) the above axiom be constantly borne in mind (ii) commonsense be brought to bear on every problem as it arises (iii) due regard be paid to the requirements of individual crops; it will be found that vegetable of every kind, and of really high quality can be grown in practically every settled area in Kenya.[46]

As every gardener knows, however much such advice is followed, crops fail: "Beginners are very apt to imagine that their first efforts in plant culture will of necessity be successful; the contrary is generally the case."[47] Such setbacks combined with order and discipline to express the moral virtues of gardening. There is no doubt why gardening was such a ready bedfellow for the temperance movement and the evangelicals.

In India order contrasted sharply with the disorder, as the British saw it, of local vegetable gardens. Jaffrey mused: "it has no doubt seemed a great mystery to many how the poorer classes of natives contrive to subsist on small incomes, this is in some measure explained when the hedges and ditches are found to team with wholesome esculents."[48] Edith Cuthell, who regarded Indian vegetables as a poor substitute for European and whose gardens scented "the neighbourhood with a forest of sweet peas," marveled at "the result of such patient microscopic husbandry – a rough basket, one iron tool, the implements, little fields sunk, and divided by raised banks, and round and about each – runnels, so carefully filled morn and eve from the well."[49] She did not pause to think why she should enjoy a large well-ordered garden, while most of the population had to make do with tiny plots. As Vikram Seth wrote in his poem "The Humble Administrator's Garden":

> This is the loveliest of all gardens. What
> Do scruples know of beauty anyhow?[50]

Despite the widespread antipathy to Indian vegetables there were some who did not share the Reverend Firminger's view that they were little better than weeds, "only being employed in their cooking merely as a vehicle for their curry-ingredients."[51] Lieutenant Lowther, who could write fondly of "Old England," considered that "the vegetable[s] natural to this part of India are few in number, but of good quality." While out on expeditions in his district he lived on them, reporting: "Are you aware the nuts of the Nelumbium [lotus] are delicious eating."[52] The Indian fruit that was universally to be found on the colonial table was mangoes that were grown widely in the tropics. In Africa and the Caribbean the banana enjoyed a similar place in the horticulturalist's calendar.

The assimilation of local plants into the colonial garden is indicative of a deep contradiction and flaw in the imagined flowers and vegetables of "Old England" because the majority were nothing of the kind. The pea that might seem a quintessentially English vegetable was introduced in the fifteenth century by the monks of the Hospital of St. Mary of Rouncival at Charing Cross. The runner bean that is grown extensively in England is a native of South America, while broad beans originate from the Middle East. The potato, by the late eighteenth century the staple of the British diet, came from America, as did the tomato or love-apple that only became an essential ingredient of the European salad in the nineteenth century. Although there are native brassicas and wild carrots and onions, most of those beloved by the British came from elsewhere, such as Brussels sprouts, savoys, Early Nantes and Spanish onions,

MICHAEL MOSS

as their names imply. The vegetable gardens of the United Kingdom were the result of continuous appropriation and experimentation that has never stopped. The very nature of Britishness that these vegetables embodied was equally dynamic and appropriated, particularly after the French wars (1794–1815) that gave Britain vast new overseas possessions. This irony was not lost on some, who realized that vegetables indigenous in other parts of the world were sometimes merely precursors of familiar British varieties that had been improved by gardeners and nurserymen, such as Carters of Holborn and Veitch & Co. of Exeter, who supplied seeds to the Empire.

There was a deeper irony in the activities of professional gardeners and plant hunters, who were busy transforming the gardens of the United Kingdom by appropriating plants as fast as they could from the colonies and Empire. Plant hunting had been a feature of British horticulture since the sixteenth century. New introductions became a flood in the late eighteenth century, fueled in large measure by the Enlightenment spirit of improvement and energetically fostered by Sir Joseph Banks, honorary director of Kew Gardens from 1772 to 1820, who "inculcated in the British a sense of botanical nationalism."[53] Kew Gardens, which had been founded by Princess Augusta, the widow of the Prince of Wales, in 1759, became the hub of horticultural endeavor in the Empire, a shining example of what the French sociologist and anthropologist Bruno Latour has called centers of accumulation and calculation.[54] Introductions from India and the Far East, particularly of rhododendrons and magnolias, were to transform British gardens. Kew was not simply a repository of information in its enormous herbarium, but actively prosecuted the exchange of economically and socially useful plant material across the Empire. The paradox was that at the same time as efforts were being made to grow Brussels sprouts in inhospitable parts of the world, the very same people were both improving strains of useful local plants and trees and experimenting with the introduction of others from elsewhere. Sugar cane, for example, was introduced into the West Indies in the eighteenth century and famously in the nineteenth century the Cinchona tree was taken from Peru to India in order to produce quinine to combat malaria. While books were busily being published on how to grow European vegetables in the Empire, others were being written on tropical agriculture and horticulture.

Perhaps the greatest paradox was that for many of those who lived out colonial or imperial lives, the countries where they were posted came to possess them through roots casually put down to evoke an imagined home. When they did eventually return home they brought back with them tropes of the time they had spent far from home: tiger skins, stuffed animals and curios, Persian rugs, a taste for gin and tonic to stave off malaria, bungalows, verandas, and plants in pots. Their homes and gardens became, as it were, imperial possessions in a gloriously ironic exchange that was beautifully observed by Louis MacNeice in his poem "Bagpipe Music":

> It's no go the merrygoround, it's no go the rickshaw,
> All we want is a limousine and a ticket for the peepshow.
> Their knickers are made of crepe-de-chine, their shoes are made of python,
> Their halls are lined with tiger rugs and their walls with head of bison.

Major General Lowther built for himself Cardew Lodge at Dalston in Cumbria that has single-storey gabled wings reminiscent of an Indian bungalow, which he stuffed with mementos of his time in Bengal, including the skin of a crocodile shot after it had eaten a man, and he planted rhododendrons and azaleas in his garden.

NOTES

1 I would like to thank Dr. Susan Stuart for suggesting this contribution, the late Bill Stowell, who learned to grow vegetables in the reign of Queen Victoria and instilled in me a passion for their cultivation, Shaun Castle for details of Cardew Lodge, Connie Robertson of the Poetry Archive, and Carcanet Press Ltd. for permission to quote from Vikrem Seth's poem "The Humble Administrator's Garden."

2 A. J. Jex-Blake (ed.) *Gardening in East Africa* (London: Longmans, Green, 1934), p. 200.

3 W. Gollan, *The Indian Vegetable Garden* (Allahabad: Indian Press, 1892), p. 25.

4 J. N. Milsum and D. H. Grist, *Vegetable Gardening in Malaya* (Kuala Lumpur: Straits Settlement Dept. of Agriculture, 1941), p. 117.

5 A. Crosby, *Ecological Imperialism: The Biological Expansion of Europe, 900–1900* (Cambridge: Cambridge University Press, 1986), p. i.

6 C. Carlton and C. Carlton, *The Significance of Gardens in British India* (New York: Edwin Mellen Press, 2004), p. ii.

7 J. M. MacKenzie, "Empire and Metropolitan Culture," in W. R. Louis and A. Porter (eds.) *The Oxford History of the British Empire, Vol. 3: The Nineteenth Century* (Oxford: Oxford University Press, 1999), p. 263.

8 D. Cooper, *A Philosophy of Gardens* (Oxford: Oxford University Press, 2006), p. 93.

  MICHAEL MOSS

9   D. McDonald, *English Vegetables & Flowers in India & Ceylon* (London: John Haddon, 1890), p. 7.

10   W. J. Tutcher, *Gardening for Hong Kong* (Hong Kong: South China Morning Post, 1964), p. 1.

11   E. Cuthell, *My Garden City in the City of Gardens* (London: John Lane the Bodley Head, 1905), p. 18.

12   A. T. Jaffrey, *Hints to the Amateur Gardeners of South India* (Madras: Pharoah, 1858), p. 34.

13   McDonald, *English Vegetables & Flowers in India & Ceylon*, p. 3.

14   Jaffrey, *Hints to the Amateur Gardeners of South India*, preface.

15   G. T. F. B. Speede, *New Indian Gardener and Guide to the Successful Culture of the Kitchen and Fruit Garden in India* (Calcutta: W. Thacker, 1848), p. 121.

16   Mrs. E. D. Butler (ed.) *Gardening for Amateurs in Malaya* (Singapore: Young Women's Christian Association, 1934), p. 60.

17   D. Tannock, *Manual of Gardening in New Zealand* (Auckland: Whitcombe & Tombs, 1916), p. 196.

18   *Transactions of the Agricultural and Horticultural Society of the Punjab* (1851): 26, 123.

19   G. Atkinson, *Curry & Rice* (London: Day & Son, 1858), pp. 157–8.

20   Speede, *New Indian Gardener*, pp. 2, 160.

21   T. Firminger, *Gardening Manual for Bengal and Upper India* (London: Thacker, Spink, 1864), p. 133.

22   F. Pogson, *Indian Gardening* (Calcutta: Wyman, 1872), pp. i–ii.

23   *Transactions of the Agricultural and Horticultural Society of the Punjab* (1851): 54.

24   Ibid., p. 23.

25   Speede, *New Indian Gardener*, p. 1.

26   Pogson, *Indian Gardening*, p. 42.

27   McDonald, *English Vegetables & Flowers in India & Ceylon*, p. 7.

28   J. Updike, "Hoeing" in *Collected Poems 1953–1993* (London: Hamish Hamilton, 1993), p. 40.

29   Cooper, *A Philosophy of Gardens*, p. 93.

30   McDonald, *English Vegetables & Flowers in India & Ceylon*, p. 9.

31   Speede, *New Indian Gardener*, p. 1.

32   W. Speck, *A Guide on Gardening in Jamaica* (Kingston: J. W. Kerr, 1891), p. 6.

33   E. C. Thompstone, *An Introduction to Practical School Gardening in Burma* (Rangoon: American Baptist Mission Press, 1913), pp. 1–4.

34   H. E. Houghton, *The Amateur's Guide to Gardening in Southern India* (Madras: Higginbothams, 1917), p. 1.

35   G. M. Woodrow, *Hints on Gardening in India* (Bombay: Thacker, 1867), preface.

36   Butler, *Gardening for Amateurs in Malaya*, p. 60.

37   Speck, *A Guide on Gardening in Jamaica*, p. 30.

38   Houghton, *The Amateur's Guide to Gardening in Southern India*, p. 2.

39   G. Elliot, "Janet's Repentance," in *Scenes of Clerical Life* (Leipzig: Bernhard Tauchnitz, 1859), p. 49.

40   Cuthell, *My Garden City in the City of Gardens*, p. 163.

41   R. Godden, *The River* (London: Michael Joseph, 1946), p. 38.

42   M. Pollan, *Second Nature: A Gardener's Education* (London: Bloomsbury, 1996), p. 156.

43   S. P. Lancaster, *An Amateur in an Indian Garden* (Alipur: S. Percy-Lancaster, 1929), p. 2.

44   W. Gowrie, *Gardening in South Africa* (Grahamstown: Grocott and Sherry, 1912), p. 15.

45   Anon., *Amateur Gardener in the Hills* (Calcutta: Thacker, Spink, 1881), p. 57.

46   Jex-Blake, *Gardening in East Africa*, p. 189.

47   Anon., *Amateur Gardener in the Hills*, p. iv.

48   Jaffrey, *Hints to the Amateur Gardeners of South India*, p. 49.

49   Cuthell, *My Garden City in the City of Gardens*, pp. 180, 186.

50   V. Seth, *The Humble Administrator's Garden* (Manchester: Carcanet, 1985), p. 11.

51   Firminger, *Gardening Manual for Bengal and Upper India*, p. 97.

52   *Transactions of the Agricultural and Horticultural Society of the Punjab* (1851): p. 121.

53   D. McCracken, *Gardens of Empire* (London: Continuum, 1997), p. 3.

54   B. Latour, *Science in Action: How to Follow Science and Engineers through Society* (Cambridge, MA: Harvard University Press, 1987).

CHAPTER 7

TRANSPLANTING LIBERTY

Lafayette's American Garden

Catherine and Caleb Cushing of Massachusetts had been in Paris for nearly two months before they had a chance to visit "that spot which, above all others," Mrs. Cushing "most desired to see."[1] This much-anticipated destination was the 700-acre estate of La Grange, home of General Lafayette, the French hero of the American Revolution. Around 11 o'clock in the morning on Friday, October 9, 1829, Lafayette's carriage picked up the Cushings at their rented rooms on the Rue d'Artois and headed east, along 35 miles of vineyards and farmlands. Lafayette kept the ride lively, regaling his guests with reminiscences of his time in America until, "at length, we approached the end of our journey, and as we entered the boundaries of La Grange, – 'Now,' cried the General, 'we are upon American ground.'"

Geographically speaking, Lafayette and his companions remained in France. But Lafayette saw the United States as his adopted land, liberal politics as his raison d'être, and La Grange as an embodiment of both. Although La Grange was the ancestral estate of his late mother-in-law, Henriette d'Aguesseau, duchesse d'Ayen, who perished on the guillotine on July 22, 1794, Lafayette had put his stamp on the property. Renovating the house and gardens consumed Lafayette's attention throughout the Napoleonic era (1799–1815), and tending the land remained a primary focus even after his return to national politics during the Restoration of the Bourbon monarchy (1815–30). Borrowing from British and American sources to implement rational principles of husbandry, Lafayette nurtured thousands of trees, myriad decorative plantings, and a wide array of vegetables, along with large quantities of comestible, collectible, and working animals. Most importantly, perhaps, Lafayette also cultivated his own identity there. Following his lead, the American papers hailed his fields, woods, and barns as the very models of self-sufficiency and good governance, while cheering Lafayette as an ideal steward of land and liberty.

Lafayette's American Plants

Although Lafayette did not devote himself wholeheartedly to agricultural pursuits until 1799, when differences with an ascendant Napoleon necessitated withdrawal from public life, his interest in plants and agriculture dates to the 1780s. Significantly, the subject first attracted his attention during a visit to the United States. For Lafayette, agriculture seems to have been bound up with political ideals from the very start.

In 1784, nearly three years after his actions in the decisive Battle of Yorktown had helped to bring about the end of the Revolutionary War, Lafayette paid his first visit to an independent United States. A highlight of the trip was a sojourn with George Washington, the former commander whom Lafayette termed his adopted father. Washington was enjoying what turned out to be a temporary retirement – between serving as Commander-in-Chief of the Continental Army and President of the United States – at his Virginia estate, Mount Vernon. Lafayette evidently whiled away his time at Mount Vernon "lunching, chatting, writing, dining, chatting, writing, and supping."[2] But Washington was far from idle: his was an active retirement, with a great deal of time, energy, and resources expended on agricultural experiments and improvements. In matters ranging from crop rotation and fertilization to threshing and breeding, Washington was in the vanguard of American farmers. For him, tending to the land was more than a hobby; it was a contribution to the wellbeing of the nation. In a letter thanking "the South Carolina Society for promoting and improving agriculture" for naming him their first honorary member, Washington expounded the civic virtues of agricultural improvement, writing "nothing in my opinion would contribute more to the welfare of these States, than the proper management of our Lands; and nothing, in this State particularly, seems to be less understood."[3]

LAURA AURRICHIO

Washington's retirement from military affairs and concomitant dedication to agricultural pursuits were widely understood at the time as twin marks of integrity that placed him in a lineage of honorable rulers dating back to the Roman general Lucius Quinctius Cincinnatus. Cincinnatus, a farmer who lived in the fifth century BCE, had been persuaded by his countrymen to lead Rome through a time of crisis. After serving as dictator in a moment of dire need, Cincinnatus refused the role of lifelong ruler and rededicated himself to his land. Texts and images likening Washington to Cincinnatus were widely circulated in the 1780s. Most notably, perhaps, the officers who had served under Washington – including Lafayette and many of his countrymen – had formed the Society of the Cincinnati in 1783. Envisioned as a means of fostering dedication to each other, to liberty, and to the fledgling United States, the society also perpetuated the connection between Washington and Cincinnatus, which was further reinforced when Washington became the organization's first president and the city of Cincinnati, Ohio, was named in his honor.

The link between Washington and Cincinnatus seems to have been on Lafayette's mind during his visit to Mount Vernon, as evidenced by a letter to his wife, Adrienne. On August 29, 1784, Lafayette wrote that he had been prompted by the example of "the true Cincinnatus" to give some thought to domestic details, such as the decoration of his study in the Paris townhouse that he had recently purchased.[4] Later on the same visit to America, Lafayette began writing about plants and shipping them to France for his own use. Writing to Adrienne from Church's Tavern, near Hartford, Connecticut, on October 10, 1784, Lafayette explained: "I must speak with you about a famous plant, known as ginseng, of which I can send only one pot, addressed to you, and which I beg you to share with Monsieur le Maréchal de Noailles and Madame de Tessé" (Adrienne's uncle and aunt, both of whom were avid collectors of plants and trees).[5] Continuing, Lafayette observed, "since this may be the only time in my life that we will speak botanically, I will add that I have discovered here a climbing plant, always green, that will yield a marvellous effect on the two walls of our terrace. When it reaches you, I ask you to please seed it and to plant a large quantity."

Notwithstanding Lafayette's belief that his 1784 letter could be his last on the subject, botanical and agricultural matters would play a large role in his correspondence in years to come. During the 1780s, Lafayette's discussions of plants were frequently bound up with expressions of interest in the United States. For instance, in 1786 Lafayette wrote to a member of the Native American federation of the Six Nations asking him to collect, and to ship to France, a range of American specimens. "Osgeanon-don-ha, my child," wrote Lafayette, "there are in your island trees that are not found in this one, and your fathers the French wish to eat of the fruits that nourish you and to lie down in the shade of the trees that cover you."[6] The letter requested that its recipient collect pecan nuts, apple seeds, and, more generally, "seeds of all sorts of shrubs and flowers from your country, and especially ginseng."

It is not clear what Lafayette intended to do with the American nuts and seeds that he solicited in the 1780s. In fact, we do not even know if he wanted them for his own use. He may, for instance, have written on behalf of his wife's botanically inclined relatives, or he may even have been serving as an intermediary between the Americans and King Louis XVI. In 1785 Lafayette had acted in the latter capacity when he wrote a letter of introduction to George Washington for André Michaux, the French botanist who had been sent to America by King Louis XVI "in order to know the trees, the seeds, and every kind of natural production whose growth may be either curious, or useful."[7] The king intended to plant these American specimens in "a nursery at a country seat of his which he is very fond of." Lafayette, however, saw Louis XVI's American plant project in terms of the transatlantic political and economic relations that he championed. "I am the more pleased with the plan as it opens a new channel of intercourse and mutual farming good offices between the two nations," he explained to Washington. Whatever the ultimate destination of these plants, his request was inextricable from his role as a living link between France and the United States – a function, one might argue, that Lafayette shared with the specimens he sought.

English Agrarian Influences

In 1791 Lafayette initiated his first large-scale agricultural project when he took steps to create a model farm at Chavaniac, the estate in the mountainous Auvergne region of central France where he had spent his childhood. Not incidentally, at a time when the French Revolution was in full throttle, Chavaniac was also a place of comparative quiet. But, like Washington's, Lafayette's turn to agriculture served not only as a respite from his political life, but also as an extension of it. Lafayette explained

LAURA AURRICHIO

his thinking in a document entitled "Note Regarding my Personal Fortune."[8] His hope, wrote Lafayette, was to "give the region an example of the best agriculture, and to raise there the most necessary types of animals. This manner of serving my neighbours would have been very useful in the interest of peace."

Two men were placed in charge of the undertaking, which was largely conducted while Lafayette was serving as Commander of the Army of the Center, based in Metz, some 400 miles northeast of Chavaniac. The neoclassical architect Antoine-Laurent-Thomas Vaudoyer spent the 12 months from mid-October 1791 through late October 1792 planning and overseeing alterations to the rustic house and grounds. Agricultural guidance was supplied by an English farmer, John Dyson of Suffolk, who joined Vaudoyer at Chavaniac for most of 1792. Dyson had been hired to survey the lands and to make recommendations regarding the selection and care of crops and livestock that would be best suited to the climate and terrain. In choosing an Englishman for the job, Lafayette was following the lead of his political ally, François-Alexandre-Frédéric, duc de La Rochefoucauld-Liancourt, who had met the English agricultural reformer Arthur Young while traveling in the British Isles. Having gained a deep appreciation of the English agrarian movement as a key to the amelioration of rural poverty, La Rochefoucauld-Liancourt had founded his own model farm, workshops, and schools.

As it turned out, however, Chavaniac never saw the improvements that Lafayette envisioned. Since the outbreak of Revolution in 1789, Lafayette had committed himself to forging a middle path between royalists, who wished to shore up the powers of the king, and republicans, who sought to replace the monarchy with a democratic government envisioned, perhaps, along the lines of the American model. Opposing both courses of action, Lafayette counted among the moderate reformers who hoped to establish a constitutional monarchy in France that might emulate the English system. However, events overtook Lafayette in June and July of 1791. By the time workers began breaking ground at Chavaniac, the Revolution was heading inexorably in a radical direction that rendered his middle-of-the-road position untenable. On August 19, 1792, with calls for his arrest emanating from Paris, Lafayette fled across the border and was promptly placed in Austrian custody. The arrest of Adrienne one month later and the seizure of Lafayette's properties by the nation put a definitive end to any hopes that Lafayette might be able to institute an English system of government in France, or an English ideal of rural reform at Chavaniac.

Transforming La Grange

During the seven years of prison and exile (1792–9) that followed his arrest, Lafayette devoted much of his time to agricultural readings. Forcibly removed as he was from his native soil, perhaps he found some solace in contemplating the land he had left behind. In this respect, Lafayette was like many members of the nobility who began to return from exile as circumstances in France permitted. Alexandre de Laborde, whose father, the financier and garden enthusiast Jean-Joseph de Laborde, had been executed during the Revolution, wrote movingly about this phenomenon in his 1808 publication, *Descriptions of the New Gardens of France and its ancient Chateaux*. Likening the experience of French émigrés to that of the biblical Jews in Exodus, Laborde describes the exiles' joy in rediscovering even the smallest corner of their fathers' lands, however reduced their circumstances might have become.

Writing from the medieval Dutch city of Vianen on May 29, 1799, Lafayette asked Adrienne for news of La Grange, to which she had already returned. He sought specifics about the house, farm, woods, and park, explaining that he was "more immersed than ever in the study of agriculture, and all the details that you will send me will give me the pleasure of comparing practices in France with those of England and Holland."[9] Five months later, now in Utrecht, he wrote again of his agricultural thoughts, which had taken a more practical turn. Lafayette now expected that, after returning to France, "my activity … will focus on agriculture, which I study with all the ardor that I had in my youth for other occupations."[10]

As Lafayette indicated, his commitment to agriculture had redoubled after reading several volumes by Arthur Young, lent to him by La Rochefoucault-Liancourt – a fellow exile. Young's French admirers sought to remedy a problem that Young had pinpointed as a key source of the searing poverty that he witnessed in his tours of rural France. The nation's absentee landlords, Young believed, managed only to stifle production and breed misery by placing demands on the peasantry that were "equally subversive of agriculture, and the common rights of mankind."[11] "The nobility in France," wrote Young, "have no more idea of practicing agriculture, and making it an object of conversation, except on the mere theory … than of any other object the most remote from their habits and pursuits."[12] Lafayette was determined to find a new way forward.

At the end of 1799, soon after his return to France, Lafayette reprised the project initiated at Chavaniac, adapting his plans to the new location

LAURA AURRICHIO

FIGURE 7.1   Isidore Deroy, *La Grange East View*, lithograph, 1826, after Alvan Fisher.

at La Grange. Again, Vaudoyer was placed in charge of the massive undertaking, which involved everything from redirecting roads and irrigating fields to redesigning the gardens and woods and renovating the chateau's interior.

The area immediately surrounding the chateau was reconceived by the landscape painter and garden designer Hubert Robert, with the purchasing and labor overseen by Vaudoyer. Robert was one of the artists who had collaborated on the creation of Jean-Joseph de Laborde's garden of Méréville, contributing to its meandering waterways, sinuous paths, and numerous follies. At La Grange, Robert seems to have reimagined the defensive moat that once ringed the chateau as an ornamental rivulet, as seen in Isadore Deroy's lithograph reproducing a painting of La Grange by the American artist Alvan Fisher (figure 7.1). Surrounded by a flowing stream and nearly overtaken by a pleasantly varied ring of densely planted trees and shrubs, the building is drained of much of its imposing character. As Fisher depicts it, the central tower looks as though it will soon be dwarfed by the young Cyprus and pine trees that frame it, and the entire medieval structure appears to rise from the water like a fairy tale's enchanted castle.

Robert also intervened in the formal woods that border the chateau. Interrupting the straight alleys of the axial plan, he generated surprising vistas by introducing irregular cut-aways, creating a large swath of open land running from the house to the southern edge of the woods, and dotting the western meadow with small, asymmetrical clusters of oak and elm trees. No less a gardener than Madame de Tessé was reported to have been "perfectly satisfied with the breaks and openings in the park."[13]

Creating these picturesque effects entailed more than clearing trees; Lafayette also undertook extensive plantings. In 1806–7 alone, he purchased more than 6,500 trees for the 134 acres of woods and park. These were mostly deciduous trees native to Europe – chestnut, maple, ash, poplar, and plane trees are among the more commonly named items in his bills of sale. Some trees, such as the four weeping willows purchased in 1806, were selected for ornamental effect – to create stunning tableaux such as that visible in Deroy's lithograph. Others, like the red elder or the sorbus, may have been selected for their colorful berries. Apple and pear trees appear to have been planted for their fruit, and in large quantity; 203 pear trees and 165 apple tree were acquired in one 1807 purchase alone.

The largest portion of the property, however, is given over not to trees but to arable fields. In contrast to Laborde's garden of Méréville, where the kitchen garden occupied only a small plot of land at the northern border of the park, La Grange featured 416 acres of fields and another 70 acres of pasture surrounding the chateau. It was this part of the property to which Lafayette dedicated most of his attention. He set himself a goal of rendering his farm as profitable as the lands of his neighbors, keeping meticulous records, in his own hand, of each year's income and expenditures. Lafayette seems also to have taken particular pride in furnishing his table with food from his own fields. Mrs. Cushing corroborated that Lafayette was able to wrest tremendous bounties from the land. Upon reaching the dining room, she wrote, "we found the table abundantly spread, with meats and vegetables almost exclusively the produce of the farm; and the fruits, which formed the dessert, were all of the General's own raising."[14]

In part, Lafayette owed his success as a gardener to the extensive library that he assembled. We are fortunate to have lists of all the books

LAURA AURRICHIO

that he owned, sold, or purchased during his time at La Grange, catego-rized by subject matter. The heading "Agriculture," alone, encompasses some 76 books, with related titles appearing in categories including "Botany," "Political Economy," and "Works in English." Together, these afford a deep understanding of plants and gardens from a wide variety of theoretical, scientific, and practical perspectives. Works like Jean-Marie Morel's *Théorie des jardins* (1776) and Uvedale Price's *Essays on the Picturesque* (1794) are complemented by catalogues describing and clas-sifying plants, trees, and flowers, as well as instructional manuals such as R. W. Dickson's *Practical Agriculture; Or a Complete System of Husbandry* (1805), and even a French translation of Virgil's *Georgics*. As one might expect, Lafayette's library also contained André Michaux's texts on American flora, the writings of Arthur Young, and periodicals, including *Annales d'agriculture* and *Mémoires d'agriculture*, which published the lat-est developments in agricultural theory and practice.

The location of Lafayette's library enhanced the connection between land and learning. The windows in the circular room offer panoramic views of the grounds, but the alcove that Vaudoyer designed for Lafayette's desk directly overlooks the farm buildings. Lady Sydney Morgan, the noted Irish author and outspoken advocate of liberal causes, drew out the intellectual implications of this arrangement in her recollections of a visit to La Grange. In an excerpt from the book *France* (1817) that was reproduced in American newspapers, Lady Morgan wrote that Lafayette's "elegant and well chosen collection of books, occupies the highest apart-ments in one of the towers of the chateau, and like the study of Montaigne, hangs over the farmyard of the philosophical agriculturalist."[15] Another American, who had visited La Grange in January 1826, recalled that the library windows "command a view of a rural domain, such as Cincinnatus or Washington would have enjoyed, and such as its own proprietor would not exchange for an empire."[16]

As he had at Chavaniac, Lafayette supplemented book learning with practical advice solicited from English experts. For instance, an "Agricultural Report of a Practical English Farmer" (1805) provided a thorough assessment of the assets, drawbacks, and needs of Lafayette's land. Its author addressed everything from the excessively loamy nature of the soil at La Grange to preferable sources of seeds to best practices in potato planting. The soil, observed the Englishman, retained too much water as a result of "too frequent dressings of argillaceous matter, in which it did not stand in need so much as of a proper Course of Crops."[17] As a corrective, three four-year cycles of crop rotations were prescribed, with the repertoire running from cabbage, turnips, and green vegetables to barley, oats, beans, and wheat.

Lafayette gathered further advice, as well as seeds, plants, tools, and animals, from the United States. Following his 1824–5 triumphal tour of his adopted nation, where he was fêted in every state, Lafayette became a regular correspondent of John Skinner of Baltimore. Skinner edited a periodical entitled *The American Farmer*, which frequently published letters to, from, or about Lafayette's agricultural endeavors. Surely Lafayette did not miss the resonances of the journal's title, which echoed that of another book in his library: the 1787 French edition of *Letters from an American Farmer*. Written by a Frenchman under the name Hector St. John de Crèvecoeur, this widely read volume cast the American farmer as a new race of man, living in a blissful state of communion with nature, and enjoying incomparable freedom and happiness. In his letters to Skinner, Lafayette fully embraced his identity as essentially American, concluding an 1826 missive with an observation written, notably, in the first person plural: "I had more to say of agricultural concerns than European politics, nauseous as their diplomacy cannot fail to be to our American taste."

While seeking to emulate Crèvecoeur's American farmer, Lafayette ensured that his property would continue to yield American fruits. Even at the end of his life, Lafayette was still collecting trees from the United States. On March 5, 1834, less than three months before Lafayette died, the American artist and inventor Samuel F. B. Morse (best known as the creator of the telegraph) made a purchase at William Prince and Sons' Linnaean Botanic Garden and Nurseries in Flushing, New York. On behalf of Lafayette, Morse paid for 25 indigenous trees, with Messieurs Prince tossing in an additional 17 plants as a gift to America's French hero. In addition to the orange, peach, and apple trees that Morse had ordered, the nurserymen shipped to La Grange several varieties of apple trees native to New York, a dozen American red raspberry bushes, described as the "finest flavor for Brandy," and one *Mespilus arbutifolia*, which the receipt terms, quite aptly, "a beautiful ornamental shrub."[18]

Planting Politics at La Grange

There is, of course, nothing inherently political, and nothing necessarily liberal, about importing plants from halfway around the world or seeking to extract as much value as possible from one's property. In fact, the author Madame de Genlis perceived only self-interest in the attention that France's nobility began to lavish upon their lands in the first decades of the nineteenth century. An apologist for the old regime, Genlis wrote that the lords of France in the post-Revolutionary era had abdicated their obligations towards the peasantry. "The peasants," she wrote, "often die from lack of care, albeit free as the air."[19]

Lafayette, however, presented his agricultural pursuits in quite a different light, as he took every opportunity to underscore the international, liberal credentials of both the land and its proprietor. The political underpinnings of the landscape were, for example, a theme of the tours that Lafayette offered to the multitude of foreign visitors who flocked to La Grange. One guest, William Taylor of Norwich, one of England's leading translators of German romantic literature, has left us a particularly insightful account.[20] While traveling through France in the late spring of 1802, Taylor spent three days at La Grange. He arrived in the evening and was shown to rooms furnished with a degree of simplicity that "struck me at first as nakedness." On the second day of his visit, Taylor remembered, "before breakfast, Lafayette took me over his farm." Describing his walk through Lafayette's lands, Taylor quipped about a recently deceased English reformer: "the Duke of Bedford's ghost might have listened with interest to our conversation, for we talked of agriculture, of liberty, and him; but he would have listened with a sneer to my agriculture, though not to Lafayette's politics."

As his words glide smoothly between agriculture and liberty, Taylor reveals a keen understanding of the political goals of Lafayette's agricultural enterprise. Perhaps we should expect nothing less of Taylor, whose cousin, John Dyson, had been charged with the ill-fated project of creating a model farm at Chavaniac. Yet Lafayette's guided tours ensured that no guest would miss these implications. For instance, nearly every visitor reports an experience very much like the following one, offered by Lady Morgan: Lafayette, wrote Lady Morgan, "took me out the morning after my arrival, to show me a tower, richly covered with ivy! – 'It was Fox,' he said 'who planted that ivy! I have taught my grandchildren to venerate it.'" Charles James Fox was an early supporter of the American and French Revolutions and, like Lafayette, fully committed to the abolition of slavery; along with Cincinnatus, Washington, and the Duke of Bedford, he was another idealized political figure whose values were said to be implanted and nurtured at La Grange. So fully did Fox's planting represent the meaning of the place that a young American, Henry Russell Cleveland, received a tour from Lafayette in 1832 and "afterwards gathered a few leaves of the ivy, as a memorial of La Grange."[21]

Through his agricultural endeavors at La Grange, and the language in which he framed them, Lafayette was able to approximate Crèvecoeur's archetypal American farmer. To Lafayette's visitors, readers, and admirers across the Atlantic and across the Channel, La Grange came to embody liberal values of self-sufficiency, beneficent stewardship, and natural rights. As Lafayette declared to Mrs. Cushing, La Grange was nothing less than an exemplary "American ground."

NOTES

1   Mrs. Caleb Cushing, "Visit to La Grange," *Literary Journal and Weekly Register of Science and the Arts* 1, 13 (August 31, 1833), p. 97.
2   Lafayette to Adrienne, August 29, 1784, Reel 31, Folder 354, Marquis de Lafayette Papers, Manuscript Division, Library of Congress, Washington, DC.
3   George Washington to William Drayton, March 25, 1786, in John C. Fitzpatrick (ed.) *The Writings of George Washington from the Original Manuscript Sources, 1745–1799*, 39 vols. (Washington, DC: Government Printing Office, 1944).
4   Lafayette to Adrienne, August 29, 1784, Reel 31, Folder 354, Marquis de Lafayette Papers, Manuscript Division, Library of Congress, Washington, DC.
5   Lafayette to Adrienne, October 10, 1784, Reel 31, Folder 354, Marquis de Lafayette Papers, Manuscript Division, Library of Congress, Washington, DC.
6   Lafayette to Osgeanon-don-ha, January 17, 1786, Feinstone Collection, American Philosophical Society Library, photocopy in Louis Gottschalk Papers, Box 65, Folder 2, Special Collections Research Center, University of Chicago Library, Chicago, IL.
7   Lafayette to Washington, September 3, 1785, in Theodore J. Crackel (ed.) *The Papers of George Washington Digital Edition* (Charlottesville: University of Virginia Press, Rotunda 2007); available online at www.rotunda.upress.virginia.edu/pgwde/print-Con03d186.
8   "Note relative à ma fortune personelle," no date (1801?), Box 6, Folder 16, Dean Lafayette Collection, #4611, Division of Rare and Manuscript Collections, Cornell University Library, Ithaca, NY.
9   Lafayette to Adrienne, May 29, 1799, *Mémoires, correspondance et manuscrits du général Lafayette publiés par sa famille*, vol. 5 (Paris: H. Fournier ainé, 1837–8), pp. 51–2.
10 Lafayette to Adrienne, Utrecht, October 28, 1799, ibid., pp. 142–3.
11 Arthur Young, *Arthur Young's Travels in France During the Years 1787, 1788, 1789*, ed. Matilda Betham-Edwards (London: George Bell and Sons, 1909), 5.18.

12   Ibid., 3.60.
13   Lafayette to Vaudoyer, 28 floréal 10 (May 18, 1802), Container 1, Folder 5, Letter 8, Marquis de Lafayette Collection, LC, Manuscript Division, Library of Congress, Washington, DC.
14   Mrs. Caleb Cushing, "Visit to La Grange."
15   This excerpt was published in at least two newspapers: "General La Fayette," *Essex Patriot* (Haverhill, MA) (November 29, 1817), p. 1; and "From Lady Morgan's 'France,'" *American Advocate* (Hallowell, ME) (November 22, 1817), p. 4.
16   This unsigned account was also published in at least two newspapers: "Lafayette at Home," *American Mercury* (Hartford, CT) (August 22, 1826), p. 2; and "Travels. Letters from Europe – No. LXXIII," *The Torch Light* (Hagers-Town, MD) (February 15, 1827), p. 1.
17   "Agricultural Report of a Practical English Farmer, in Consequence of a View and Examination of the Grange Estate of Monsr de Lafayette, in the Department de Seine & Marne. Made in October 1805," Reel 51, Marquis de Lafayette Papers, Manuscript Division, Library of Congress, Washington, DC.
18   "List of plants for General Lafayette," Box 4, Folder 12, Dean Lafayette Collection, #4611, Division of Rare and Manuscript Collections, Cornell University Library, Ithaca, NY.
19   Madame la Comtesse de Genlis, *Dictionnaire critique et raisonne des etiquettes de la cour*, vol. 2 (Paris: Mongie, 1818), p. 14.
20   William Taylor to John Dyson, May 15, 1802, reprinted in *The Life and Writings of the Late William Taylor of Norwich*, ed. J. W. Robberds (London: John Murray, 1843), pp. 404–10.
21   George S. Hillard, *A Selection from the Writings of Henry R. Cleveland* (Boston: Freeman and Bolles, 1844), p. 234.

CHAPTER 8

COCKNEY PLOTS
Allotments and Grassroots Political Activism

Over the past decade, people all over the industrialized world have taken a renewed interest in food security and food safety, organic production, and locally grown food. We are probably now all familiar, for example, with the "100-mile diet" or the growing organic section in the grocery store.[1] In today's global economic crisis, as we currently struggle to keep food costs reasonable, environmental impacts low, and product quality high, community gardening seems all the more relevant.

Allotment gardens have historically, as I will illustrate, assisted lower-income citizens to better engage in political processes, prompted socialist movements, and improved the overall health of those who have participated in them. Allotments, particularly in cities, remain one of the few ways urban dwellers can grow and control their own food. A political philosophy of cooperation, solidarity, and active citizenship still runs through every allotment site like an unwavering current as it did one hundred years ago. Indeed, many of the historical struggles for permanency and access to land, which will be examined in this essay, continue to plague plot holders across the United Kingdom. Allotments are frequently replaced by large-scale building developments, tossed aside as relics of the past or symbols of harder times. However, those who have fought for them, whether in the past or the present, envision their usefulness beyond times of hardship or war and possess an ethos of concern about the state and accessibility of food. This essay will consider that struggle in a historical context in the old East London borough of Poplar (now part of Tower Hamlets) from the close of the nineteenth century to the end of World War I. Working-class men's participation as gardeners, organizers, secretaries, and activists enhanced their political and civic lives and created a more effective and meaningful brand of citizenship.

Historically, the provision of allotments was part of a larger middle-class scheme to improve the social conditions of the working classes. However, over time allotments became an integral part of working-class culture and politics, an activity synonymous with being a laborer. In the East End of London, and in particular the borough of Poplar, allotments existed from about the 1890s. Poplar housed a great number of dock workers and other laborers due to its location on the Thames and the proximity of the ports. This made it a fitting borough for the development of an allotment movement. The plot itself fostered the development of local horticultural knowledge, collective identity, and cultural pride, and provided a healthy social space largely dictated by its members' needs. Allotment sites were overwhelmingly masculine spaces where the dreariness of working-class life could be temporarily left behind. Allotments, then, connect us to the working man's preserve; this was a green space strictly for him, whereas the typical English square was not. These gardens were meaningful places where men produced their own food, experimented with different growing methods, and recycled all kinds of materials from manure to sheet metal, all within a spirit of cooperation.

East End men participated in allotment gardening in many different ways and to varying degrees. Many simply enjoyed gardening and chose not to participate in the political aspects of allotments. The majority, though, formed or joined associations which often had almost full control of setting up, running, and maintaining the allotment site. For all of these men, their participation in the allotment movement drastically changed the level of their political activity and the nature of their political philosophies. Allotments brought them in contact with local councils, the London County Council, the Port of London Authority, the Board of Agriculture, and even Parliament. Under few other schemes were working-class men able to fully participate in community planning and policy. The duties and functions of the allotment societies varied, but most took part in letter writing campaigns for better facilities and usually petitioned for more plots. Most societies organized lectures and seminars and held monthly meetings which most of the plot holders attended. For many of the allotment holders, dealing with the local council was beyond their everyday experience. The borough councils in turn developed unique relationships with the men living and working the land within their boundaries. Initially, these relationships remained on shaky ground, as both sides negotiated their positions within existing class and power structures. What emerged was a new, more balanced relationship characterized by an evolved working-class political consciousness and engagement.

During the war period, most of the work done by the allotment associations involved petitioning the local council and Parliament for permanent allotments. In 1916, by the time the effects of war were no doubt felt, Parliament passed the *Cultivation of Lands Order* which allowed that all vacant land could be appropriated for the purposes of allotment cultivation. Football grounds, parks, graveyards, and vacant land were all transformed into vegetable gardens. Yet, all of this activity failed to provide allotment holders with any security; they would spend the next few years fighting for the permanency of their plots. Plot holders organized protest meetings which many attended and produced petitions with thousands of signatures. Allotment associations fought excessive rental rates, made applications for site improvements, met with borough councillors, and participated in a complex relationship with the local council and the Port of London Authority. This participation fostered a sense of community and gave working-class men some autonomy over their affairs. They also learned other skills such as accounting and public speaking, which later served their community on other social and political campaigns. Allotments helped East Enders gain a lasting political confidence and maturity in two ways: through the process of their politicization and in virtue of the new relationships they built with government officials.

Allotment Associations

The cultivation of allotments was first and foremost a self-help movement. Not only did working-class men practice self-help in the action of gardening, but also by becoming politically active they helped determine their community's direction and future. This was achieved by belonging to an allotment association, which was the hub of all allotment activity across the United Kingdom. Associations extended the democratic process to a largely disenfranchised population in East London. Julia Bush has said of East Enders that they were "deprived of political self-expression and political motivation," making their experience in the allotment association all the more meaningful.[2] Working men in the East End, and particularly in Poplar, also lived in some of the poorest neighborhoods in the country. Their poverty was further entrenched by the difficulties of living in an overcrowded, unsanitary, and polluted urban environment. Extremely high food prices during the war added to the already difficult life London's East Enders endured in the early twentieth century. For them, participation in an allotment association was particularly transforming. It was a community group that mixed leisure and politics, learning and improvement. At the same time, it offered members a piece of ground on which to ease the financial and emotional burden of feeding the family. Most importantly, the association gave the working man some power over both his and his community's affairs. By the end of World War I, allotment associations had become fully functioning, self-sufficient, and autonomous grassroots political bodies with active memberships and efficient executives.

Allotment associations in the East End offered their members participation in a political process at many different levels. The member was free to choose how much or how little work he would perform for the association. Allotment associations fostered many skills working-class men would not have learned elsewhere (aside from the trade union which in East London tended not to succeed due to poverty and the casual nature of work). The key functions of an association were to manage the allotments site(s), maintain membership and plot holder lists, write letters and run campaigns, organize protests, hold meetings, sponsor horticultural and legal lectures and seminars, manage funds, and elect the executive. Learning and perfecting these skills led working men to further politicization by regaining control over their affairs, participating in a democratic process, gaining voice and autonomy, building confidence with officials, advocating the community's needs, and expressing their individuality while working within a collective. Individual political autonomy was hard to come by for working-class men; many did not secure the vote until 1918, most struggled to own property, and certainly all remained outside the norms of Victorian middle-class masculinity and liberalism. They were always stronger collectively, defining themselves by class. Allotments offered an opportunity to promote not only the interests of the community but also of the self. Men's participation in these organizations benefited the whole community: working-class women and children now had a voice in their more effective fathers, husbands, brothers, and sons. As part of the self-help ethos of the allotments movement, working-class people could better safeguard their affairs. Frederick Impey wrote in 1886 of the "desire of men everywhere to have something beyond their labour to depend upon – to occupy land on their own accord."[3]

Gerald Butcher of the Vacant Land Cultivations Society maintained that the most significant aspect of the allotments movement was "the democratic influence which it has exercised upon the minds of the people."[4] Indeed, this democratic extension occurred in all areas of the East End where there were allotments, but particularly in Poplar. Equally profound was the patriotic urge to contribute to the war effort, especially by 1916 and the *Cultivation of Lands Order*. Butcher claimed that while patriotism was key to the vigor with which people picked up the spade in 1916, so too was their nostalgia for better times and a lost life on the land:

> True patriotism, no doubt, induced many to take up the arduous and, occasionally, disconcerting task of cultivating allotments, but, while the motives of nearly all war-time allotmenteers were prompted by a patriotic impulse, there is indisputable evidence to show that the movement which seeks to place amateurs in possession of land was really animated and made possible by the awakening of a long-latent land-hunger in the hearts of the people.[5]

Nostalgic and idyllic memories of easier times occurred frequently in the East End psyche precisely because life was so difficult and often unpleasant in comparison. Butcher himself said that allotment holders, "recognizing the patriotic nature of their employment, strenuously devoted their time either to office routine or to making out and allotting new plots."[6]

In early 1917 working-class men in the borough of Poplar set about the task of forming allotments associations. In February the borough council formed itself into an allotment society they called the Poplar Borough Allotments Society. This was only to be temporary though, for one week later the council held a meeting to call for the formation of an allotment society among its residents – they formed the Cubitt Town Allotments Society. The name was later changed to the Millwall and Cubitt Town Allotments Association. The Mayor chaired this inaugural meeting as a plea to the residents of the borough and offered advice to prospective plot holders; the advice would encourage those who were

ELIZABETH A. SCOTT

unsure about the possibility of growing food in London to apply for a plot. That day, the new association signed up nearly 100 new plot holders "where Millwaller after Millwaller signed the necessary form and invested in some cheap and very informative literature showing how to get the maximum quantity of produce from a few square yards of ground."[7] The *East End News* reported that the vigor with which the new society worked was most impressive: "It is … gratifying that the Borough Allotment Society, though born only a week or two ago, would appear to have become a most promising infant … its youthful enthusiasm has inspired quite a small army of Millwallers."[8] The *Vacant Lots and the Allotment Holder* newspaper also cheered on the men in Poplar. They reported that the first meeting was "enthusiastic and inspiring."[9] The paper also confirmed that the men elected a chairman, secretary, treasurer, and committee; the first decision was to secure the necessary fencing for the allotments sites under their auspices. They also ensured that the water supply was satisfactory and sometimes even provided tools to the plot holders.

Within a matter of hours, then, at least 100 working-class men participated in a democratic election, advocated for their community's need for food and proper allotments sites, and learned practical and theoretical horticultural knowledge to apply to their gardens. Few associations, societies, or clubs offered such a diversity of political opportunities to working-class men. Allotment associations in Poplar continued to mature throughout 1917. In March the association raised £8 for fencing and successfully requested a further £24 to complete their project from the borough council. The negotiation with the borough council was professional and carefully calculated and shows working-class men drawing on the literacy and mathematical skills required to engage in political dialogue.

The Allotment Site

The allotment site provided East End men with further opportunities to develop their political awareness. Allotment holders learned how to manage land so that it was of benefit to the entire collective. While there was a "good-natured rivalry" between gardeners, the men had to learn how to work cooperatively, not just individually. For instance, tools were often held collectively and so planning a schedule for use and learning to fairly execute the rotation of tools and supplies was in itself an act of community bonding that forged stronger relationships between individuals. These relationships would later translate into the willingness to advocate for the community on various other social and political issues. Evidently, in working an allotment in the war period there was an element of moral responsibility to the community, both to the local working-class community and to the country as a whole. Alternatively, working an allotment, especially one that sat on a vacant lot, was also a way to improve the aesthetic of the neighborhood, thus increasing community pride; the Allotments Society aimed to turn their site into "a beauty spot and a credit to the borough."[10] Beautification was particularly significant for East End allotmenteers because of the aesthetically deprived urban conditions in which they were forced to live. For East End men, the opportunity to participate in a scheme that fostered creativity and individual expression helped them better define their cultural parameters and escape from the daily monotony of their paid work.

The physical act of gardening was in its essence a positive and healthy activity that strengthened working-class men's self-esteem. Allotment holders were said to be "happily at work on ... newly acquired garden plots" throughout London in the war period.[11] Furthermore, Londoners observed that "many people who had hitherto taken no interest in the commons and parks ... now love to doddle among the potatoes and the marrows."[12] Certainly, working-class men had other opportunities to be physically active; they played football, cycled, swam, and danced; they walked in the local open spaces, and enjoyed cricket, boxing, and tennis. It was the particular brand of physical activity that the allotment site offered that is noteworthy. The physical act of cultivating one's own food as a member of the disadvantaged class created lasting intellectual and philosophical results. By growing food on an allotment, the East End man eased the emotional and financial burden of feeding his family. His physical labor allowed him to regain some control over his financial affairs on top of his low or casual wages. This recovery of autonomy was a powerful force and led allotment holders to fight for the permanency of their plots later in 1918. In no other way did working-class men in the East End of London draw power and wealth from the land. The small 10-rod plot returned to its worker a long-lost sense of self-sufficiency, self-worth, and pride.

Tending an allotment was no easy task and demanded a high level of responsibility and dedication. These were qualities that working men in the late nineteenth and early twentieth centuries continually had to prove they possessed to their middle-class critics. The allotment fostered responsibility among its participants – a quality essential to becoming a more politically effective member of society. Allotments tested the men who worked them; growing food in the polluted East End was difficult and so learning about horticulture and growing methods was essential. Horticultural knowledge and learning was one of the most significant ways in which working-class men strengthened their literacy skills, expanded their thinking, and their participation in wider society. Consequently, working an allotment was also an exercise in expressing and developing the image of respectable working-class masculinity. He was a man who learned, participated, and worked hard without necessarily aspiring to leave his social position. His ability to provide for his family further earmarked him as a competent and respectable man. Indeed, the primary mark of rising to the middle class was a man's ability to earn enough that his wife would not have to work.

New Relationships: Councillors and Gardeners

The nature of the relationships that developed between plot holders and borough councillors in the early twentieth century suggests that the allotments scheme in East London encouraged working-class men to become active in local politics and enhance and practice the skills they learned in the association and on the plot. In Poplar, allotmenteers and councillors developed a relationship exhibiting a great degree of solidarity; from the beginning, the council encouraged and advocated for its plot holders. In a recent article, Alan Johnson has identified the origins of many of the Poplar borough councillors from 1919 to 1925. He found that the vast majority of local councillors had been longtime residents of the borough and were members of the working classes: "Stevedores and housewives, toolmakers and dock labourers, corn porters and railwaymen, labourers, postmen and engineers, ran the council chamber and the street protests."[13] This is critically important and, as Johnson suggests, narrowed the usual gap between working-class resident and middle-class administrator. Johnson describes the leadership of the Poplar council on various social issues as involving a "conversation rather than a lecture."[14] By 1921 the borough council in Poplar had its residents' needs at heart when it refused to submit its rates to the London County Council over the policy of equalization of the poor rates. Rates were twice as high in

Poplar as they were in the West End simply because of the high proportion of laboring poor in the East End; George Lansbury, MP, said "the poor were paying for the poor."[15] Known as the Poplar Rates Rebellion, six councillors were imprisoned over the affair. Their actions suggest that the relationship I have identified for the allotment movement existed in other forms and was made possible by what Johnson calls a political leadership that was "organic to the Poplar working class."[16] Finally, Johnson further explains, as have others, that the councillors in Poplar were in "active contact" with residents on labor issues and that in this context residents formed "an unusually active and participating electorate [who] came to political meetings of all kinds, were stirred by what they heard, raised their voices, were drawn in and consulted and, from time to time, were filled with excitement and a sense of purpose."[17] Clearly, the people of Poplar were active in the administration of their affairs and the allotment movement provided them with a significant and valuable link to local government.

As early as 1910, the local council was closely involved with allotments and horticulture in Poplar. The *East London Observer* reported in September of that year that the Mayor of Poplar "last Friday, opened the second show held under the auspices of the Millwall and Cubitt Town Horticultural Society," and he, along with the judges, "expressed genuine approval of the quality of the cauliflowers, onions, cabbages, carrots, beans, and beetroots that were exhibited."[18] Naturally then, by 1917 the council was fully implementing the 1916 *Cultivation of Lands Order* and spent a great deal of time setting up allotments in the borough to meet residents' needs. In January 1917 the General Purposes Committee, after lengthy deliberation on the opening of some of the first wartime allotments in Cubitt Town, decided to appoint an executive committee to carry out the proposals. The prudence with which the council dealt with allotments points to a more general concern over the wellbeing of the residents and is early evidence of an emerging relationship between the plot holders and the councillors.

By the summer of 1917 the council was doing everything in its power not to increase allotment rents to cover costs. The motion to pass a rent for second-year holders was withdrawn, suggesting the council sympathized with the plot holders. In September the council minutes reveal one of the first meetings recorded between a councillor, in this case Councillor Thorne, and a group of allotment holders. The meeting was held to address allotment rents and was successful – the allotment holders agreed to pass the rent only because it would benefit the site and

ELIZABETH A. SCOTT

people were willing to pay. Councillor Thorne's attendance at the meeting gave allotment holders in Poplar the chance to directly engage in political dialogue with a member of the council. These meetings created significant bonds between the two groups that proved necessary once the threat of eviction loomed large in 1918.

At the Millwall Mudfield, the Port of London Authority operated 224 allotments and dealt directly with its members. However, in May 1918 the Authority approached the council on a fencing matter where it is recorded that the borough council would continue to act in a middleman role between the plot holders and the Authority. The advocacy demonstrated on the part of the council indicates a relationship that acted to protect allotment holders' interests with other governing bodies and to help them better voice their concerns. It could be interpreted as a somewhat paternal relationship, or at least protective in some capacity, but I would argue that the council created a partnership with the plot holders in Poplar. The Allotments Society reported to the Vacant Land Cultivations Society in June 1917 that they were "grateful to our local council and borough surveyor for the encouragement and financial help rendered by them," illustrating once again Poplar's dedication to the plot holders' work.[19] The partnership between the council in Poplar and allotment holders is evident in the support, encouragement, and commitment described above and evokes friendly rather than paternal comparisons; the council did not dictate how the plot holders should run their sites, nor did they assume to be experts on allotments. They evidently stood in solidarity with each other on many matters.

The relationships identified above are significant for several reasons. First, and most importantly, they provided working-class men with a tangible political connection to government. These connections fostered a better appreciation of political activism in that working men in East London could see the results of their involvement. Second, class relations in the East End were never as strained internally as they were externally; that is, tensions between members of one class were never as difficult as between members of two different classes. Nonetheless, working men were considered of a lower order than those on the councils. The relationships I have outlined here suggest the beginning of a change in class relations in East London, at least in Poplar. A diminished importance was placed on class as is shown by the solidarity of the allotment holders and councillors. Class, while it was still most certainly present, was not the most important category in which borough councils discussed allotment holders' concerns. First and foremost was their attention to the direct and specific needs of the allotment community. Finally, working men's participation in allotment politics in the period studied reveals the maturation of their political conscience. When we consider the vigor with which allotment holders fought for the permanency of their plots after 1918, we can clearly see that the previous period of political growth allowed for a more articulate and informed campaign. Participation in allotment associations led working men to voice their concerns on other local matters equipped with the knowledge and skills they had secured through allotments.

Conclusions

The right to grow one's own food is fundamental to our existence, yet we rarely consider it at risk. Community gardens and allotments have provided, and still do provide, a grassroots solution to this threat. Allotments represent the struggle to access the power and wealth that lies in the land, a struggle in which East Enders fully participated, in the least likely of places. What we can take from the experience in Poplar is that the social and political dynamics that result from participating in community initiatives strengthens local bonds and enfranchises those citizens who often struggle to find equal footing. Likewise, we can begin to better grasp the philosophical results of returning to the land for our most basic provisions. Food grown by our own hands instils self-sufficiency and control, concepts especially meaningful for people in lower-income brackets who through history have relied on others for often meager wages and subsistence. Today, the allotments movement has evolved to reflect current social concerns and its trajectory has shifted in response to the demand for organic and locally grown produce. Allotments can and do connect people in a complex web of political and social relationships that can have lasting meaningful results for communities and individuals. Class difference can narrow, advocacy can develop and bring about change, and communities can achieve solidarity. As David Crouch and Colin Ward have suggested, allotments "have been the result of municipal socialism, conservative paternalism, [and] liberal civic pride."[20] They may be small in size and deceivingly unassuming places, but allotments have the power to encourage unexpected growth both in physical and human nature.

ELIZABETH A. SCOTT

NOTES

1 A. Smith and J. B. McKinnion, *The 100-Mile Diet: A Year of Eating Locally* (Toronto: Random House Canada, 2007). Also see M. Pollan, *In Defense of Food: An Eater's Manifesto* (New York: Penguin, 2008) and T. Pawlick, *The End of Food* (Fort Lee: Barricade Books, 2006) for commentaries on the state of the modern food supply, access to food, and general concern about our ability to feed ourselves in healthy ways both physically and politically.

2 J. Bush, *Behind the Lines: East London Labour 1914–1919* (London: Merlin Press, 1984), p. 2; see also S. Pennybacker, *A Vision for London 1889–1914: Labour, Everyday Life and the LCC Experiment* (London: Routledge, 1995), pp. 4, 9.

3 F. Impey, *'Housed Beggars', or The Right of the Labourer to Allotments and Small Holdings* (London: Swan Sonnenschein, 1886), p. 7.

4 G. W. Butcher, *Allotments for All: The Story of a Great Movement* (London: Allen and Unwin, 1918), p. 32.

5 Ibid.

6 Ibid., p. 25.

7 "Allotments for Poplar," *East End News* (February 16, 1917), Tower Hamlets Local History Library and Archives, Allotments File No. 630–1.

8 Ibid.

9 "Branch News & Notes," *Vacant Lots and the Allotment Holder*, March 1917.

10 "Branch News & Notes," *Vacant Lots and the Allotment Holder*, June 1917.

11 "Our Widening Horizons," *Allotments & Gardens*, January 1918.

12 "The Fight for Permanency. Monster Petition to the LCC," *Vacant Lots and the Allotment Holder*, November 1917.

13 A. Johnson, "The Making of a Poor People's Movement: A Study in the Political Leadership of Poplarism, 1919–25," in M. Lavalette and G. Mooney (eds.) *Class Struggle and Social Welfare* (London: Routledge, 2000), p. 102.

14 Ibid., p. 103; see also P. P. Bober, "Rate Capping and 'Poplarism,'" *Contemporary Review* 249, 1448 (1986): 139.

15 Johnson, "The Making of a Poor People's Movement," p. 97.

16 Ibid., p. 101.

17 Ibid., p. 104.

18 "Cubitt Town Paradise," *East London Observer* (September 3, 1910), Tower Hamlets Local History Library and Archives, Allotments File No. 630–1.

19 "Branch News & Notes," *Vacant Lots and the Allotment Holder*, June 1917.

20 D. Crouch and C. Ward, *The Allotment: Its Landscape and Culture* (Nottingham: Five Leaves Publications, 1997), p. 271.

PART III

THE FLOWER SHOW

CHAPTER 9

HORTUS INCANTANS

Gardening as an Art of Enchantment

 While digging in a garden, a young woman stares in breathless wonder at the immense beetle writhing in the clump of mulch that she holds in her hand. While sitting in a garden, an old man is startled by the sudden recollection of a warm summer afternoon spent building sand castles with a long-forgotten childhood friend. While strolling in a garden, a scholar of Byzantine poetry suddenly grasps the meaning of a particularly cryptic passage that has eluded her for nearly three months.

This essay considers the garden as a setting that calls forth such varied moments of enchantment – a category of experience that political philosopher Jane Bennett has described as "a momentary immobilizing encounter; it is to be transfixed, spellbound."[1] Enchantment is rooted in wonder, which Plato famously claimed as the beginning of all philosophy, and which Descartes esteemed to be the most fundamental of all human passions, "because if the object presented has nothing in it that surprises us, we are not in the least moved by it and regard it without passion."[2]

Enchantment involves a peculiar combination of bodily responses and a state of heightened sensory perception. It is also a complex emotional and cognitive state, which Bennett characterizes as "a pleasurable feeling of being charmed by the novel and as yet unprocessed encounter," mixed with "a more *unheimlich* (uncanny) feeling of being disrupted or torn out of one's default sensory-psychic-intellectual disposition." Enchantment

FIGURE 9.1 The Pebble Garden at Dumbarton Oaks, viewed from the terrace of the Green Garden, suggesting the layering of "garden rooms" that comprise the gardens of Dumbarton Oaks.

thus includes an undercurrent of anxiety, but this distress is tempered by a feeling of joyful fascination. "The overall effect of enchantment," Bennett writes, "is a mood of fullness, plenitude, or liveliness, a sense of having had one's nerves or circulation or concentration powers tuned up or recharged – a shot in the arm, a fleeting return to childlike excitement about life."[3]

To be enchanted is to be absorbed by something that strikes us as incredible, perhaps even supernatural: a dandelion puff that floats through the air as if guided by its own volition; a stone figure that shifts its gaze as we pass by; the eerie feeling of being led along a path by some unseen spirit or ghost. Rather than appealing to reason and science to explain away the enchantment effect, in this essay I take such experiences as invitations to consider an alternate view of what a garden is and how it works its magic. Any garden may invite such contemplation, but the account that follows was inspired by some of my own encounters with the garden at Dumbarton Oaks in Washington, DC. To enter this garden is to step into

ERIC MACDONALD

a world that cannot be ascribed to the categories of "nature" or "culture," a space where inert objects become animate, walls speak, and voices from the distant past reverberate through the present (figure 9.1).[4]

Gardens and Enchantment

Enchantment is a prevalent, if underappreciated, theme in the modern European tradition of garden design. The writings of Pliny the Younger and other classical sources provide us with marvelous accounts of Roman gardens that were filled with exotic plants and animals, as well as statuary and mechanical devices that were intended to delight and enchant. These traditions were revived in the palatial gardens of the Renaissance, where statues evoked pagan deities and classical myths amid spectacular fountains, water-powered automata, and "water jokes" that elicited surprise and astonishment from garden visitors. Such devices were commonplace in courtly gardens throughout Europe during the Renaissance and Baroque periods, and they evoked a sense of wonder capable of sparking philosophical and scientific inquiry. Descartes's investigation of the cause of rainbows in his *Météores*, for example, was inspired by his contemplation of the "artificial rainbows" produced by fountains he had admired in several European gardens.

Rainbow fountains and similar garden embellishments worked their magic by provoking uncertainty about the boundary between nature and artifice. The great landscape gardens built in England during the eighteenth century likewise skirted this boundary, although they relied on a different set of techniques to produce an effect of magic. English landscape gardeners manipulated landscape forms, vegetation, and architecture to alter the ordinary perception of space and time. They labored to create idyllic settings that fostered the illusion that one had suddenly stepped into a painting by Claude Lorrain or a poem by Virgil. Since at least Roman times the various modes of Western garden design have exemplified the kind of art that anthropologist Alfred Gell characterized as a "Technology of Enchantment" – a technology that mediates social life through the "manipulation of desire, terror, wonder, cupidity, fantasy, vanity, an inexhaustible list of human passions."[5]

By the nineteenth century gardening also had become a technology that was involved in a larger narrative about the nature (and culture) of *dis*enchantment in the modern world: a story of how modern science, materialism, and instrumental rationality had progressively stripped nature of wonder, mystery, and divinity, leaving humans adrift in a cold, meaningless world. This view of modernity was concisely articulated in 1917 by sociologist Max Weber, who soberly concluded that "[t]he fate of our times is characterized by rationalization and intellectualization and, above all, by the 'disenchantment of the world.'"[6] Gardens and designed landscapes became a means for countering this trend. Public landscapes such as New York City's Central Park were conceived as places for reacquainting urban populations with nature's "charms" and repairing the psychic and spiritual damage caused by everyday life in the modern industrial city. By the beginning of the twentieth century the notion that gardening nurtured a spiritual connection with nature and restored a sense of mystery and magic to a disenchanted world had become a prevalent theme in popular garden literature.

Modern strategies for cultivating the enchantment in gardens varied. Some writers urged gardeners more closely to observe and imitate nature, promoting "wild gardening" as a practice for nurturing a deeper, mystical connection with the non-human world. Others sought to lead modern gardeners back to earlier forms of European garden art, hoping to both revitalize a dispirited civilization and rekindle a sense of mystery and reverence for the natural world. The American novelist Edith Wharton, for example, sought inspiration from the great flowering of humanism known as the Italian Renaissance. In 1904 Wharton published *Italian Villas and Their Gardens*, a book that she hoped would reacquaint modern readers with the "garden-magic" of Italian Renaissance villas. "The traveler returning from Italy, with his eyes and imagination full of the ineffable Italian garden-magic, knows vaguely that the enchantment exists; that he has been under its spell, and that it is more potent, more enduring, more intoxicating to every sense than the most elaborate and glowing effects of modern horticulture," wrote Wharton.[7] The practitioner of "modern horticulture," who was too inclined toward analytical reduction, was ill-equipped to uncover the source of this enchantment, Wharton believed. The experience of enchantment could not be analyzed scientifically and it could not be causally linked to any single element or combination of elements, such as the blueness of the sky, or the luxuriant green of clipped hedges. Italian garden-magic, Wharton argued, emerged from the way in which garden spaces related to the architectural geometry of the house and the manner in which they accommodated the shape of the land and incorporated views of the surrounding countryside. Garden-magic, in other words, was not reducible to a material property. It was instead

ERIC MACDONALD

a relational effect that emerged from drawing disparate elements into harmonious association with one another. Indeed, the first great development in Renaissance garden art, Wharton wrote, "was the architect's discovery of the means by which nature and art might be fused."[8]

Dumbarton Oaks: A Fusion of Nature and Art?

The notion of gardening as an act of resistance to a disenchanted, fragmented modern world is a theme that threads through the history of Dumbarton Oaks. Formerly the private estate of diplomat Robert Woods Bliss and his wife Mildred, Dumbarton Oaks is today a public garden, museum, and research institution that promotes scholarship in Byzantine, Pre-Columbian, and garden and landscape studies. Located atop the highest point in the Georgetown district of Washington, DC, the 53-acre parcel that the Blisses purchased in 1920 included an old brick mansion, several farm buildings, and steep wooded hillsides traversed by service roads and cow paths. Shortly after acquiring the property, the Blisses hired Edith Wharton's niece, landscape gardener Beatrix Farrand, to help them create an ideal "country place" in the city. During the 1920s, Farrand and Mildred Bliss collaborated on the design of the estate and its gardens, a work that Bliss once described as the realization of their "mutual dream."[9]

Both Bliss and Farrand were knowledgeable of European garden traditions, and they looked to contemporary and historic gardens in Italy, France, and England for inspiration. They transformed the steeply sloping ground north and east of the house into a connected complex of terraces and garden rooms. The general plan of the garden employed orthogonal geometry, but it was carefully adapted to the terrain as well as to a framework of existing tall trees. Pathways, openings, and enclosures were carefully arranged to create a sequence of tightly defined and expansive views, subtly guiding one's movement through the garden. Design details, garden architecture, and ornament were meticulously developed from careful study of European precedents. Although Farrand's involvement in the garden's design diminished after the late 1940s, Mildred Bliss continued to develop the garden with the assistance of Farrand's former assistant, Ruth Havey. At the time of Bliss's death in 1969, Dumbarton Oaks exemplified the kind of endeavor that Wharton had upheld as an art of "garden magic."

Dumbarton Oaks, however, became more than just a single, private act of resistance to the disenchantment narrative. It became an institution dedicated to preserving the values of humanism that, to Mildred Bliss, the garden so beautifully embodied. During the late 1930s, as a second world war seemed all but imminent, the Blisses began making arrangements to transfer their estate to Harvard University for use as a library, museum, and research center. In 1940 Dumbarton Oaks began its new life as an oasis for humanities scholars. "If ever the humanities were necessary ... it is in this epoch of disintegration and dislocation," wrote Mildred Bliss to a Harvard official.[10] As she continued to develop the gardens of Dumbarton Oaks during the 1950s and 1960s, Bliss increasingly began to view gardening and garden scholarship as a necessary part of this mission. In 1947, with Farrand's encouragement and assistance, she began collecting books and manuscripts on gardening and horticulture, and in 1963 a new building was constructed to house the Dumbarton Oaks Garden Library. She encouraged Harvard administrators to think of Dumbarton Oaks as an institution to "advance garden design and ornament through example, not just operate botany courses," and she pressed them to establish a research program in the history of gardens similar to those in place for Byzantine and pre-Columbian scholars. In the preamble to her will, Mildred Bliss called upon the university

> to remember that Dumbarton Oaks is conceived in a new pattern ... that it is home of the humanities, not a mere aggregation of books and objects of art.... Those responsible should remember ... that gardens have their place in the Humanist order of life; and that trees are noble elements to be protected by successive generations and are not to be lightly destroyed.[11]

Gardens were essential to Mildred Bliss's vision of Dumbarton Oaks as a sanctuary for humanism. In a disintegrating and disenchanted world, the garden was needed because, unlike Byzantine or pre-Columbian studies, it explicitly held the potential to restore both nature and culture. The garden, itself a harmonious synthesis of humans and nature, was a form of work that might rescue a culture that was becoming increasingly alienated and estranged from nature. At the same time, the garden held the promise of saving nature by leading humans toward a more nurturing and reverent appreciation of the "nobility" of trees and other forms of life. The garden thus had a kind of impossible double mission: itself a hybrid of nature and culture, the garden was nonetheless to become a vehicle for achieving both a purified nature and culture. Such an account thus leaves us with a rather puzzling depiction of the agency of gardens. Yet it highlights the central paradox that underlies much modern commentary on gardens and gardening: in a world made of only two kinds of ingredients – humans on one side, and non-human "nature" on the other – gardens may be explained only as the result of some manner of interaction between the two. In some narratives, as in the fortuitous fusion of art and nature sought by Wharton, the mixing of humans and nature occurs as a harmonious partnership. In other tales, the drama unfolds as a kind of unending battle, with the human gardener heroically struggling to exert dominion over the unruly and hostile forces of nature. In either case, our stories about gardens are limited by this dualistic way of thinking.

If we abandon the time-worn notions of nature and culture, how else might we describe the human experience of gardens? Perhaps we might posit that the world is simply made up of vast assemblages of things – organisms, machines, humans, institutions, and so on – entities that don't have to be designated as either "nature" or "culture," or conceived as some kind of nature-culture blend. These assemblages, or networks of entities, are constantly changing and, as a result, their capacity to act – their degrees of agency – also evolves. Because we can never fully account for all of the entities that are linked together, they frequently perform in ways that surprise us. Thinking about a garden as a network, then, might help us become more attuned to moments when we glimpse the surprising relationships among the various things that the garden connects together. It might yield an alternative view of the rare encounters that comprise the experience of "garden-magic." Drawing upon this premise, the account below focuses on three types of enchanting experiences – crossings, complexity, and circuits – to contemplate just what a garden like Dumbarton Oaks might be, as well as some of the ways in which it might enchant.

Dumbarton Oaks as a Site of Enchantment: Crossings, Complexity, and Circuits

In seeking to revive the magical dimension of this art, writers like Edith Wharton promoted gardens as a sacred kind of haven in a disenchanted world, the sort of place where it might be possible to once again become attuned to the mystery and wonder of life. The gardeners of Mildred Bliss's generation, embracing the view of garden design expressed by Wharton, were inclined to regard "garden-magic" as a product of "the deeper harmony of design" achieved by successfully fusing nature and art. This strategy also was exemplified in the individual elements that enlivened the grand old European landscapes that these gardeners admired: fountains that produced rainbows, perspective effects that made faraway places seem near, sculptural figures that moved as if they were alive – all of these devices crossed the boundary between nature and artifice. Designing a garden was thus an exercise in producing marvellous nature-culture hybrids.

To the extent that we remain wedded to a picture of the world that distinguishes humans and nature as belonging to separate realms of existence, it is perhaps not surprising that those who design and manage gardens continue to see the production of novel nature-culture hybrids as a source of enchantment. Indeed, this tradition persists at Dumbarton Oaks. During the summer and fall of 2009, for example, visitors to the garden encountered a bizarre inflorescence protruding from a wisteria vine in an area of the garden known as Arbor Terrace. This alien entity, looming overhead in a shadowy corner of a wooden arbor, seemed to be part animal and part vegetable, with a flesh-coloured "skin" that was swathed in places by a twisted band of tiny clay "bricks." This strange and grotesque hybrid, entitled "Growth," was part of a temporary exhibition entitled *Landscape/Body/Dwelling* that featured artworks by American sculptor Charles Simonds. Placed throughout the Dumbarton Oaks gardens and museum, many of Simonds's sculptures resemble beings that are undergoing a process of transformation. Their forms are ambiguous, often fusing elements in ways that confuse boundaries between earth, animal, and vegetable. Some of the pieces, like "Growth," were stealthy, almost blending seamlessly with their surroundings, appearing at once familiar and alien, disturbing and beautiful. They are wonderful examples of the kinds of objects that Jane Bennett characterizes as "crossings": entities that appear to "morph from one category of being to another."[12] Like the mechanical automata that once evoked wonder in Renaissance and Baroque gardens, Simonds's sculptures charm by presenting themselves as entities that provoke uncertainty about the relationship between art and nature, humans and non-humans. Indeed, they seem capable of eliciting reflection about the ambiguous status of the entire garden as a hybrid. As Michael O'Sullivan remarked in a review of the exhibition for the *Washington Post*:

> Dumbarton Oaks' tended roses are also a mix of nature and artifice. That's the essence of almost any garden: It's both born and made. In the light of

ERIC MACDONALD

Simonds's hybrid sculptures – part earth, part plant, part animal – our attempts to tame and train what is, by nature, wild and ever-changing are laid bare.[13]

The sculptures of *Landscape/Body/Dwelling* presented visitors with perplexing and sometimes disturbing "crossings," accentuating the garden's ability to act as a site that calls into question the relationship between humans and nature. In other words, artworks like "Growth" surprise and provoke a sense of wonder because they expose the paradox that lies at the heart of a world in which humans and nature inhabit distinct realms. Yet, as O'Sullivan's comment suggests, Simonds's evocative sculptures are not the only hybrid entities in the world around us. Indeed, we might take seriously the suggestion that everything around us – even we ourselves – are "hybrids." Like "Growth" and the "tended rose," we all exist and do what we do by virtue of becoming mixed and entangled with many other things, some of which are human and some of which are not. The tended rose need not be seen as a thing of nature, a human artifact, or even a "fusion" of nature and art. Rather, it may be a network of plant DNA, gardeners, hybridizers, soil, water, insects, pesticides, ticket-buying garden visitors, and numerous other entities. Everything in the garden is an imbroglio, a knot that ties together humans and innumerable other things.

In a garden, conceived not as a synthesis of nature and culture but as a dynamic and complex assemblage of humans and non-human entities, unexpected things like "Growth" are constantly showing up. *Landscape/Body/Dwelling*, for example, was initiated by the arrival of a new human actor: John Beardsley, who became Director of Garden and Landscape Studies at Dumbarton Oaks the previous year. Beardsley brought with him expertise in contemporary environmental art, extensive experience as an art curator, and personal connections with the art world, including a longtime friendship with the artist, Charles Simonds. *Landscape/Body/Dwelling* materialized as but one instance of what is constantly going on in a garden: the arrival of new actors creates a ripple effect as they forge unforeseen alliances with both human and non-human entities. These shifts in the composition of the garden allow it to behave in astonishing ways. We never really know for sure how many humans, plants, animals, and other entities are interacting within the garden, and this uncertainty is perhaps a fundamental source of enchantment. Moments of wonder may occur as glimpses of previously unseen or new components of the assemblage: a strange insect, or an enveloping fog. Or they may arise from encounters with entities that behave in surprising ways: a bird performing a curious "dance," a once-solid hillside that is now saturated with gurgling water, on the verge of melting into the streambed below.

The sudden appearance of any of these things – the bug, the bird, the fog, and the dissolving hillside – highlights the sheer complexity of the assemblage that envelopes us. The garden is not just complicated – that is, made of many parts – it is complex, meaning that the individual components are related in ways that make the garden's "performance" something that can never be entirely predicted. The garden, in other words, may achieve the appearance of coherence and stability, but it is never static. It is in a state of constant flux. Moreover, some of the entities have been drawn together in ways that make them practically invisible. Consider, for example, the network of water pipes that underlies the garden terraces. It consists of a vast array of components – water, pumps, gauges, pipes, couplings, etc. – yet we rarely see the essential "work" that this assemblage performs in making the garden possible. The water system, buried, invisible, and undocumented, silently and reliably does its job until one day ... a pipe leaks, the hillside becomes saturated with water and begins to lose some of its solidity. The garden can no longer be experienced as a serene, verdant oasis. The garden reveals itself as composed, in part, by a machine that sometimes behaves badly – a machine that spurs members of the Dumbarton Oaks maintenance crew into frantic action. As they search for the source of the leak, the garden becomes a confusing and complex multiplicity of potentially faulty pipes, valves, and couplings. For people who love mechanical devices, who delight in deciphering complex systems and take pleasure in making things operate smoothly, a leaking pipe can be a source of vexation, exhilaration, and enchantment. In such moments we may wonder at the sheer complexity of something that once seemed so simple, revel in the surprise of just what a taken-for-granted entity might be made of, and gasp at the flurry of human activity that is now swarming around it.

Enchantment arises from the sense that we can never fully account for the action that unfolds before our eyes. Hence, the experience of enchantment may spring from a sudden awareness of the complexity of things that at first seemed simple, or from encounters that jolt us out of our normal sense of the distinctions between humans and non-human things. A garden like Dumbarton Oaks is filled with such entities – material objects that have the ability to take on capacities that we commonly assume to be uniquely human, such as the ability to speak. Consider, for example, a wall in a section of the garden known as Arbor Terrace. The wall bears the Latin inscription, "Those who in old time sang of the Golden Age, and of its happy state, perchance, upon Parnassus, dreamed of this place."[14] The passage, selected by Mildred Bliss from Dante's *Purgatorio*, is rendered in decorative lead letters set in a simple stone plaque. Who is it that speaks in the Arbor Terrace? Dante? Mildred Bliss? The artisan who crafted the plaque? The wall itself? The wall carries the speaking of, at least, all of these. The wall, with its inscription, is an assemblage that links together all of these entities, and they all collaborate to speak in a way that also links together different spaces and times. Dante, Mildred Bliss, and the artisan are nowhere to be seen. Yet in this particular garden wall, their thoughts, words, and actions reverberate through the present.

The garden thus weaves together many actors, some of whom have long since vanished from the scene. Its walls and walkways, sculptures and inscriptions act as circuits that constantly connect us with the past, sometimes in surprising or uncanny ways. For instance, garden historian Michel Conan has described how many visitors navigate Dumbarton Oaks' carefully planned sequence of spaces and views, all the while feeling as though someone or something is "guiding one's steps in ways one does not even realize are happening."[15] Such intuitions reveal that a garden path is never simply a linear shaft of space that is experienced as a single moment in time. It is a material construction that transfers past actions forward into the present, so that today we walk where Mildred Bliss and Beatrix Farrand walked, and we follow the path they carefully mapped out for us. They really *are* our guides, as the path mediates between us and them and connects the past to the present. In those rare moments when we sense this circuit, the effect can be enchanting.

The abundance of such linkages in a garden like Dumbarton Oaks ensures that the past is never wholly lost, "back there," forever inaccessible and growing ever more remote with each tick of the clock. Everywhere, objects abound that, given a certain state of affairs, might shift us out of a linear temporality. Indeed, much of the work of maintaining a garden like Dumbarton Oaks is devoted to preserving the circuitry between past and present. Trees, walls, pathways, sculptures, and other material elements of the garden are meticulously conserved, but so is an immense and ever-growing assemblage of plans, accounts, letters, diaries, receipts, paintings, sketches, and photographs. Each document becomes a link back to the past, and the garden archive becomes yet another site where one might appreciate the peculiar ability of artifacts to preserve the most ephemeral instances of human experience: a candid photograph captures the bond of affection felt between two friends, or a letter conveys the super-charged emotion of a heated dispute between two adversaries. The photograph and the letter translate only some tiny fragment of the social exchange, but in doing so – in becoming material – the fragment gains both durability and mobility. Some sliver of a persona, emotion, and thought escapes the precise place and moment of its enactment so that a researcher, today, may become enraptured in tracing the unfolding of a conversation that occurred in 1953.

The discovery of an old letter, photograph, or sketch – perhaps the spine-tingling discovery by a historian working in the garden library – creates a new assemblage, as the historian forges new connections with some of the innumerable entities that comprise Dumbarton Oaks. Who knows what effect the historian, together with her documents, will have on the future of the garden? Perhaps they will join forces in a research report or an academic seminar. Perhaps they will enter into a lively debate about historical truth and fiction, or whether a certain garden feature ought to be conserved, removed, or replaced. If we follow the action that unfolds, we may become more attuned to the magical power of material things – their uncanny ability to become fully entangled in the lives of humans, to carry and mediate human action and to influence what humans do and how they feel. We might also wonder at the tremendous power of the garden itself – how it has the ability to make people do all kinds of surprising things. What kind of magic might be possessed by an entity that compels people to devote untold hours to digging, weeding, and pruning, or moves them to toil with such urgency to fix an unruly water system, or inspires them to create artworks that flout the distinctions between animal, vegetable, and mineral – or, for that matter, to write accounts about the enchantment of gardens? There is no way of knowing for certain what a garden is made of, and no way of knowing for sure what it can do.

Cultivating Enchantment

In depicting Dumbarton Oaks as an artful assemblage, I have ventured an account that is, I hope, more inspiring than one that describes gardening as a ceaseless "battle" between humans and nature, and more fruitful than a tale that renders it as a mysterious "fusion" of art and nature. Indeed, much of the action that unfolds within a garden is cause for

ERIC MACDONALD

wonder, yet our sense of magic is obscured when we use verbs such as "battle" and "fuse" to characterize the art of gardening. A great garden like Dumbarton Oaks presents us with something much more interesting and astonishing: a vast, entangled web of humans, water, rock, trees and flowers, electrical circuits, filing cabinets, computers, documents, accounting techniques, and innumerable other things connected in associations that may or may not hold together for very long. We may suspect that Dumbarton Oaks even exceeds the aspirations of Mildred Bliss and Beatrix Farrand in its capacity to stand against the disenchantment of the world – not as an artful fusion of nature and culture, but as an endless, speculative exploration of an assemblage, a constant testing of what will hold with what, and a hopeful weaving of relations that are traceable and durable.

For the humans involved in this endeavor, the uncertainty about what is (or may be) drawn together, and the rare moments of enchantment that erupt when some of the hidden connections are glimpsed, must be among the chief joys of gardening. Indeed, perhaps wonder is the beginning not only of philosophy, but also of gardening. Perhaps, too, we might begin to think more seriously about cultivating gardens as sites of enchantment, for such experiences may open us to the strangeness, vitality, and beauty of the world. Jane Bennett argues that enchantment can have this effect, and she suggests that cultivating an awareness of wonder may enable one "to respond gracefully and generously to the painful challenges posed by our condition as finite beings in a turbulent and unjust world."[16] Indeed, "without modes of enchantment," Bennett writes, "we might not have the energy and inspiration to enact ecological projects, or to contest ugly and unjust modes of commercialization, or to respond generously to humans and nonhumans that challenge our settled identities."[17] In light of this possibility – the slim chance that a garden might reveal some of the surprising connections that tie together the world – we might renew again Voltaire's declaration, "We must cultivate our garden."

NOTES

1 J. Bennett, *The Enchantment of Modern Life: Attachments, Crossings, and Ethics* (Princeton: Princeton University Press, 2001), p. 5.
2 R. Descartes, *The Passions of the Soul*, trans. S. H. Voss (Indianapolis: Hackett, 1989 [1649]), p. 52.

3 Bennett, *The Enchantment of Modern Life*, p. 5.

4 This essay draws selectively from some of the key premises of actor-network theory (ANT), a body of thought that has emerged since the 1980s through the work of scholars of science and technology such as Bruno Latour, Michel Callon, and John Law.

5 A. Gell, "Technology and Magic," *Anthropology Today* 4, 2 (April 1988): 7.

6 M. Weber, "Science as a Vocation," in *Max Weber: Essays in Sociology*, ed. and trans. H. H. Gerth and C. Wright Mills (New York: Oxford University Press, 1946), p. 155.

7 E. Wharton, *Italian Villas and Their Gardens* (New York: Century, 1904), p. 6.

8 Ibid., p. 7.

9 R. Karson, *A Genius for Place: American Landscapes of the Country Place Era* (Amherst: University of Massachusetts Press, in association with the Library of American Landscape History, 2008), p. 153.

10 Inscription outside the Dumbarton Oaks Library, quoted from a letter written by Mildred Bliss to Harvard professor Paul Sachs.

11 Mildred Barnes Bliss's will, quoted in S. Tamulevich, *Dumbarton Oaks: Garden into Art* (New York: Monacelli Press, 2001), p. 200.

12 Bennett, *The Enchantment of Modern Life*, p. 13.

13 M. O'Sullivan, "At Dumbarton Oaks, a Bold New 'Landscape,'" *Washington Post* (June 12, 2009).

14 The inscription quotes lines 139–41 of Canto XXVIII of Dante's *Purgatorio*. The translation given above is by Charles Eliot Norton. See L. Lott and J. Carder, *Garden Ornament at Dumbarton Oaks* (Washington, DC: Dumbarton Oaks Research Library and Collection, 2001), pp. 35–6.

15 S. Tamulevich, P. Amranand, and P. Johnson, *Dumbarton Oaks* (New York: Random House, 2002), p. 98.

16 Bennett, *The Enchantment of Modern Life*, p. 160.

17 Ibid., p. 174.

CHAPTER 10

GARDENS, MUSIC, AND TIME

 The eighteenth-century philosopher Immanuel Kant is often considered to be the father of modern aesthetics. In the *Critique of Judgement* he suggests a taxonomy of the fine arts (beaux arts) of his time, dividing them into three: the arts of speech, the formative arts and, as he described it, "the art of the beautiful play of sensations." He then further divides the formative arts into plastic art (sculpture and architecture) and painting, and painting into "painting proper" and "landscape gardening."[1] Painting proper involves "the beautiful portrayal of nature" and landscape gardening involves "the beautiful arrangement of its products."[2] Kant goes on to say that gardens, or at least landscape gardens, are "for the eye only, just like painting,"[3] and that, like any work of fine art, a beautiful garden is one that meets a certain aesthetic standard. Kant's classification of landscape gardens as works of visual art reflected the commonsense view of his time. They were works of art because their creation required skill and planning and because they aspired to be beautiful to look at. The view that gardens were primarily works of visual art persisted and was strengthened by successive historical and aesthetic events such as the rise in importance of the picturesque as an aesthetic quality, the continuing influence of the Beaux Arts tradition, and the influence of modernism as the dominant aesthetic theory during much of the last century. The belief that gardens are works of visual art like painting

has endured since Kant's time and it is only in the last few decades that the belief has come under scrutiny.

We will not challenge the claim that gardens can be understood and appreciated as things that are "for the eye" and that aspire to be lovely to look at. Understanding gardens as a subcategory of painting is a valid way to understand their value, as far as it goes. Gardens can be appreciated as pictures. However, appreciating them in this way affords only an incomplete experience of them. Our purpose is to argue that gardens have visual dimensions that painting, sculpture, and architecture lack. In particular, we will develop a suggestion that gardens present the passing of time visually in a way that is analogous to the way in which music presents the passing of time audibly, notwithstanding certain differences between their respective forms of presentation. We will argue that appreciating this aspect of gardens supplies a reason for conceptualizing them as a distinctive category of art that offers a unique kind of experience.

Mara Miller defines gardens as "any purposeful arrangement of natural objects (such as sand, water, plants, rocks, etc.) with exposure to the sky or open air, in which the form is not fully accounted for by purely practical considerations such as convenience."[4] We will adopt this as a working definition while sharing Miller's concerns about its limitations. We agree with her clarification that the point of many historical and contemporary gardens is to produce food and medicinal supplies and their form is dictated by these and other practical considerations. Moreover, we agree that many gardens incorporate unnatural objects as elements – sculptures made of fiberglass, ceramic birdbaths, glass, mosaics, etc. However, Miller's definition is adequate for our purposes because our focus is on gardens as works of art and her definition comfortably includes paradigmatic art gardens, such as Monet's garden at Giverney, the gardens at Stourhead, the Ryōanji gardens at Kyoto, and Jencks's Garden of Cosmic Speculation in Scotland. Like Miller, our interest is in these art gardens, their visual components and the arrangement of them. However, we are concerned with the temporal implications of these visual phenomena.

Change and the Arts

Changes are essential to gardens in a way that implies gardens are unlike the other objects Kant placed in the category of formative arts. This is because gardens are made of natural objects and, especially, living

ISMAY BARWELL AND JOHN POWELL

organisms, which are arranged to be objects of aesthetic experience. Gardeners expect changes in the organisms they arrange and intend these changes to be among the features of gardens to which attention is directed and in which pleasure is taken. In particular, relations in and between the sequences of events that constitute the lives of plants, and between these sequences and those that are changes in inorganic objects that are also parts of gardens, are features that supply reasons for the aesthetic judgments involved in appreciation of gardens. Gardeners arrange or employ inorganic and organic elements in the expectation that characteristic changes will occur in them and with the intention that relations in and between these changes will be the object of aesthetic attention and pleasure. Flowering, as well as flowers, the unfurling of fronds as well as the fronds, sprouting and decaying, fruiting and seeding and relations between these events are to be noticed and enjoyed.

Paintings, non-kinetic sculptures, and buildings do change and painters, sculptors, and architects expect them to do so, but from an aesthetic point of view few of these changes are desirable. For example, a painting's varnish may darken and its color fade, a sculpture's marble may chip or discolor, and a building's steel may rust or its paint peel off. Ideally, objects of these kinds should remain as they were first painted, carved, cast, or built, apart from changes, such as the acquisition of a patina, that are perceived to increase their aesthetic qualities and enhance their aesthetic value. This is why the point of restoring a painting, a sculpture, or a building is to return it to its original condition, or to that which is considered to be most beautiful. In both cases it would be aesthetically desirable for the object to remain in the condition to which it has been returned. Aesthetic attention to paintings and sculptures is attention to relations between objects in a static configuration.

Gardens are not ideally static. Although gardeners resist some of the changes that are characteristic of the living organisms that are the material of gardens by, for example, mowing lawns and clipping hedges, they plan for and encourage others. Gardens should develop, not remain as they were when first created. Aesthetic appreciation of gardens that is confined to the way they appear only at particular moments and that does not take account of the relation between these appearances and those that precede and succeed them misses out a whole dimension of aesthetic experience.

Changes are also essential to performances because performances are sequences of events. Typically, the events constituting performances are actions of agents following instructions supplied by a script, a score, or a choreography. These actions or their products are intended to be that to which attention is directed and in which pleasure is taken. In dance performances these are the movements of the dancer. In dramatic performances they are the actions of actors, the story they tell, and the way in which they tell it. In musical performances they are sequences of sounds produced by the performers.

However, the changes essential to performances are unlike those essential to gardens in a crucial respect because the objects in which the changes occur are not performers. Crocuses, for example, sprout in the winter or early spring, produce flowers and die down during the summer. These events are what crocuses do. Crocuses are not, however, performing and they are not carrying out instructions even when in sprouting and flowering they realize a gardener's intentions.

Events are changes in objects and changes involve time. An object changes when the properties it has or the relations in which it stands at one time differ from the properties it has and the relations in which it stands at another time. This means that changes cannot occur without time passing. Time and change are therefore inextricably linked. Time and change are essential to gardens because they are essential to a garden's objects, and therefore J. D. Hunt is correct when he says that time makes a "fundamental contribution" to "the being of a garden" and a garden "not only exists in but also takes its special character from four dimensions."[5]

For the purposes of this essay we assume that time is a basic concept, i.e., that it is not dependent on any underlying concept, and that it is linear. Time and its passage exist and can be experienced in different modes. The first of these modes is measurable, predictable time, the time of science and clocks. In this essay we call this chronological time. The second mode is experiential time. This is time as individual humans experience its passing. It is not objectively measurable: it slows down and speeds up according to our individual experience of it in the context of some external or internal event or object. "Time flies when you're having fun" is a cliché that succinctly expresses an opinion about the passage of experiential time. The third mode of time is musical time. This is the time created in a musical work. It is a product of the complex interplay between pulse, meter, and the composed temporal units in a work. This time is different from the time taken for a musical performance, which can be declared accurately in terms of chronological time, and it is different from how long the musical composition seems to a listener. It will be discussed more fully later in the essay.

Time and the Arts

Works of art can be divided into three groups based on the way in which they involve time. As we said in the previous section, paintings and sculpture are works whose temporal aspects are only marginally, if ever, the objects of aesthetic attention. Aesthetic attention to them is not attention to events or processes, but to static configurations. However, some paintings and sculptures are like novels in that they have a temporal dimension because they represent either single events or narratives. The time taken by the events they represent is chronological time. The time taken to look at them or read them is also chronological time. It is variable and largely unconstrained by them. A long novel takes longer to read than a short one, but how long it takes to read depends on factors such as how quickly someone reads and how much time she wants to spend reading. However, aesthetic attention to events or narratives in painting and sculpture cannot be directed to any temporal aspects of those representations; in these arts aesthetic attention can be directed only to static configurations and not to events or processes. In these arts, therefore, aesthetic pleasure in any representation of narrative cannot be pleasure in any (non-existent) temporal aspects of the representation.

The second group includes opera, dance, theatre, and readings of poetry. They have a temporal dimension because they are performances and performances are temporally ordered sequences of events. They take place in chronological time and so does the experience of them. The time taken to experience a performance is constrained by the time the performance takes. Watching a play or dance and listening to an opera begins when the performance begins and ends when the performance ends. In addition, most works in this group represent sequences of events that take place in chronological time. They tell stories. Usually, the time taken by the performance differs from the time taken by the events it represents. A play that lasts two hours might represent events that occur over twenty years. A dance that lasts five minutes might represent the week-long life of a butterfly. Because the passage of time is a constitutive component of these arts, aesthetic attention to them is attention to time's passage. Aesthetic pleasure is taken in temporal aspects of the way in which they represent their stories.

The third group includes music and, as we shall see, gardens. Musical performances generally do not *represent* events. As a consequence, the time taken performing them is not to be contrasted with the time taken by the events they represent. In these works the essential artistic activity is the creation of temporal patterns that *present the passing of time to the ear*. As we will argue, music does this by creating patterns in sounds through rhythm. Aesthetic attention to musical performance includes attention not only to the pitch, timbre, and amplitude of the sounds; it must also include attention to the temporal aspects of the performance's sounds.

When we experience gardens as paintings we experience them as we experience members of the first group that do not represent events or tell stories. We attend to them as static arrangements and ignore their temporal aspect altogether. However, when we experience them as *presenting the passing of time* we experience them as objects whose temporal qualities are as important as their pictorial qualities. Our experience of them is analogous to our experience of musical performances. We will now argue that gardens present the passing of time to the eye by presenting visible patterns in changes occurring in and to organic and inorganic objects. The patterns are perceived to be rhythmic just like patterns in sound. They can be the objects of aesthetic pleasure and supply reasons for aesthetic judgments just as audible rhythms can be.

Time and Change in Gardens

Gardens cannot literally make time visible; even sundials and floral clocks cannot do that. But noticing changes that take place in gardens makes awareness of time possible and noticing patterns in and between these changes makes aesthetic appreciation of time possible. Gardens present visual evidence of the passage of time or evidence of a gardener's or garden designer's attempts to resist the changes brought about by it.

We are aware of change in gardens in two different ways. Firstly, we are aware, to a greater or lesser degree, of the changes that occur continuously in all natural objects and that are clearly exhibited in a garden since such objects are the material of which it is made. For instance, the individual plants in a traditional herbaceous border look completely different in midwinter from the way they look in midsummer. Secondly, insofar as gardens are designed, we may be aware of the designer having composed, contrasted, or otherwise articulated types of change in gardens in order to highlight the passage(s) of time(s) in ways that may be interesting and attractive.

ISMAY BARWELL AND JOHN POWELL

The passage of chronological time is evident in gardens in three ways. There is firstly the time of geology and geomorphology, the time spans over which rocks, landforms, and soils are made, changed, and eroded. There is secondly biological time, the time spans over which individual plants and parts of plants live, die, and reproduce. Thirdly, there are diurnal and seasonal cycles. The time the changes and the cycles take is the same as the time experiencing them would take, if we were to watch them continuously. This is a way in which changes in gardens are like performances. However, we do not usually sit and watch the grass grow or oak trees mature. This is because we would feel that the experience was taking even longer that the time it does take. We would experience it as intolerably long because it would be very tedious. This is an example of the difference between experiential and chronological time.

We have already claimed that it is in the nature of gardens that they change constantly, the most change occurring in the plants of the garden. Change is essential to all living organisms and the changes that constitute their lives are responsible for the richness and complexity of the experience of time that gardens offer. Moreover, it is the use of plants as materials that makes the art of gardening distinctive and that makes the aesthetic experience of gardens different from the experience of paintings.

Plants are always either growing or dying, and sometimes different parts of the same plant can be growing and dying at the same time. Plants grow, set seed, senesce, and die according to their internal biological clocks. You cannot usually see a mature kauri in a newly established garden and nor can you see camellia flowers in summer. You have to wait while the kauri takes its own time to grow and you have to wait for the appropriate season to see the camellia in flower.

The speed of change varies greatly between different plants. Petunias and radishes have brief lifespans. The flowers of daylilies and moonflowers are particularly ephemeral, although the plants are not. Some aloes mature over several years and then die as soon as they flower. Oaks endure for centuries but change quite markedly each year in tune with the seasons.

The fact that different plants, different parts of plants, and natural materials all have different rates of change presents aesthetic opportunities to the gardener in the way she chooses to combine plants and natural materials. For example, an oak tree grows slowly, its leaves grow and decay relatively quickly, a drift of crocuses underneath the oak appears and disappears at a different rate, and a surrounding lawn is managed so that it looks the same all year round. Such a combination of plants affords visual interest, but at the same time it creates a complex rhythm of life cycles, growth, and decay that may interest, excite, calm, disturb, or reassure an attentive visitor. Similarly, rhythms of change and decay are also present to be noticed by the observant and informed where the passing of geological and geomorphological time is manifest in the shape of the ground itself, and in the shape, color, and composition of rocks, gravel, sand, and soil.

All of this means that the passage of time is inescapable in gardens. There is always evidence of it: flowers opening, worms working the soil, leaves changing color and falling from the trees, fern fronds unfurling, leaves and petals folding for the night, and even whole gardens maturing or senescing. Gardens do not merely *happen* to exhibit time's passing: they *must* do so. Any garden is living; it must change and with that, time must pass, no matter how subtly. The patterns in these changes are there to be seen. They are visible and they are the fundamental artistic material of gardens. We will now argue that they are like patterns in sound in that they are rhythms. They are visual rhythms produced in a way that is analogous to the way in which audible rhythms are produced.

Music Makes the Passage of Time Audible

Susanne Langer developed a detailed philosophy of the arts in *Philosophy in a New Key* and *Feeling and Form*.[6] She was comprehensive in her treatment of music, but she did not discuss gardens in any detail. Some preliminary ideas about how she might have treated landscape and garden design were developed in John Powell's *Thawed Music?*[7] Langer described in detail how the individual arts function as symbolic forms. Each art involves an "illusory field." Music's illusory field is time. She claimed that "music makes the passage of time audible."[8] We agree with the spirit of this claim, but our account of *how* music does this, while it owes a debt to her, differs from hers.

Music cannot literally make time audible but, by organizing sounds rhythmically, it can draw listeners' attention to its passing. Musical time, which rhythm articulates, is a complex product of the interactions between pulse, meter, and what we term "composed temporal units." In a composition a composer divides objectively measurable chronological time into a regularly recurring pattern called pulse. A composer then organizes pulses into a meter, which is also usually regular and recurring.

ISMAY BARWELL AND JOHN POWELL

PULSE

allegro con brio

etc

METER

allegro con brio

etc

COMPOSED TEMPORAL UNITS

allegro con brio

etc

FIGURES 10.1   Examples of pulse, meter, and rhythm derived from the opening of Beethoven's Symphony No. 5.

When we tap our feet or clap our hands in time to music it is often in accordance with elements of a composition's meter. Pulse and meter are indicated by a composition's tempo indication (e.g., *allegro* or *andante*) and its time signature (e.g., 2/4 or 3/4).

Rhythm is created in a composition when a composer invents composed temporal units, or rhythmic motifs, that are articulated and experienced in relation to the meter (figure 10.1). The temporal events that constitute rhythms are usually linked to melodic units, but this is not always the case. Melody is not necessary. Music requires only rhythm to exist.

Musical time, which rhythm articulates, is not objectively measurable chronological time and nor is it experiential time as defined earlier in this essay. It is, however, *like* experiential time in that it can appear to slow down, speed up, fragment, or even stop. Just as excitement, boredom, or shock can make human experiential time appear to pass quickly, drag, or stop, so too can a composer manipulate her materials to create a range of temporal effects for our direct experience (figures 10.2 and 10.3).

FIGURE 10.2 Although the pulse and meter remain constant, musical time appears to speed up in this example.

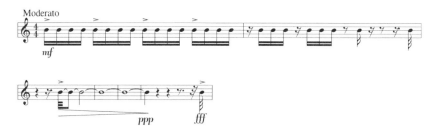

FIGURE 10.3 Musical time starts regularly and predictably in this example but gradually it becomes fragmented, erratic, and unpredictable.

Music uses the passage of this musical time as its fundamental artistic material. Music creates its own experiential, audible time world and offers us the opportunity to pay attention to it. Although we experience musical time as being different from objectively measurable, chronological time we inevitably experience the former time in relation to the latter because that is the only way we can experience rhythm and thus experience sound as music at all. Perhaps just as a *cantus firmus* (fixed song) provides a melodic structural element around which a polyphonic musical composition is heard, so too chronological time can be said to provide a temporal structural element, a *rhythmus firmus*, against, or more accurately, parallel to which, a piece of music is heard.

Gardens Make the Passage of Time Visible

The relevant patterns in and between the changes that occur in gardens are visual. These visual patterns are rhythms produced in a way that is analogous to the way in which rhythms are produced in sound. They are

ISMAY BARWELL AND JOHN POWELL

patterns in the movements essential to gardens. All growth is movement: sprouting, unfurling, flowing, and fruiting are movements, and so are dwindling, drooping, falling, and decaying.

In gardens, as in music, chronological time provides a *rhythmus firmus*. In a garden the continuum of chronological time divides itself into regular, recurring patterns experienced as diurnal and seasonal cycles. These cycles set up what we described in music as pulse and meter. It is important to note that in gardens this pulse and meter are not selected by the designer but are provided by nature itself.

Rhythm is created in a garden when a designer organizes natural objects into perceptual units. If they are plants then they bring with them the patterns of the events that constitute the lives of their kinds. For instance, oak trees grow from acorns, each year they lose all of their leaves, grow new leaves, flower and produce more acorns. Crocuses grow leaves and flowers in spring and then die down and lie dormant until the next spring. The patterns in these events are given, not created, and there is a limit to the extent to which a gardener can alter or influence them. These patterns are experienced in relation to each other and to the background provided by the pulse and meter of diurnal and seasonal time, which are themselves stretches of chronological time. When we experience these patterns in this way we experience them as rhythm.

Just as in music, time in gardens is a complex product of the interactions between pulse, meter, and selected perceptual units. But there is an important difference: all the elements of garden time are chronological time elements. Unlike musical time, chronological time cannot be slowed down or speeded up, reversed, fragmented or stopped. Gardeners use the passage of chronological time as a fundamental artistic material, but in so doing they create their own complex arrangement of temporal patterns and thereby offer us opportunities to think about the implications of time and its passage.

In music and gardens our experience of rhythms depends not only on our memory of what has preceded what we see and hear, but also on our expectation of what may follow what we see and hear. For instance, when deciduous trees are bare in gardens in winter we know that at a certain distance in time in the past the trees were covered in leaves and we know that at a certain distance in time in the future they will again have leaves. Similarly, in music, our experience of the silence in bar three of the Beethoven example above is influenced by what we know we heard in bars one and two, and this knowledge in turn influences what we may expect to hear later in that bar and in the following bars. Thus, in both music and gardens, these experiences are based on knowledge. But there is a difference. In music our sphere of knowledge is generally restricted to the composition in progress and to the composer's compositional style. However, in gardens our knowledge may be of that particular garden, or one of its plants, a few minutes or a year ago, or it may be a much broader knowledge of living materials and natural processes in gardens or nature generally.

Because people are living organisms, human responses to a garden's rhythms may be especially interesting, evocative, and resonant. In gardens we are faced with patterns in real chronological time, rather than the "play" time of music. These patterns may lead to reflections on time and its effects. By providing designed real-time worlds, gardens can offer us opportunities to observe painlessly, and to meditate on and experience, time's passing. In gardens we see birth, senescence, and death; we see slow and fast cyclical changes, and we see "offspring" and "parents." These experiences enable reflections on the human condition, its permanence or transience, stability or instability, on mortality or regeneration, growth or decay, health or sickness. They allow us to reflect on the vagaries of human as well as plant life.

Our experiences of gardens may direct our attention to time itself, to its irreversibility, its unidirectionality, its cyclic nature, its inevitability, its fleetingness and its inexorability. They may direct our attention to our comfort when we embrace time's passage or to our discomfort when we struggle against it. Some gardens, such as the so-called "timeless" Zen-style raked sand gardens, and other gardens that highlight geological or very slow moving time, may invite us to reflect on eternity. They may offer us the opportunity to step out of our own time, to lose ourselves, to release ourselves from our human time and escape temporarily to a realm where time appears to stand still. In gardens we are both spectators and participants. We observe and we dance in the garden of time.

NOTES

1 I. Kant, *The Critique of Judgement*, trans. J. C. Meredith (Oxford: Clarendon Press, 1952), section 51, p. 187.
2 Ibid.
3 Ibid., section 51, p. 188.
4 M. Miller, *The Garden as an Art* (Albany: State University of New York Press, 1993), p. 15.

ISMAY BARWELL AND JOHN POWELL

5 J. D. Hunt, *Greater Perfections: The Practice of Garden Theory* (Philadelphia: University of Pennsylvania Press, 2000), p. 15.

6 S. K. Langer, *Philosophy in a New Key: A Study in the Symbolism of Reason, Rite, and Art* (Cambridge, MA: Harvard University Press, 1957); *Feeling and Form: A Theory of Art* (London: Routledge and Kegan Paul, 1953).

7 J. Powell, *Thawed Music?* Dip. L.A. dissertation, Lincoln College, 1988.

8 Langer, *Feeling and Form*, p. 110.

CHAPTER II

THE PRAGMATIC PICTURESQUE
The Philosophy of Central Park

New York's Central Park is one of the world's iconic works of landscape architecture. The park has achieved global recognition through its representations in film and photography; it is visited by millions every year and every sunny day sees a procession of engaged or newly married couples having their official photographs taken against the background of its picturesque scenery and monumental structures.

In the twenty-first century it may sound slightly odd to consider Central Park as a form of gardening, but the eighteenth-century founders of modern aesthetics and the philosophy of art would have called it a garden or park. Horace Walpole spoke for the age in saying that "poetry, painting & gardening, or the science of landscape, will forever by men of taste be deemed three sisters, or *the Three New Graces* who dress and adorn nature."[2] Walpole was thinking of the great English landscape gardens or parks constructed on private estates. Poets like Alexander Pope and critics like Joseph Addison were enthusiastic garden designers whose poetry and prose explored the meanings of the art. In Immanuel Kant's *Critique of the Power of Judgment* (1790), generally taken to be the founding text of modern aesthetics, landscape gardening is classified as a form of painting, which differs from the two-dimensional canvases we respectfully visit in museums only in its use of the medium of actual plants, land, water, and sky.[3]

Yet gardening did not maintain its place among the fine arts. There is a story to be told about how around 1830, as a recent, distinguished historian of landscape design puts it: "Garden encyclopedias replaced treatises on aesthetics."[4] G. W. F. Hegel, whose monumental lectures on aesthetics set much of the pattern for thinking on this subject in the nineteenth century, treated gardens as a minor appendix to architecture, and remarked that however pleasant a walk through a garden might be, one would never be tempted to visit the same one twice.[5] To put it briefly, gardening was marginalized among the arts when it came to be seen as a private, individual, and domestic avocation, and the marginalization, as is so frequently the case, was accompanied by feminization, assigning the art to women whose real or imagined activity was confined to the home.

I agree with a number of recent critics who believe that this marginalization needs to be remedied, and that what are variously called gardens, parks, earthworks, or perhaps most generally land art should be acknowledged once again as major forms of art.[6] This essay argues that Central Park is a major work of this type and attempts to show the aesthetic principles that contributed to its design and its continuing appeal. If I am right, then we can say that Frederick Law Olmsted, the park's co-designer (with Calvert Vaux), is the most influential American artist.[7] Certainly, more people have toured or viewed Central Park or others which Olmsted designed, like Brooklyn's Prospect Park, or the parks of Boston, Buffalo, the Chicago area, the Stanford University campus, and the Biltmore estate (and the list goes on), than are familiar with the paintings of Thomas Cole or Georgia O'Keefe or the architecture of Frank Lloyd Wright. And who has been more influential in constructing models emulated in other parks, gardens, campuses, and corporate landscaping? But it is more than a question of numbers. Around 1900, Harvard President Charles Eliot Norton said of Olmsted that of all American artists he stood "first in the production of great works which answer the needs and give expression to the life of our immense and miscellaneous democracy."[8] Perhaps Olmsted has been a victim of his own success in adapting, popularizing, and spreading the picturesque style across the continent. For the desired picturesque effect of a pleasing mix of open meadows, changing elevation, occasional wooded areas, irregular bodies of water, and the succession of new and sometimes surprising views encountered on a stroll along one of Olmsted's serpentine walkways has been taken to be the "natural" form in which landscape presents itself. This was precisely the effect that the style sought to achieve, but it does so through planning, design, and construction. Like other arts it involves the imposition of form and invites its audience to approach it in specific ways.

The Invention of the Picturesque Style

To understand the artistic principles of Central Park and of Olmsted's work, it is necessary to see how the picturesque style of landscape design arose and flourished. Until the advent of the picturesque, gardens were typically enclosed, walled structures. The Persian word which is the root of the English "paradise" conveyed the idea of an enclosed garden. Enclosed gardens were often laid out in relatively formal, geometric patterns, along straight axes and with clearly centered structures. Even when there were no walls, and the garden trailed off ultimately into the countryside, as in André Le Nôtre's great garden at Versailles for Louis XIV, the garden retained or even intensified such a formal structure. There was no doubt that the garden was quite distinct from the surrounding world. Since throughout most of human history the natural world was understandably seen as threatening or hostile, the garden was felt to be a place of safety and refuge, sometimes conceived as an analogue of heaven. It was culture as opposed to nature.

In the eighteenth century, and especially in England, this changed. People were placing less hope in the afterlife and focusing more on how this world could be made more appealing and fulfilling. Economic and social developments presented new opportunities to English landowners. Enclosure of lands and the dispossession of local people were taken to be aesthetically and politically legitimate since aristocratic gardens were seen as representatives of British liberty, in contrast with the monarchical, centralized, and geometrical gardens of the Sun King at Versailles.

What we call the picturesque in respect to the English garden or park actually involves a series of stylistic variations. John Dixon Hunt has pointed out a significant change in the practice and aesthetics of garden design around the middle of the eighteenth century. The exemplary gardens of the century's first decades (e.g., Castle Howard, Stowe, Stourhead) are symbolic and allegorical: they are structured by temples and other monuments that recall Roman republicanism and British tradition and have a strong political import. They require interpretation or what recent philosophers call hermeneutics. To say that these parks were picturesque meant that they resembled "history paintings" that depicted significant human actions.

Then philosophical empiricism (John Locke and his successors) replaced a culture of interpretation; meaning was understood as a function of sensory impressions and ideas constructed from them, rather than on the model of interpreting texts. Gardens were created for the taste of landowners who were not so firmly grounded in classical culture as their predecessors. In just a few years the "picturesque" acquired its later meaning – Hunt calls it "vulgar" – in which it is the shape and disposition of the landscape that is crucial. Parks were now laid out on the whole to present pleasing images of "nature," and while designers continued to use painting as a model for their work, they tended to concentrate on paintings (or those aspects of paintings) that represented landscapes with little or no allegorical and symbolic meaning.[9]

The ideal was now that of a total landscape, one in which the boundary between the property and the surrounding world was blurred or obscured. This aesthetic required an artful veiling of the difference between nature and culture, accomplished by destroying any visible boundaries to the park, such as traditional walls or obtrusive structures in the distance. Borrowed scenery blurred the distinction between private property and a view of the world. Trees were planted and earth moved to screen unwanted reminders of the limits of the property, but practical requirements (keeping some animals in, while excluding others and human intruders) dictated some substitute for walls. The great aesthetic invention of the picturesque was its discovery of the ha-ha, the ditch or sunken pit which is the hidden frame of the park. Together with artful planting and leveling or building up of the earth, the ha-ha contributed to producing what Joseph Addison called a "landskip" that presented "an image of liberty, where the eye has room to range abroad, to expatiate at large on the immensity of its views."[10] As Gina Crandell succinctly expresses it: "what is designed and owned is composed to give the illusion of being natural, when in fact it is maintained as an enclave."[11] This is an instance of what the philosopher Jacques Derrida suggests is a paradox necessarily arising from the fact that all works of visual art have a frame, yet the frame is neither simply inside nor outside the work. Just as a picture frame both detaches a painting from the gallery wall while attaching it to the same, so the invisible frame of the park's grounds (plantings, ha-has, etc.) performs this double function. The eighteenth-century English picturesque garden is an exemplary case of the paradox of the frame, because it must, in its founding gesture, disguise the frame which is essential to it. The undecidability of the frame's position – is it the core of the work or something which the work erases? – is only intensified by the practice of the picturesque. This frame does its work of framing by concealing itself. The frame is both internal and external to the park. It requires boundaries and limits and yet also must create the impression that it is continuous with the world.

The picturesque aesthetic was elaborated by British writers like William Gilpin, who produced guides to English scenery, and Uvedale Price, a landowner who both designed his own park and produced a lengthy treatise on the picturesque which linked it very closely to painting, although Price reduces painting, at least for these purposes, to the representation of landscape, unlike the designers of a generation or two earlier who took history painting as their model. Sightseeing manuals by Gilpin and others advised viewers how to frame ideal views, preferably with the aid of the "Claude glass," an optical device with which the spectator looked at the scene behind her with a handheld rearview mirror. The mirror provided both a frame, comparable to a painting, while tinting the color to resemble the model paintings of the picturesque movement. Olmsted took the works of these two men to be the finest guides to landscaping aesthetics, and so put them immediately into apprentices' hands. They were, he thought, superior to "any published" and he instructed his pupils: "You are to read these seriously, as a student of law would read Blackstone."[12]

We can think of the English theorists of the picturesque as developing a diagram of visibility that enabled experiences of intricacy, complexity, and shifting perspectives. Following the philosophers Michel Foucault and Gilles Deleuze, I think of the diagram not simply as an outline sketch or blueprint, but as a dynamic arrangement of structures and forces, which channels and focuses human activity to specific ends. Around the same time that the English picturesque was flourishing, the philosopher Jeremy Bentham was elaborating the diagram of what he called the Panopticon, the plan of an architecture of total surveillance, to be used most famously in prisons, where inmates were given the impression that they were objects of observation and inspection by hidden guards in a central tower.[13] Having to assume that they might be under observation at any time, they were encouraged to become their own guards, imposing on themselves the discipline of the institution (Bentham intended that his model could also be extended to schools, factories, and other disciplinary sites). This diagram can be thought of as a machine – a complex

GARY SHAPIRO

arrangement of architectural structures, human action, expectation, observation, and self-observation – that produces a holistic effect of discipline in its subjects. If the Panopticon is the diagram of the *gaze* – focused and objectifying vision – at its extreme, the English picturesque garden, designed for those who regard themselves as very much at liberty, is the theatre of the *glance* – the passing, perspectival, and partial look. While the diagram or frame of the Panopticon oppressively structures its enclosed world, that of the ideal park frames the territory by producing the illusion that there is no frame. Where Bentham offered a diagram for total visibility with relatively fixed positions for observed and observer, Price laid down principles for exploiting the moving body's multiplicity and complexity of orientations and views; he was exploiting the concepts of the threshold and horizon. This optical machine has a political dimension: the impression of unlimited views and a horizon receding into infinity are thought to be congruent with the educated spectator taking a wide, impartial view not only of the landscape, but also, by analogy, of the public good of the nation.

Olmsted and Central Park: Ethics, Politics, Aesthetics

Olmsted published his *Walks and Talks of an American Farmer in England* in 1852, offering an account of his tours of the English countryside and parks. Guided in his taste by classic thinkers and critics of the picturesque (like Gilpin and Price), Olmsted also saw new possibilities for adapting the style to the life of the modern, urban, democratic population he saw emerging in the United States. He was especially impressed by Sir Joseph Paxton's design for the People's Garden in the Liverpool suburb of Birkenhead, one of the first public parks.

By 1858 Olmsted and Calvert Vaux had been successful in the competition to produce a plan for what was to be Central Park. The park's site was determined by the city authorities, the city having committed itself to a grid pattern of building which left little choice by that time. Olmsted regretted the park's rectangular dimensions and its isolation from the rivers and waterways that bound Manhattan. The park was framed as a pastoral island within a maritime island. This also required that the traffic of the city somehow flow through the park. At the same time the central position of the park opened it up to the maximum number of people.

In designing Central Park Olmsted and Vaux turned the diagram of the English park inside out, transforming it to respond both to the specific nature of the site and the emerging urban society to be served by the park. The inversion of the diagram can be described in formal terms, but the choice of the form is governed both by an analysis of the social and infrastructure needs of the emergent American metropolis and an ethical and political vision of the life of a democratic citizenry. Inspired by the perfectionism of Carlyle and Emerson, and working in the same climate of ideas that nurtured the classic American philosophy of Charles Peirce, William James, and John Dewey, Olmsted devised the innovative approach to urban life that I call the "pragmatic picturesque." The formal innovation can be described succinctly, but must be integrated with Olmsted's perfectionist and pragmatic view of public life. That the designers wanted to create the impression of "naturalness" is clear, and they did so by following the diagram of the picturesque, which calls for intricacy, variety, and a multiplicity of thresholds leading on to new views and perspectives. They sketched this diagram in their Greensward Plan. Although the diagram of the picturesque is decidedly different from that of the walled Italian Renaissance garden or the intensively centralized schema of a park like Versailles, which echoes the forms of monarchical power, it is still a diagram, a way of delimiting, inscribing, marking, and coding a territory, and indicating forms of movement appropriate for the bodies which move within or through it. In the exemplary picturesque park the hidden frame created the impression of unlimited space, while actually laying claim to an exclusive and private domain. Central Park has a clearly defined and visible rectangular boundary, a low stone wall punctuated by a series of entries, called gates by the designers and given specific titles (e.g., All Saints Gate, Mariner's Gate); the surrounding city cannot be hidden, and even in the few places where the New York skyline is not visible, the city is never far away because of our awareness of the urban multitude. The movement of the city enters into the park, not only through its openness to walkers and cyclists, but because its design, from the beginning, incorporated carriageways (now roadways and a few remaining ways for horses, carriages, and occasional pedestrians).

While the private park celebrated the liberty of the glance of the landowner and privileged guests, the Olmsted park enables citizens to encounter one another in a mutual recognition that minimizes the competition and crowding of urban life. The frame is explicit rather than hidden. Rather than the illusion of the natural and pastoral, far from the city, Central Park opens itself up to urban traffic while artfully concealing

GARY SHAPIRO

most of the roadways by bridges and other architecture. In many cases the roads pass below the ground level of the park, so becoming the analogue of the picturesque ha-has. In Robert Smithson's 1972 essay on "Frederick Law Olmsted and the Dialectical Landscape" he calls this interaction of the park and the city a form of "dialectical materialism," emphasizing the fluid nature of the exchange. Rather than the park being maintained as a closed site as in the aristocratic English model (which disguised this isolation), Central Park interacts with its urban surroundings. It does this spatially by admitting people and traffic, and historically in the way that the park and the city engage in mutually influenced alterations over time. Smithson claimed that Olmsted was "America's greatest earthworks artist"; he was himself a pioneer in the new forms of this genre that took shape in the 1960s.[14] Smithson's essay seems to be the first theoretical analysis of the park's diagram (after Olmsted's own). Smithson was highly critical of gardens and their aesthetics because he thought they generally obscured the truth of change, entropy, and ruin. They promoted an illusion of eternity, something ingredient in the garden through its many transformations from the enclosed Persian form, through classical gardens of the Versailles type, to the English "natural" model. In contrast he praised Olmsted for creating a fluid work, that opened itself up to interchange with its surroundings, and did not need to hide the facts of historical or geological change and becoming.

Olmsted attempted to explain the social and political horizon of public parks in his extensive writings on cities and urban planning; these could very well be introduced into the canon of American philosophy. Writing in 1870, using the model of Central Park to convince Bostonians of the need for analogous public spaces, Olmsted produced what we could call a Platonic argument to explain the necessity and function of the park. Like Plato in the *Republic*, he asks how life in the city, life together, can be strengthened and supported, and contribute to human excellence. Like Plato he is intensely conscious of the importance of aesthetic education, including the mostly unconscious influence of the citizens' aesthetic surroundings.[15] Unlike Plato, of course, the assumed political form of the city is democratic, and rather than imagining that a new utopian city can be constructed from scratch, he pragmatically accepts given social and economic conditions as a starting point, and just as pragmatically asks how they can best be directed and focused.

Olmsted argues that the principle of the city (especially on a naturally bounded site like Manhattan island) is density and concentration. This leads to specific hazards to physical health and the need for fresh air.

More than that, unrelieved congestion and crowded street life requires the city dweller to be constantly wary of others, and to assess the character and motives of strangers. Olmsted notes that the very structure of the city promotes a practical and political skepticism about the possibility of community and cooperation. In the modern metropolis where we encounter unknown people with suspicion and reserve, Olmsted says: "Our minds are thus brought into close dealings with other minds without any friendly flowing toward them, but rather a drawing from them."[16] Yet a flourishing democratic state must allow and encourage other means of social interaction which reinforce inclinations for mutual respect and a sense of communal identity.

Plato developed a set of categories and distinctions with respect to the gymnastics and music (including poetry) appropriate for forming the character of the city's guardians; Olmsted distinguishes two basic forms of recreation, "exertive" (strenuous sporting activities) and "receptive" (relatively passive and spectatorial activities). He divides the receptive into the neighborly (gatherings of small groups that encourage personal friendliness) and the "gregarious," which involve a large number, generally unknown to one another. Here the multitude comes together with "evident glee," Olmsted says, with "all classes largely represented, with a common purpose, not at all intellectual, competitive with none, disposing to jealousy and spiritual or intellectual pride toward none, each individual adding by his mere presence to the pleasure of all others, all helping to the greater happiness of each."[17] Olmsted's "Platonic argument," then, is also pragmatic: a democracy requires the sense among its citizens of their mutual trustworthiness, of their ability to engage in noncompetitive social interaction, and an acceptance of their belonging together beyond such distinctions as class, religion, and ethnicity. The diagram that he and Vaux created for Central Park brilliantly transforms the picturesque genre, as it enables new forms of recognition and self-knowledge in the park's visitors.

"The Gates" and the Meaning of the Park

While we know that this is an idealized picture, the ideal approached actualization when millions of people turned out in the depths of winter 2005 for "The Gates." This work of Christo and Jeanne-Claude involved placing 7,500 gates – steel bases with striking orange saffron fabric

GARY SHAPIRO

panels – along 23 miles of the park's footpaths. The artists needed 26 years to gather support for the project and overcome resistance to it, which included not only practical worries about damage to trees and vegetation, but the more philosophical claim that "The Gates" would desecrate the original artwork designed by Olmsted and Vaux.[18] Seen from the perspective of what I have been calling the pragmatic picturesque, "The Gates" is not an unprecedented intervention in the park, but a contemporary technological variation of the diagram which the nineteenth-century designers adapted from eighteenth-century parks and their theorists.

What the twenty-first century artists accomplished was to focus specifically on two aspects of Olmsted's idea for the park: the refreshing experience of landscape and the pleasure of seeing and meeting others in a generous atmosphere encouraging mutual recognition, affirmation, and joy. I accepted the invitation of "The Gates" thresholds in February 2005 and spent the better part of two days following the paths that were laid out through the snowy park. Having ignored the park in winter before, these walks were a revelation. The sheer multiplicity of the visitors in all their diversity, and the shared enthusiasm for the collective experience, seemed in keeping with the designers' (Olmsted and Vaux as well as Christo and Jean-Claude) broad expectations for their work.

Viewed from a height – as from a tall building, especially in the winter season of bare trees and unobstructed views – the gates marked the serpentine paths of the park as a machine for walking. On the ground, following the walkways, passing through the gates, you felt drawn in, welcomed, invited. You were not observing an artwork but entering one. And you were not alone.

With two old and dear friends I joined the multitude attracted to "The Gates." There was, first, the time of walking, a walking with no other goal than exploring, observing, whiling away the time, lingering with the elements, enjoying the crowd. The artists say they chose Central Park for this project because more people walk here than any place else (they have lived in New York since 1964). We should place equal weight on the activity of walking and on the presence of the multitude. The time of humans on the earth is a time of walking, despite the technology of speed, from auto to air, that can abbreviate or eclipse this fundamental form of mobility. The saffron banners wafting, fluttering, blowing, or billowing in the breeze marked the walkways of the park; they were invitations to stroll beneath them, along with the people thronging the park on those cold days.

"The Gates" takes its name from those which Olmsted and Vaux gave to the park entrances. This naming discloses the project's structure, building on the park's basic diagram. Unlike the great private English gardens, the park has always been open. Unlike what is called a "gated community," the gates invite rather than exclude. The time of hospitality and invitation can be distinguished from the time of work, which is a function of economic constraints. It is, we say, leisure time. But we seldom have the leisure time to think about leisure. The Greeks called this alternative time *scholé*, and the Romans *otium*, thinking that nothing would better occupy a time freed from necessity than study, contemplation, and friendship. It is the time of the Muses, more specifically a musical time, as Olmsted perceived when he compared walking through a park to listening to music. The park offers a time with its own rhythm and movement. "The Gates" offered the gift of time. It is also a *gift* to the park and the city, for the project was totally self-financing, leaving no credit or debt. It's as if Christo and Jeanne-Claude were saying: "Here is your time, a precious two weeks, a unique event, now and only now." You knew that the work was up for only two weeks, so the lived duration of your stroll bore a close relation to the finite time of the work. You were not given a thing, you were *given time*. To know that the work endures only for a specific, limited period, is to experience time otherwise than we do when returning to a painting or a sculpture that we expect to be preserved in a condition as close as possible to its original one. You were not gazing at the eternal beauty of an immortal work, as in the classical museum, but living your time on earth in and with the work.

The time of the visit opens on to *other times*, to a multiplicity of layered times, that the thinkers of the picturesque (from the eighteenth century to Smithson) would have understood. There is meteorological and atmospheric time, marked by the weather of the day or hour, the play of the elements (including several snowfalls), plays of light and shade, and the changing, floating, billowing movement of the banners, stirred in different directions by each breeze. As the artists discovered in their earlier *Running Fence* project, it was impossible to anticipate that neighboring sections of the fabric fence might simultaneously puff out in different directions, because the swirling eddies are more complex than we imagine. So the very nature of simultaneity becomes a focus of temporal attention. The time of the park is also geological, as Smithson stresses in his Olmsted essay; it is the remnant of the last ice age, a swathe of land shaped by retreating glaciers. "The Gates" are also invitations to natural and historical time. The park's diagram, then, as elaborated by Olmsted and distilled in "The Gates," intensifies the experience of time as well as space. Olmsted compared the experience of strolling through the park to music, suggesting such a transformation of temporality.

Since those February days in the park, I've sought out some of the responses to "The Gates"; among the most significant, I think, are the many Youtube videos of walks, solitary or in the crowd, in varied weather and times of day or night. Almost all are accompanied by music, in (probably unwitting) homage to the work's evocation of the multiple times of the earth and those who walk it.

NOTES

1   Thanks to Dan O'Brien for help with pruning and cultivating prose, and to Karsten Struhl and Olga Bukhina for illuminating conversation as we explored "The Gates."
2   Cited by J. D. Hunt and P. Willis, *The Genius of the Place: The English Landscape Garden 1620–1820* (Cambridge, MA: MIT Press, 1988), p. 11.
3   I. Kant, *Critique of the Power of Judgment*, section 51.
4   E. B. Rogers, *Landscape Design: A Cultural and Architectural History* (New York: Harry N. Abrams, 2001), p. 314.
5   G. W. F. Hegel, *Aesthetics*, vol. 2, trans. T. M. Knox (Oxford: Oxford University Press, 1975), pp. 699–700.
6   The literature on this theme is enormous. A good place to start is J. Kastner and B. Wallis (eds.) *Land and Environmental Art* (London: Phaidon Press, 1998). A valuable collection of philosophical essays can be found in S. Kemal and I. Gaskell (eds.) *Landscape, Natural Beauty, and the Arts* (Cambridge: Cambridge University Press, 1993).
7   In this essay I generally refer simply to Olmsted. He and Vaux collaborated on Central Park and Prospect Park, while Olmsted went on to do many more projects on his own and with others.
8   Quoted in R. Smithson, *The Collected Writings*, ed. J. Flam (Berkeley: University of California Press, 1996), p. 168.
9   J. D. Hunt, "'Ut Pictura Poesis': The Garden and the Picturesque in England (1710–1750)," in M. Mosser and G. Teyssot, *The History of Garden Design* (London: Thames and Hudson, 1991), pp. 231–41.
10 J. Addison, *The Spectator*, 1712, number 412.
11 G. Crandell, *Nature Pictorialized* (Baltimore: Johns Hopkins University Press, 1993), p. 130.
12 Quoted in Smithson, *Collected Writings*, p. 159.
13 The classic account of Bentham's Panopticon, with references, is to be found in M. Foucault, "Panopticism," in *Discipline and Punish*, trans. A. Sheridan (New York: Vintage, 1979), III.3, pp. 195–228.

14 Smithson, *Collected Writings*, pp. 157–71; cf. G. Shapiro, *Earthwards: Robert Smithson and Art after Babel* (Berkeley: University of California Press, 1995).

15 Plato, *Republic* (London: Penguin, 1955), Books II and III.

16 F. L. Olmsted, *Civilizing American Cities: Writings on City Landscapes*, ed. S. B. Sutton (New York: Da Capo, 1997), p. 65.

17 Ibid., p. 75.

18 See the lectures and interviews in Christo and Jeanne-Claude, *On the Way to The Gates* (New Haven: Yale University Press, 2004), pp. 127–96.

PART IV

THE COSMIC GARDEN

CHAPTER 12

ILLUSIONS OF GRANDEUR

A Harmonious Garden for the Sun King

The French monarch Louis XIV was, like most men of his age, relatively short in height. Measuring only five feet three inches, he managed to increase his stature by wearing a towering black wig and red high-heeled shoes. His eulogists called him "Louis-le-Grand" or "Louis the Great," and indeed he loomed large on the European political stage. But the French word *grand* also conveys the idea of grandeur, and in that most ostentatious period of Western history, the Baroque, no one had a better fix on grandiosity than the Sun King. For proof we need only enter the garden at Versailles, at first glance vast and overpowering, but then seductive in its appeal to the senses. Ultimately, the grandeur of Versailles lies in the august idea that it embodies – nothing less than the sublimity of Louis XIV's place in the universe. This chapter aims to uncover the myths hidden at Versailles by inviting the reader into its sheltering groves.

Upon coming to power in 1661, Louis XIV inherited numerous royal palaces and châteaux, including the Louvre in Paris, but he immediately lavished his attention on the old hunting lodge at Versailles, favored as a retreat by his Bourbon predecessors. Gradually, he enlarged the buildings and the domain, designating it the official capital of the realm in 1682, just as France achieved the status of the premier political power in Europe. The site, initially vilified by contemporaries as a rough and inhospitable swamp lacking soil, woods, and water, nonetheless yielded to the collaborative efforts of a design team working under the royal gardener, André Le Nôtre. Armies of workmen moved vast quantities of earth to form a series of suspended terraces along the garden hillside in order to accommodate the many lawns and ramps, while hydraulic engineers diverted water from the Eure and Seine rivers and channeled it to hundreds of cascades, jets, and sprays. It was here that the art of gardening attained a status comparable to that enjoyed by painting, sculpture, architecture, theatre, music, and dance as a visual art used by the Crown to project an image of the king. All gardens reflect the philosophical ideals of their time, but the French formal garden is a particularly persuasive example because of the highly stylized reformatting of nature and its capacity to embody abstract ideas. Many historians consider the Versailles garden as an analogue to the theoretical principles of the French philosopher, scientist, and mathematician René Descartes.[2] Certain garden features – the dynamic central *allée*, the seemingly limitless periphery, and the rigorous geometrization of natural elements – seem to echo Descartes's theories on the relationship of space and matter. In his youth Le Nôtre studied geometry, optics, and perspective, and thus he was able to conceive *jardins d'intelligence* expressive of basic concepts in Cartesian logic: that all movement consists of boundless axial extension, and that space, however vast, can be charted as a series of points on a grid.

Like the overall scheme of the Versailles garden, the smaller features within it also demonstrate the close alliance between design and theory in the French formal garden. By way of a case study, this essay offers a new interpretation of the Bosquet de la Colonnade, one of fifteen retreats hidden within the Petit Parc, the grove located midway between the palace and the Apollo Basin (1684–8; figure 12.1).

Exceptionally, it was not Le Nôtre but Louis XIV's principal architect, Jules Hardouin-Mansart, who devised the circular white-marble arcade supported by 32 colored Ionic columns and buttressed by a circle of piers decorated with pilasters. When the fountains are playing, tall jets of water spurt from each of the marble tables located beneath the arches. The water splashes back down into a shallow pool on the tabletop and then overflows onto the stone platform below, filling a channel around the circular space, thus creating a ring of water (figure 12.2).

Marble sculpture is located in two places: the keystones at the apex of each arch and the spandrels bridging the arches. The space, which measures some 131 feet in diameter, is not flat but is moderated in levels by means of five recessed circular steps in the center. Nature is fully visible, not only in the water but in the abundant greenery of the trees that enclose the Bosquet behind a transparent trellis wall.

ROBERT NEUMAN

FIGURE 12.1   Jules Houdouin-Mansart, Bosquet de la Colonnade, Versailles, 1684–8. Print by Jacques Rigaud, ca. 1730. Paris, Bibliothèque Nationale de France.

The Colonnade had several functions: it served as a focal point within a network of promenades explored by moving participants; it was an amphitheatre in which stationary spectators watched a musical entertainment or enjoyed a light supper; and it conveyed a message about the king that could be easily comprehended by the contemporary viewer. My aim in this essay is to recover that message, which operates on many levels but ultimately centers on the philosophical idea of harmony, overseen in the universe by Apollo and on earth by Louis XIV. I will show that in designing the structure, Hardouin-Mansart referenced two ancient building types – the circular temple and the imperial villa – in order to create a symbolic Temple of Apollo while drawing an analogy between Louis XIV and the greatest of Roman emperors, Hadrian. Furthermore, Hardouin-Mansart's use of simple ratios in the design of the arcade derives from contemporary interest in the Pythagorean system of proportions that embodies the ancient notion of the harmony of the spheres. I will also demonstrate that while the sculptures call to mind many of Apollo's roles as pagan deity, they emphasize his position as god of music and creator of cosmic order. It is well known that images of Apollo appear throughout Versailles, but historians have failed to recognize his presence in the Colonnade, which uses the typical Baroque devices of metaphor and allegory to praise the Sun King.

FIGURE 12.2   Detail of the Colonnade, Versailles, showing the table fountains, the circular water channel, the spandrels, and a keystone mask. Photo: Stephanie Leitch.

A Temple of Apollo

In designing the structure, Hardouin-Mansart consciously borrowed from two ancient building types, the circular (peripteral) temple and the Roman imperial villa. This had the purpose of attaching the associational value of historic buildings to the new Bosquet. In the case of the peripteral temple, Hardouin-Mansart used the basic elements of a circular plan

ROBERT NEUMAN

enclosed by a colonnade to create a symbolic Temple of Apollo suitable for both the Sun God and the Sun King. Several details confirm my thesis. Renaissance and Baroque architects were familiar with ancient circular temples dedicated to Apollo; in his *Four Books of Architecture*, for example, Palladio describes the Temple of the Sun in Rome, remarking on its plan, as broad as it is long, implying that the circular form represents the movement of the sun in the heavens. Furthermore, both the inner ring of Ionic columns and the outer ring of buttressing Ionic piers are built of richly colored and veined French marble in brilliant tones of red and gold. Significantly, by using columns and colored marbles in a circular plan, Hardouin-Mansart responded to the famous description of the Sun God's Solar Palace in Ovid's *Metamorphoses*: "The soaring palace of the Sun, with all its giant columns, was ablaze with gold and bronze, as if aflame; its pediments were crowned on high with polished ivory; and glowing silver graced the double doors."[3] Ovid goes on to describe the fictive sculpted reliefs decorating the doors, which represent the universe, using words that reverberate in the alternating circles of land and water at the Colonnade: "the world's wide sphere, the reach of all the seas that circle the dry land, and, too, the skies that overhang earth's span." We will see below that Ovid's list of the inhabitants of the earth – tritons and nereids in the sea, nymphs and rural deities on land – is duplicated in the Colonnade keystones.

Circular temples are normally experienced primarily from the outside; at Versailles that concept is turned inside out. Of course, in a real temple the columns would support a roof. Casual observers at Versailles often refer to the structure as a "sham ruin" because the arcade is non-supporting, and indeed the building does have something of the character of an ancient ruin invaded by nature. One further point should be made about the plan. Renaissance theorists eulogized the circle as the most perfect geometric form: lacking beginning or end, corners or edges, the circle symbolizes harmony. Here the circular plan specifically symbolizes the unitary nature of the Sun God, and, as I will show, contributes to the cosmological theme also present in the Bosquet.

The sole painting commissioned by Louis XIV to commemorate the Bosquet corroborates further my point that this symbolic temple is dedicated to Apollo. Shortly after completion of the Colonnade, Jean Cotelle II painted the *View of the Colonnade* as part of a series of 21 vistas of the Versailles garden that hung in the king's retreat on the north side of the domain, the Grand Trianon (1688–90). A unique aspect of the series was the incorporation of mythological figures within the realistic views.

Appropriately, in this painting, Apollo inhabits the Colonnade refreshed by the nymphs after the labors of the day; their poses reflect the sculptural group of *Apollo Served by the Nymphs* by François Girardon and Thomas Regnaudin, originally installed in the Versailles Grotto (1660–75). With the dismantling of the Grotto to make way for a new wing of the palace, the king initially planned to move the sculptures to the site of the Colonnade; ultimately, he routed them to the Bosquet de la Renommée. In short, the painting confirms the notion of the peristyle as a "shrine" to Apollo.

Quoting the Roman Garden Villa

In addition to using motifs from the peripteral temple, Hardouin-Mansart also incorporated ideas from ancient Roman villa gardens to provide another layer of meaning for the Bosquet. A standard feature of such gardens was the colonnade (peristyle), visible in extant ruins and documented in ancient literary descriptions of lost structures. Circular colonnades in particular piqued the interest of Baroque architects, such as the elaborate aviary described by the Roman writer Varro, which consisted of a ring colonnade surrounding a circular canal facing a round colonnaded pavilion. Another instance was the description in the letters of Pliny the Younger of the colonnade in his Laurentian Villa.

Only one example of a ring colonnade in an ancient Roman villa garden has survived, and the ruins were well known to the French by the end of the fifteenth century: the so-called Maritime Theatre (also called the Island Enclosure), one of many independent gardens linked by a peripatetic circuit within Hadrian's Villa at Tivoli (begun 118 CE). This remarkable garden consisted of three principal features, all built on a concentric plan: on the perimeter a colonnade of 40 columns; an adjacent shallow channel of water; and in the center, an islet pavilion that functioned as a private retreat. Some relief sculptures decorating the friezes are extant, and their subjects, drawn from classical mythology, include sylvan and marine deities and cavorting winged cherubs.

I propose that Hardouin-Mansart synthesized the concept of the villa colonnade with the peripteral temple colonnade while adding another major element of Hadrian's scheme, the circular water channel. The resulting configuration refers not only to Apollo but also to Hadrian, thus enriching further the meaning of the Bosquet. It should be remembered that ancient Rome provided the standard by which Baroque monarchs were judged, and that throughout Versailles Louis XIV appears not only in the guise of Apollo but also as a Roman emperor in full military regalia. Hadrian was a significant choice because as ruler of vast territories and victor at battle he was a worthy model for Louis XIV, who aspired to equal and even surpass him. Moreover, like Louis, Hadrian claimed a special affinity for Apollo, his chief divine protector, who had named Hadrian his representative on earth and to whom the emperor dedicated several temples.

There is one further reason why Hardouin-Mansart referenced the Maritime Theatre: he would have understood the symbolic character of its plan and decoration. The concentric circles of water and earth, the radial expansion from a central core, and the division into four zones all point to the presence of an underlying cosmological scheme. Hadrian was an avid student of Pythagorean ideas, and it may be that they underlie the layout of the Tivoli structure. Scholars have recently argued that Pythagorean principles determined the conception of some of Hadrian's buildings, in particular the Pantheon in Rome, but there is no definitive interpretation of the Maritime Theatre. Nevertheless, I will demonstrate shortly that Pythagorean themes are integrated with Apollonian ones in the architecture and sculpture of the Versailles Colonnade in a way that is noteworthy for Louis XIV, and this makes Hardouin-Mansart's reference to the Maritime Theatre all the more relevant.

Harmonic Proportions

The peristyle of the Bosquet de la Colonnade, with its refined Ionic order and simple rhythm of arcaded bays, operates in tandem with the circular ground plan in representing ancient ideas regarding harmony. Looking at the elevation, we see that Hardouin-Mansart used a series of simple relationships in determining its dimensions: for example, the ratio of the width of each bay to its height is 1:2. Lacking original measured drawings or written evidence, we cannot be entirely certain of Hardouin-Mansart's intentions in using a particular numerical system to draft the design. But it is significant that during the years of the Colonnade's conception, French royal architects believed that the harmonic and mathematical proportions governing the natural world could be used to produce beautiful and meaningful buildings. These architects were part of a diverse group of intellectuals that included painters, sculptors, musicians, philosophers, and mathematicians who from the mid-fifteenth through the seventeenth century investigated the theory of universal harmony rooted in the Pythagorean-Platonic system of numbers. The source of this tradition was the sixth century BCE mathematician and philosopher Pythagoras, who posited that relative lengths of a stretched string, or monochord, produced harmonic musical intervals in the proportion of 1:2 (octave), 2:3 (fifth), and 3:4 (fourth). Plato in the *Timaeus* further deduced that musical harmony was equivalent to the harmony of the universe, both being based on the same geometrical progression of numbers. Realizing that use of classical elements in architectural design required knowledge of proportions, Renaissance and Baroque architects sought to determine the ancient systems of numerical ratios.

Only a few years before the creation of the Colonnade, the French Oratorian René Ouvrard published a treatise, *Architecture harmonique ou application de la doctrine des proportions à l'architecture* (1679), in which he followed the lead of Italian theorists by promoting the idea that the numerical relationships shared by beautiful buildings and music are earthly manifestations of divine harmony. Ouvrard's points were reiterated in a chapter in the *Cours d'architecture*, published in 1683 by François Blondel, director of the newly established Academy of Architecture, where the Pythagorean musical analogy was elucidated. Hardouin-Mansart was familiar with these ideas, and it seems reasonable to suggest that he incorporated them at the Colonnade. The serene character of the structure is based on simple ratios that are perceptible to the eye. Contemporaries would have considered the perfection of this architecture as an embodiment of the numerical harmonies of the world. One further link is meaningful: like Louis XIV and Hadrian, Pythagoras held a special connection with Apollo. Aristotle tells us that the Sun God was the only deity worshipped by the philosopher, who became known as the immortal son of Apollo, worthy of veneration in his own right. These interwoven imperial, Apollonian, and Pythagorean systems of meaning are consonant with the iconography of the Colonnade's sculptural program, to which we now turn.

The Sculptural Program

Current scholarship attributes the design of the decorative sculpture to Pierre Mignard, and the sculpting to a team that included

Antoine Coysevox, Jean-Baptiste Tuby, Louis Le Conte, Simon Mazière, and Pierre Granier.[4] In inventing the sculptural program, the members of the Petit Académie, the committee charged with formulating the royal iconography, logically wished to complement the themes of the structure. The original program did not include the freestanding sculpture in the center, François Girardon's *Rape of Proserpina*, set up in 1699.

Below the cornice a series of 32 keystone masks (faces) were installed at the height of each arch. Sculpted in 1685, the masks are identified by two early sources: an article in the court circular, the *Mercure Galant*, of November 1686, which calls the faces those of "the pastoral and marine deities, such as nymphs, naiads, dryads, hamadryads, sylvans, etc.," and a surviving annotated plan that specifies the identity and sculptor for each.[5] As in the antique past, for example at Hadrian's Villa, the incorporation of satyrs, nymphs, and sea creatures suggests the ideals of pleasure, abandon, and fertility in the context of a garden. The connections with Apollo are apparent: the pastoral creatures relate to the Sun God's position as protector of flocks and herds, while the watery denizens of Thetis' abode beneath the sea refer to Apollo's rest after the labors of the day.

The 32 triangular bas-reliefs mounted on the spandrels date from slightly later (1686–9). Each spandrel features a pair of rambunctious cherubs (putti), most winged and carrying a variety of symbolic objects, such as flowers and birds. The equivalent of the untamed nature deities of the keystones, boisterous children were also a common decorative feature in ancient Roman gardens, as at Hadrian's Maritime Theatre. Although Apollo is not literally shown in the spandrels, his presence is implied throughout the reliefs. Most obvious are the representations of 31 musical instruments in 18 reliefs, which refer directly to the god of music: eight strings, fourteen winds, and nine percussive instruments. The lyre, which appears three times, is Apollo's most recognizable attribute, and its sister strings, the harp and the violin, often shown in post-classical images of him, also appear (figure 12.3).

In addition, several bows, arrows, and quivers allude to Apollo, the god of archery (figure 12.4), while the many branches and wreathes of laurel are associated with his rule over the arts.

And as the god entrusted with the care of flocks, Apollo is referenced twice by the musette, a pastoral wind instrument that developed out of the bagpipe in the early seventeenth century.

The sculpture in Spandrel 16, where the putti hold a lyre and a pan-pipe, is of particular significance, because it calls to mind two ancient

FIGURE 12.3   Antoine Coysevox (attributed), Spandrel 16, putti with lyre and panpipe, the Colonnade, 1686–8. Photo: B. de La Moureyre.

FIGURE 12.4   Louis Le Conte (attributed), Spandrel 14, putti with firebolt, bow, arrows, and quiver, the Colonnade, 1686–8. Photo: B. de La Moureyre.

legends, the comical contest between Apollo and the satyr Pan and the tragic contest between Apollo and the satyr Marsyas (figure 12.3). According to the first story, Pan, having fashioned the panpipe, foolishly challenged Apollo to a contest. Apollo's divine inspiration and his ability to sing while playing made him the winner. The other story resulted from the invention of the reed pipe by Athena. Despite its pleasant sounds, the gods poked fun at her facial distortions and puffy cheeks, so that she placed a curse on the flute and threw it away. Marsyas retrieved it and challenged Apollo to a match. Crowned the victor with a wreath of laurel, Apollo enacted a cruel punishment – tying Marsyas to a pine tree and flaying him alive. Significantly, the heads of both Pan and Marsyas are included among the keystone masks in the Colonnade, and the 32 pinecone vases surmounting the cornice refer to Marsyas' demise. These two ancient narratives traditionally embodied the eternal conflict between two musical realms, the Apollonian stringed instruments, with their clear, harmonious, plucked tones, and the Dionysian winds and percussion, shrill and strident. On a higher plane, this clash epitomized the dichotomy between the principles of reason and of passion. The ancients interpreted the mythological challenges to the lyre as attempts to overthrow the universal order. Apollo's terrible punishment of Marsyas, therefore, was justified, and the lyre became a visual symbol for the principle of intelligence, control, and reason.

At this point we must return to the Pythagorean/Platonic tradition of universal harmony discussed earlier in connection with architecture. Building on Pythagoras' ideas, Boethius and other intellectuals identified the seven musical tones of the octave with the seven strings on Apollo's lyre and the seven planets overseen by Apollo-Helios. The sounds produced by the movement of the planets, which were overseen by the Sun God, were called the Harmony of the Spheres. Accompanying Apollo's lyre, the Muses sang the Music of the Spheres while their dancing propelled the planetary orbits. As in the case of the post-medieval treatises on architecture and harmony that used the ancients as a model, French theorists, like Descartes in his *Compendium Musicae* (1618) and Marin Mersenne in his *Harmonie universelle* (1636), expounded on the relationship between musical and universal harmony. Moreover, they adopted ancient philosophical ideas, especially the writings of Plato, that linked musical performance with the harmony of the state. As Mersenne proclaimed, "kings and all the greatest powers on earth can draw from the utility of our harmonic treatises."[6] Historian Robert Isherwood summarizes the prevailing point of view as expressed by the poet Rault de Rouën in the October 1680 issue of the *Mercure Galant*:

> Harmony is a divine creation. It expresses the notion of the planets and the essence of nature. In creating musical harmony, the composer, therefore, is providing humanity with the principle of life itself. Indeed, he is providing the basis of government. This truth, so clearly perceived and explained by the ancient philosophers and churchmen, has been recognized by Louis XIV, who alone is responsible for reviving the musical *spectacles* of the ancients and for restoring political and musical harmony to the world.[7]

Thus the spandrel employs the traditional analogy between Apollo, who oversees the Harmony of the Spheres, as represented by the lyre, and the Sun King, who brings peace to France and harmony to Western nations.

To us the notion that the visual pairing of a lyre and panpipe would evoke so grandiose a concept may seem esoteric. But the Baroque age believed that a simple image or emblem could convey complex ideas better than a lengthy text, and this is proven by the great number of treatises on symbols and emblems published in the seventeenth century. The stories about Apollo were well known at the French court, and Mignard had previously painted the two mythological contests on the ceiling of the king's apartment at the Tuileries Palace, Paris (1660s); the court historiographer André Felibien confirmed that these were allegories of the king's deeds. Widely circulated engravings illustrated the theme of Louis-Apollo regulating the harmony of the universe through musical performance. For example, the frontispiece to the royal *Almanach* of 1679 represents the figure of France displaying Louis XIV's portrait while distributing olive branches to the assembled nations of Europe, who signify accord by singing and playing instruments in symphonic unison.

Expanding the Theme of Harmony

As ruler of universal harmony, Apollo safeguarded the turning of the Four Seasons and the equilibrium of the Four Elements: Earth, Fire, Air, and Water. These quaternaries, so beloved by the Pythagoreans, appear frequently throughout Versailles, most notably in the sculptural project for the West Parterre (Grande Commande, 1674) and in a pair of tapestry cycles designed by Charles Le Brun (1664). In choosing suitable objects to be held by the putti, the designers of the Colonnade sculptures followed the prescriptions for symbolic attributes recommended in the 1644 French translation of Cesare Ripa's handbook of emblems, the *Iconologia*. In a few cases, a single attribute conveys multiple meanings. The Seasons appear as follows: flowers (Spring), a bolt of fire (Summer), a horn of plenty (Fall), and again a fire bolt (for warmth in Winter) (figure 12.4). The Elements take the following guise: flowers and horn of plenty (Earth), fire bolt (Fire), birds and bubbles (Air), and an urn (Water). Besides its abundant presence in the fountains, water also appears in the Vitruvian wave pattern running along the classical frieze. Not only do these symbols refer to Louis-Apollo in the cosmic sense, but they also pertain to the control he imposed on the seemingly intractable site of Versailles; as the bishop of Fréjus remarked: "Our King, having conquered entire provinces, has tamed all of the elements, having forced the land and the air to nourish and protect the most odiferous plants, which in the past could not endure the cold of this country."[8]

The theme of harmony versus discord in the Colonnade is accompanied by the symbols of peace versus war. In Spandrel 31 a triumphant putto supports himself on a sword and a helmet, the attributes of Mars and of military victory. Moreover, a group of instruments share martial connotations. Three trumpets possess a dual association with war and the concept of fame. As Mersenne confirmed, the trumpet's "principal usage is destined for war," as commanders "would prepare the heart and mind of the soldier for going to war, for attacking, and engaging in combat."[9] The kettledrum represented in Spandrel 15 was paired with the trumpet in court and military music, being used in marches, flourishes, and fanfares, in addition to battle signals. Other emblems held by the putti refer to the concord brought about by the monarch's victories: the dove, palm branches, laurel wreathes, and horns of plenty.

The martial theme is reinforced by the presence of dancing putti in several spandrels. In Baroque France, as in antiquity, the dance was commonly considered a method of preparing the male body for war. In establishing the Royal Academy of Dance in 1661, the king emphasized that "[t]he art of the dance has always been recognized as one of the most respectable and most necessary to train the body and to give it the first and the most natural dispositions to every kind of exercise, to that of the arms among others."[10] The whirling putto in Spandrel 20 holds cymbals, an ancient instrument used by dancers, and his companion bears a triangle. In Spandrel 4 a dancing cherub clacks a pair of castanets, while his cohort beats the rhythm with a tambourine. The art of the dance was closely associated with the Muses and thus with the harmonious movement of the planets. According to the Pythagorean/Platonic philosophy of numbers, human dance was a reflection of the celestial dance. Seventeenth-century dance theory depended on the writings of the Greek rhetorician Lucian, who maintained that "the concord of the heavenly spheres, the interlacing of the errant planets with the fixed stars, their rhythmic agreement and timed harmony, are proofs that dance was primordial."[11] Contemporary French historians of dance, Claude Menestrier and Jacques Bonnet, claimed that in both ancient and modern society dance served as a means of portraying great events and of stimulating moral behavior, a point of view adopted by the Sun King in commissioning court ballets that commemorated his rule.

All of the instruments depicted in the sculptures were likely played within the Colonnade at one time or another during the reign. It should be remembered that Louis XIV was particularly fond of music and dance, having performed in both mediums, and he oversaw a successful musical establishment at court. Like the great rulers of the past, he realized the usefulness of the arts to project an image of the benevolence, heroism, and brilliance of the monarchy. His imperial ambitions, evident in his military campaigns, were represented by ancient Roman motifs in the architecture of the Colonnade, while the concord he claimed for France and Europe was symbolized by the gracious proportions of the structure and the sculpted symbols of Louis/Apollo as overseer of universal harmony. In sum, the Colonnade operated as both a place of delight, where nature's wonders orchestrated a spectacle, and a place for contemplation, where the artifacts of man revealed a metaphysical view of the world.

NOTES

1   Many people contributed to this essay: in particular I wish to thank Françoise de la Moureyre, Thomas Hedin, Christiane Joost-Gaugier, Ian Wardropper, Jack Freiberg, Patricia Stanley, and Lois Bonjoine. Beverley Beard introduced me to the musicological literature and shared her analysis of the musical instruments in a paper, "Musical Iconography in the Gardens of Versailles," for the Southern Chapter of the American Musicological Society, 1991. Stephanie Leitch and Paul van der Mark kindly shared photographs of the site.

2   A. S. Weiss, *Mirrors of Infinity: The French Formal Garden and 17th-Century Metaphysics* (New York: Princeton Architectural Press, 1999); E. B. Rogers,

Landscape Design: A Cultural and Architectural History (New York: Abrams, 2001), pp. 165–7; C. Mukerji, *Territorial Ambitions and the Gardens of Versailles* (Cambridge: Cambridge University Press, 1997), pp. 248–79.

3 *The Metamorphoses of Ovid*, trans. A. Mandelbaum (New York: Harcourt Brace, 1993), p. 37.

4 F. De La Moureyre, "Les enfants de la Colonnade de Versailles: Attributions à Coyzevox, Tuby, Le Hongre, Le Conte, Granier et Mazière," *Bulletin de la Société de l'Histoire de l'Art Français* 103 (1984): 89–103.

5 T. F. Hedin, "Le Nôtre to Mansart: Transition in the Gardens of Versailles," *Gazette des Beaux-Arts* 139 (December 1997): 253–5.

6 R. M. Isherwood, *Music in the Service of the King: France in the Seventeenth Century* (Ithaca: Cornell University Press, 1973), p. 2.

7 Ibid., p. 38; for a full discussion, see ch. 1, "Musical Philosophy," and pp. 162–9 on Louis/Apollo and harmony.

8 C. Goldstein, *Vaux and Versailles: The Appropriation, Erasures, and Accidents That Made Modern France* (Philadelphia: University of Pennsylvania Press, 2008), p. 215.

9 M. Mersenne, *Harmonie Universelle: The Books on Instruments*, trans. R. E. Chapman (The Hague: Nijhoff, 1957), p. 331.

10 Isherwood, *Music in the Service of the King*, p. 153.

11 *Lucian*, 8 vols., trans. A. M. Harman (Cambridge, MA: Harvard University Press, 1962), 5:221; quoted in S. R. Cohen, *Art, Dance, and the Body in French Culture of the Ancien Régime* (Cambridge: Cambridge University Press, 200), p. 86.

CHAPTER 13

TIME AND TEMPORALITY
IN THE GARDEN

Nothing is more obvious in a garden than change. Even at what seems to be the moment of perfection, a butterfly shows up. When the walk is swept, everything finally tidy, a leaf drops. We sweep again.

For some of us, creating those moments of perfection is the point of the garden: enjoying the illusion of timelessness, the illusion of paradise. But gardens are in a constant process of change – or rather, of several different processes. Many of these changes are welcome processes that affect us directly, for their own sake – and emotionally. But they also make evident the passage of time, reveal the structures of time itself.

Time is not just one thing. It is many. And gardens do not just happen into it, passive victims like everyone and everything else. By means of their styles, they structure time itself, and they make its structures evident to us, juxtaposing different structures for our consideration, for contrast. They do it in ways that allow us to understand both time itself, and time as one of the media of their own artistry.

Gardens deal with six basic and equally common but profoundly different notions of time: (1) scientific time, (2) objective time, (3) *kairos*, (4) subjective time, (5) temporality (the individual's inner experience of time passing – or not), and (6) historical time, both of society's and our own personal histories. Gardens in all cultures structure time for the visitor: it is one of their most important and least studied contributions. While the garden's structuring of time has rarely been analyzed by scholars or designers, most visitors feel it, experience it, intuit it, in all gardens, whatever their style or country of origin. Time may seem abstract, constantly with us yet hard to know. (In the words of Augustine of Hippo, "What then is time? If no one asks me, I know what it is. If I wish to explain it to him who asks, I do not know.")[1] Yet contrasting types and modalities of time provide fundamental structures for both the activities of gardening and our experiences of gardens.

Chronos and Kairos

The ancient Greeks used two contrasting notions of time. *Chronos* is familiar to us: measurable and sequential, part of the natural laws within which human life takes place, the times of day and of the year; it is quantifiable, undifferentiated, interchangeable and exchangeable in the sense that three hours of labor, now, or by Mary, is equivalent to three hours at another time or by Sally. If we estimate a task will take ten minutes, we expect it to be the same no matter which ten minutes we choose. (This of course suggests traffic jam time is not *chronos*!)

Kairos was a recognition of the appropriateness of a time and an event or act; the right or opportune moment, referred to in Ecclesiastes:

> To everything there is a season,
> and a time to every purpose under the heaven:
> A time to be born, and a time to die;
> a time to plant, and a time to pluck up that which is planted.[2]

For gardeners, the distinction between *kairos* and *chronos* is crucial – a matter of life and death. It is far more important to plant (most) seeds *after the last frost*, whenever that may be! (*kairos*) than on "May 10–14" (Boulder County, Colorado) or "April 23" (Evansville, Indiana) (*chronos*). (The Indiana dates come from the Victory Seed Company's website; Boulder County's from my memory of the recommendation printed in the Boulder *Daily Camera* circa 1998.)

Chronos and Scientific Time

In modern life, *chronos* has become split into scientific time, which is quantifiable and divisible into units of uniform length (seconds, minutes, hours, days), and objective time (discussed separately, below).

Scientific time is the type of objective, quantifiable time used by scientists and such social institutions as courts and judicial systems. It is directional (philosophers speak of "time's arrow," which never reverses course or repeats), interchangeable, and uniform (at least under specific conditions); it "moves" from the present into the future, and the trajectory of its arrow begins in the past. (The physicists' version, however, includes forms of relativity and variability with which geologists and biologists rarely deal.)

Scientists' time may be the least important for garden design, since it is rarely of aesthetic interest. Yet because it is crucial to plants' survival, it must be reckoned with constantly, whether intuitively or explicitly: considering the number of days till germination, of hours of sunlight required for a plant to fruit, and so on.

On a small (biological) scale, scientific time is of vital interest to gardeners, who would be unbearably frustrated by a new variety of rose that reversed itself into a bud instead of flowering, or by berries that refused to ripen and stayed forever green and small. To be sure, there is for gardeners a vibrant interplay between scientific time and subjective time. The desire for plants to bloom or ripen may make us experience time slowing down (subjective time), but that is in sharp contrast with the plants' scientifically predictable timing.

Astronomers' time, marking out the seasons, is equally germane to gardeners, both for its practical applications and its relevance to aesthetic considerations. For planting, we need to be able to predict the seasonal changes at least roughly. The notion of a "growing season," essential for predicting the survivability of a crop in a particular place, is a function of the amount of sunlight the place receives – although significantly, this is also a function of place (latitude and altitude). For farmers in non-scientific societies, even the phases of the moon may be considered highly significant for planting, as they may also be for gardeners affected by tides, near an ocean shore, salt-water estuary, or wetland.

The duration and intensity of sunshine affect every aspect of garden design: placement of plants, seating, dining tables, and white stones or metallic sculptures. These are not always aesthetic matters only. Both plants' lives and our ability to carry out certain activities depend on them. Siting of a hot tub or bench for moon-viewing is also a function of the celestial calendar. (All of these are also, of course, dependent upon culture as well; upon the society's gardening ideals and general aesthetics. Do Westerners even consider moon-viewing?)

This brings us to meteorologists' time, for the moon has an intimate relationship with clouds. Meteorologists' time moves faster and more unpredictably than astronomers' time – and again, there is little we can do about it! And it too deals with matters of life and death for gardens. Do we take the drastic and expensive steps to prevent frost in the orange grove? Do we water or wait for rain? There are overall patterns of consistency on this level, but we frequently find ourselves rushing to prevent damage, shaking off four inches of snow from the plants if there's more coming before this melts.

Climate and Garden Aesthetics

Climate is the result of complex interactions between time (the seasons) and the place (local topography and the larger geology). It may be the single most important determinant of garden styles. Consider the popularity of peristyle and courtyard gardens in cultures as diverse as Persia and Mughal India, Rome, and New Orleans. In hot locales the desire to view the garden while escaping the heat is as intense as the need for social and physical privacy.

The local climate provides the foundation upon which the garden builds its two-sided aesthetic system of opposition and accommodation. The basic purpose of gardens is to counteract the undesirable aspects of the environment (in all its manifestations: social, physical, climatic). When the climate is hot, we want something cool; when it's cool or windy, we want warmth; if it's rainy, we want protection from the rain; if it's dark and overcast, we want bright color; if it's dry, we want water features.

At the same time, we gardeners exploit the advantages of our climate. This, it seems to me, is less common than the desire to contradict climate, but it is fundamental nonetheless. Exploitation of the climate and the seasons depends upon our culture and our "cultural literacy" within it. The Japanese garden for four seasons, but before their knowledge and customs spread around the world, gardening for winter was rare in Europe and North America.

Subjective Time

Also important to garden design is "subjective time" – time as it *feels* to us. The fifteen minutes of a physicist and the last fifteen minutes of a student's school day are very different quantities indeed. There are three issues here. First, this is partly a difference between the measured time of the scientist and the felt or experienced time of our impatient student. Oddly, the quality of time is often felt as a difference in its quantity – its length or duration.

Second, subjective time varies for each individual, too. It is not like subjective differences in people's sense of taste or color, which tend to be standardized more or less for each of us over time, but rather varies first with our age (as Lessing shows below) and, second, with our modes of engagement with our environment, with what we are doing, and sometimes with our pleasure or pain. Ten minutes of dental work feels as if it takes longer than an hour reading a mystery novel. Yet fifteen minutes looking at my plants may feel like an hour of relaxation.

Yet, third, the variability in individuals' experience of time is also shared in some respects and therefore predictable and in some sense "objective." Doris Lessing describes this:

> The main reason, the real one, why an autobiography must be untrue is the subjective experience of time. The book is written, chapter one to the end, in regular progress through the years. Even if you go in for sleights of hand like flashbacks or *Tristram Shandy*, there is no way of conveying in words the difference between child time and grown-up time, and the different pace of time in the different stages of an adult's life. A year before you are thirty is a very different year from the sixty-year-old's year.
>
> When scientists try to get us to understand the real importance of the human race, they say something like, "if the story of the earth is twenty-four hours long, then humanity's part in it occupies the last minute of that day." Similarly, in the story of a life, if it is being told true to time as actually experienced, then I'd say seventy per cent of the book would take you to age ten. At eighty per cent you would have reached fifteen. At ninety-five per cent, you get to about thirty. The rest is a rush – toward eternity.[3]

Lessing here is *talking about* differences in temporalities, not demonstrating them or trying to get us to experience them. But these latter tasks have been taken up by many poets, novelists, and filmmakers, particularly with respect to childhood and old age, altered states of consciousness, and particular emotions such as anxiety, fear, or anticipation.

(Proust's *Remembrance of Things Past* is such an endeavor, as are Ingmar Bergman's films *Fanny and Alexander* and *Wild Strawberries*.)

Gardens facilitate for us different experiences of subjective time. There are culturally specific ways of doing this. (In *English Gardens*, for example, David Coffin discusses the ways in which seventeenth-century English gardens raised for viewers issues regarding their own mortality.)[4] But it may also be a "natural" process to some extent. By eliminating loud noises, fast motions, and the dangers they signal, gardens permit us to focus on details and on beauties – of various kinds. They allow us to immerse ourselves in the moment, completely unfocused or in chains of reverie or intense concentration. We might even speak of this capacity of gardens as an "affordance," the concept biologist James Gibson introduced to refer to spatial forms that both facilitate and entice a certain behavior from an organism, like plant stalks (of particular shapes and proportions) that encourage snails to scale them.[5] Do certain kinds of gardens stretch or alter subjective time for us? If so, do their gardeners plan it deliberately? We can imagine that those who position a bench for watching the sunset or moonrise or a slow-flowing brook intend their visitors to have certain kinds of temporal experience – quite different from those with programmed fountains that force a particular kind of attention, for instance. Although different gardening styles emphasize particular varieties of time and consciousness over others, we rarely see such questions addressed explicitly.

Objective or Shared Time

"In between" scientific time and purely subjective temporality are a variety of forms of shared or "objective" time. Particularly for modern technological societies, objective time and scientists' time overlap considerably, for our society's general shared understanding of time is largely based on scientists' studies and measurements by instruments they have devised. I would like, however, to use the term "objective" or "shared" to denote something that is a little harder to get at than physicists' time; namely, a widely shared form of subjective time – any widely shared form, regardless of the specific content or structure.

So by "objective" or "shared" time, I mean that which is experienced and understood by many people within some group (although not necessarily every single person or any single person all the time). Scientific time applies to everyone, regardless of whether we understand it or not. It may well be beyond the range of our understanding, even though we use it constantly to navigate our modern societies. But objective time is the experience of time common within a society. Since it is experienced or felt, it may be described on the one hand as subjective. But given that this particular form of experience is also widely shared, it is also objective. (This is a category of time for which our usual dualistic ways of thinking are not helpful. Perhaps we should say that the terms "subjective" and "objective" as used here are not mutually exclusive.)

Objective or shared time is both taken for granted, that is, effective on a pre-reflective level, and rational in the sense that it is capable of being understood by most people, given some discussion or explanation. (There is nothing mystical about it, nor is it specific to only some individuals.)

For example, in order to justify his reign at a time when challenges to monarchy were being felt around Western Europe, Louis XIV's gardeners at Versailles reconciled familiar daily and annual changes within nature's cycles with the seemingly eternal constants of the celestial realm by juxtaposing themes from the four seasons and the course of the sun through the sky with Apollo and other figures and themes from classical mythology.[6] These correspondences between nature and monarchy, and between sun (Apollo) and God and king, were not purely for his and his courtiers' enjoyment; Versailles was open to the public and intended to be seen by subjects (not yet citizens). The garden thus propagates a shared apprehension of time as simultaneously eternal and historic and recurring, simultaneously divine and mundane.

Another example may be taken from eighteenth-century England, where it became necessary for the purposes of development of capital and industrialization to have a relatively large population that could plan and think in the long term – longer than, say, traditional agriculture called for, which is typically one year. Capital investment for long voyages and for manufacturing presupposes the ability to delay gratification, to carry out plans over years without seeing any results. Now the new English landscape garden, to be sure, served many purposes. But one of the most significant was inculcating the habit of using large trees on a spatial scale previously quite rare (accomplished especially through the designs of Lancelot "Capability" Brown). But actually planting copses of large oaks is not feasible for most on a large scale; you plant them when they are small. Such landscape gardens demand of the planters, therefore, a long vision into the future (some of these landscapes didn't mature

MARA MILLER

until the early twentieth century). This is precisely the kind of vision so valuable in early capitalism. At the same time, on the political front, this coincided with increasing constraints on the power of the monarchy and increasing responsibilities and rights on the part of citizens, especially the upper classes. (That we have not outgrown our need for it is evident from the current deterioration of the environment and the state of much city planning; but the habit of long-range planning is not easy to instil.) In this way, the fast-growing eighteenth-century taste among landowners for large-scale redesign of their estates can be seen as an exercise or form of adult "play" that teaches new skills in thinking about time that were needed for changing social, economic, and political conditions.

Other kinds of shared time are the shared varieties of historical time as understood by a particular culture. In Ming and Qing China, in Renaissance Italy, seventeenth-century France, eighteenth-century England, nineteenth-century United States, and in twentieth-century Japanese gardens in North America (among others), the use of historical quotations and allusions in gardens helped to make the past present, to integrate an understanding of the relevance of history for the present day – even as they often instruct us as to how to experience time itself. Coffin tells us a sundial at Stanwardine Hall, dated 1560, was inscribed: "In the hours of death God be merciful unto me / For as tyme doth haste / So life doth waste."[7] Many delightful if fictional examples are provided by Cao Xuiqin's eighteenth-century novel *The Story of the Stone* and by Mark Mills' novel *The Savage Garden*, set in a fifteenth-century Italian garden:

> A weather-fretted stone bench was set before the trough, facing the amphi-theater. It bore an inscription in Latin, eroded by the elements, but just possible to make out:
>
> ANIMA FIT SEDENDO ET QUIEXCENDO PRUDENTIOR
>
> The Soul in Repose Grows Wiser. Or something like that. An appropriate message for a spot intended for contemplation.[8]

Cyclical Time

An even more widespread form of objective time than linear historical time is cyclical time. This is the "eternal recurrence" analyzed by Mircea Eliade: the time of the seasons, of the life cycles of animals (including human beings), of agriculture.[9] Inhabitants of modern and postmodern societies, too, are familiar with cyclical time: the liturgical year, the fiscal and academic years, the seasons, the cycle of holidays, and our family calendars of birthdays and anniversaries.

Gardeners integrate the cyclical time of their plants' internal calendar and the seasons with scientific time. Cyclical time profoundly affects both the creation and enjoyment of gardens. Although European and American gardens commonly ignore gardens as plants die during the autumn and during winter's dormancy, Japanese and Chinese gardens celebrate all four seasons (without the sense of mourning Eurocentric society associates with fall and the sense of winter as punishment we have derived from Genesis). They focus on the beauties of snow and rain, using stone lanterns with broad caps to catch the snow, and encouraging through poetry the appreciation of the sounds of dead lotus pods rattling in the wind.

Twenty-first-century societies have seasonal transitions, based on a civic calendar of government-instituted holidays, superimposed upon the calendar of the children's school year (derived from the agricultural calendar). Memorial Day, Independence Day, and Labor Day signal barbeques, picnics, fireworks, and pool parties in public or private gardens.

The Garden's Times

To look at a garden is to see lain out before you things of many different ages, with histories of their own and different patterns and rates of change. Plants grow at different speeds, some so slowly you barely notice for years. (Does anything grow slower than a wisteria vine whose first flowering you're waiting for?) Others change drastically within the course of a day or two. Our new native hibiscus in the corner of the *lanai* (a Hawaiian patio or largish balcony) finally began to flower yesterday afternoon; the darned flower had closed for good by evening! You go out to pick the raspberries that were almost ripe last evening and discover them eaten already by mice or birds. The butterflies enter for moments only, altering the color scheme, then departing and leaving the garden as if they have never been. Not so the cherry blossom petals that remain scattered on the ground longer than they were on the tree, it seems. Dragonflies seem equally unpredictable. (Dare I say "flighty?") The fireflies come out for much longer than the butterflies and dragonflies, though it's only a few hours at most, at dusk. They hang out for weeks, then decamp for another ten months.

Quickest changing of all is the sun itself, continuously changing position. Going about our daily work we scarcely notice this until it's time to turn the lights on. In our modern cities there seems to be just two times of day: day and night (sun on, lights off; or sun off, lights on). But try to place a couple of pots of flowers in the sun and you begin to see how complex this is. What seems to be "full sun" to you is only five hours (or two hours in a city of skyscrapers) to what will soon be your dying, sun-deprived plants. "Partial shade" is really only a light dappling for others. And put yourself in a garden to read and you really get a shock. The sun is perfectly placed at your side, then in no time it's in your eyes. You readjust your chair (and perhaps the little table with the iced tea). It's moved again. You readjust your chair (setting the iced tea on the ground this time). The perfect plan, you realize, is one of those plastic tulip-shaped glass-holders on a metal rod that you thrust in the ground. You will be ready for it the next day! You set it up the next morning, and realize the sun is now on the other side and will be in your eyes. It goes on....

This constant passage of the sun across the sky – not really constant since its angle is different every day of the year – accounts for the impossibility of permanence in any garden. Even those without plants, like the dry rock gardens of Ryōanji, evince constant change on a scale apparent to the visitor who sits still for fifteen minutes (though this is not easily done these days at Ryōanji, whose unremitting press of visitors requires constant flow of the crowds). The play of light against pale sand, or a white or ochre-colored wall unrelieved by decoration, allows us to perceive shadows (of clouds even where trees are absent) and the subtle changes in the intensity of the sunlight as clouds shift or their density changes.

These constant instantaneous changes become a background against which we notice our own relative changelessness. Against these obvious changes, awaiting the return of that butterfly, the reemergence tonight of the fireflies, and noticing the flutter of the shadows of leaves on the wall as the wind passes, we are a constant. We notice ourselves. Not for our accomplishments or any characteristics we might have, not for the things others are always pointing out to us – we're always running late, our pants are too short, we play well with others – but simply as the one who is noticing. I am the one who is here. I see and feel and smell and hear this. Like Descartes' *cogito*, it is a confirmation of our existence: "I think, therefore I am" here becomes "I notice, therefore I am."[10]

But there is a distinctive quality, a peculiar pleasure, to this noticing, that makes it quite unlike the satisfaction Descartes must have felt as he realized that he was thinking and that this thinking and his awareness of it could serve as the basis for knowledge. That was an intellectual pleasure, no doubt, and one quite different from our noticing.

In the garden, I take my place among the myriad things that are always the same and always changing, each of us at our own paces and in our own rhythms, each of us noticing our own things. I and the bee each enjoy that morning glory. He gathers nectar. I merely look. My neighbor Jane, also very fond of morning glories, has written out some poems by Basho and Issa on morning glories and slipped them through our mail slot. Our first cat particularly enjoyed their shade.

We notice ourselves noticing; it is one of the great pleasures. We can never get enough. (That is one of the problems with doing nothing – it takes so long because you never know when you're done.)

In a dry rock garden, we, the rocks, the plants, each with a shadow, a side that's catching the light. Now each is like a tiny mountain. We observe the crevasses between them. We enter the miniature landscape. This ability to enter the landscape in imagination is a valuable tool for looking at Asian miniature gardens and landscapes in every format: bonsai, paintings, framed slices of stone whose coloration depicts a landscape, small rock landscapes like the one at Daisen-in, and larger landscapes big enough to walk around but meant to be viewed from a veranda and modeled on the vastness of the Isles of the Immortals or of Japan itself. We have taught ourselves a valuable skill of imagination. We are learning the interpenetration of microcosm and macrocosm.

The different scales of seasonal and diurnal recurrence interweave. The brick or stone of walls and paths seem unchangeable; only over the course of years do you notice they have begun to wear or to chip. The fireflies arrive annually, come out each evening and go in before we want them to (reminding the parents it's the children's bedtime, if they hadn't noticed already). During their visit they light and extinguish, each in a rhythm of its own, but not regular. The mosquitoes have a much longer stay, and are out for much longer each day, following us inside to continue their feasting, as willing as we are to ignore the natural cycle of light and dark. The birds in many climates fly south in one season and north in another. If you are at one end or the other of a species migration, it is an annual event for you. If you are in the middle, you meet them twice a year, in spring and fall. (Tropical climates have seasons of their own: monsoon or hurricane, wet and dry, warmer and cooler.) These rhythms pick up resonances of their own. The geese and ducks flying south in the fall – this is the onset of winter, the sad time, the season of loneliness – cry to each other, forming migration groups, becoming as they leave us the very symbol of our being left. The ducks mate for life – the symbol, in Korea and Japan, of marital fidelity, of love.

We become aware of ourselves as the ones who know this, who have noticed; who have been taught to notice, been taught the poems or seen the gift duck on the chest, the wedding present. We become, in part, these links to our own noticing, our memory, and to the noticing and recording of these noticings in the poetic and artistic currencies of our culture.

We are enmeshed.

Moving Through the Garden

So far we have talked as if one only stays still in gardens. Certainly, encouraged indolence is one of gardens' great blessings. But most gardens are also intended to be moved through. (There are important exceptions, of course, such as municipal display beds of annuals, Japanese dry rock gardens, suburban lawns (in many localities), and often the gardens of hotels or schools.) Not only the directions visitors move in but the very ways they move, their speed and types of movement, may be deliberately orchestrated by the designer.

At one extreme is the utterly unregulated unconfined movement in any direction and at any speed implied by a flat area of grass or a playing field, or the fields of snow for snowmobiles in national parks in winter. The paved sidewalks and black-topped roads of modern parks and golf courses permit high speed travel by motor vehicles as well as pedestrians – although they facilitate this only along certain routes. Many nineteenth-century parks boast horse trails. In England there are medieval (or possibly earlier) mazes, worn permanently into the turf from being danced, that were incorporated into gardens of Tudor estates. Many were erased under the ambitious plans of eighteenth-century designers seeking to destroy everything that did not look "natural," but a few, like the one at Chenies Court, remain. Waterways are enormously important courses of movement in gardens, for fish and for us, by swimming or boating – as an activity and a spectator sport.

At the other extreme are the uneven, irregularly spaced stepping stones in Japanese tea gardens, designed to require the walker to pay attention to her every step – and thus to shed the worries from ordinary life outside the garden that would otherwise preoccupy her. Even in other types of Japanese gardens, there may well be areas with this sort of constraint on physical movement, regulating the visitor's attention, enforcing a sort of mindfulness meditation. We become more aware of the earth, of our placement of our bodies in space on the surface of the stones. We become more aware of the idiosyncrasies, of the specialness, of the "this-ness" of the moment. This is one form of Buddhist mindfulness – the immersion in the present moment, ignoring past and future. It is a specifically Buddhist notion of time in this kind of garden which invites us to this mindfulness.

Experiences of Time in the Garden

In addition to all this, historical gardens make accessible the internal experience of the original owners and visitors. The gardens themselves orchestrate our experience of time through their arrangement of spaces for walking, resting, picnicking, and theatrical and musical performances. And because this experience of moving through the garden (or resting) may be much the same for most visitors, regardless of the year or era in which we move, we gain something of our predecessors' sense of internal time. We may not walk in their shoes, but we follow their paths, and in doing so we become aware of them. There is, in other words, a sense of historical time in a garden. This is superimposed upon our awareness of the cycle of the seasons, the cycle of day and night, and the history of the developments of the plants in their own life cycles. It is a specifically human history.

The forms of time in a garden are many. While some can be ignored, ignoring others, such as the time for watering or protection from frost or searing sun, would result in the death of the garden! As a result, all gardeners are keenly aware of time, and of different kinds of time relevant to the garden. But this practical attention is only one dimension of the impact that time has on gardens. Simply paying attention to the variety of kinds of time juxtaposed in gardens can be enormously rewarding – and whether we realize it or not, is the source of some of the garden's great pleasures. Yet few of us – as garden designers or visitors – fully exploit the capabilities of gardens for exploring time and its various modes of significance for our lives. How is the orchestration of subjective or historic time to be achieved in our garden? What artistic innovations might we make? It should be recognized that the conscious appreciation, manipulation and celebration of time is as important in the garden as in music, dance, theatre, and calligraphy.[11]

NOTES

1   St. Augustine, *Confessions*, trans. R. S. Pine-Coffin (London: Penguin, 1961), X, 35.

2   Ecclesiastes 3: 1–8, quoted from the King James version of the Bible.

3   D. Lessing, *Under My Skin: Volume One of My Autobiography, to 1949* (New York: Harper Collins, 1994), p. 109.

4   D. Coffin, *English Gardens* (Princeton: Princeton University Press, 1996).

5   J. J. Gibson, "The Theory of Affordances," in *Perceiving, Acting, and Knowing*, ed. R. Shaw and J. Bransford (Mahwah: Lawrence Erlbaum, 1977); J. J. Gibson, *The Ecological Approach to Visual Perception* (New York: Houghton Mifflin, 1979).

6   M. Baridon, *A History of the Gardens of Versailles* (Philadelpia: University of Pennsylvania Press, 2008); R. W. Berger, *In the Garden of the Sun King: Studies on the Park of Versailles under Louis XIV* (Washington, DC: Dumbarton Oaks, 1958).

7   Coffin, *English Gardens*, p. 9.

8   M. Mills, *The Savage Garden* (New York: G. P. Putnam, 2007), p. 39.

9   M. Eliade, *The Myth of the Eternal Return or Cosmos and History* (Princeton: Princeton University Press, 1971 [1954]).

10 R. Descartes, *Discourse on Method* (1637) and *Principles of Philosophy* (1644) in *The Philosophical Writings of Descartes*, 3 vols, trans. J. Cottingham, R. Stoothoff, A. Kenny, and D. Murdoch (Cambridge: Cambridge University Press, 1988).

11 Some of these ideas appeared in M. Miller, *The Garden as an Art* (New York: State University of New York Press, 1993) and M. Miller, "Time and Temporality in Japanese Gardens," in J. Birksted (ed.) *Between Architecture and Landscape* (New York: Chapman and Hall, 1999).

CHAPTER 14

CULTIVATING OUR GARDEN

David Hume and Gardening as Therapy

Gardens are seen as having metaphysical and theological significance. Many think of the Garden of Eden as the first garden, and the four rivers in Eden, mentioned in both the Bible and the Quran, are represented by four watercourses in Islamic royal gardens and by four paths in the cloister gardens of Christian monasteries and churches. Japanese Zen gardens are designed to aid meditation on eternity, and so-called paradise gardens are earthly attempts to model the celestial gardens of the gods. In this volume, Robert Neuman explores how the garden of Versailles was designed as a reflection of the divine, laid out according to principles of Pythagorean and Cartesian philosophy. This rationalist tradition continues today in the Garden of Cosmic Speculation in Scotland, where the design reflects the "birth, laws, and development of the universe"; the "garden ... in part, a speculation about the underlying truths"; the gardener involved in "translating the insights of science and philosophy into workable objects."[1]

The English picturesque tradition rejects such a formal approach and the laying out of gardens according to precise geometric rules. The British empiricists of the seventeenth and eighteenth centuries saw the mind as consisting of a flux of thoughts derived from experience, rather than as a collection of innate ideas planted in us by God. This empiricist focus on experience can be seen in English landscape gardens of the time. Gardens are not a reflection of divine structures, but rather, places that are designed in order to affect the flow of our sensations. The focus is on sensation and experience, rather than reason. Here, Elizabeth Rogers notes how gardens can bring about such changes:

> The power of ruins to inspire a mood of elegiac melancholy, of dark-toned vegetation to turn the thoughts into paths of sombre reflection, of bright green meadows to soothe the agitated soul, of sunny fields reminiscent of harvest revels to raise the spirits to the level of gaiety, of still brooks and placid lakes to speak of peace and serenity, of loud tumbling waterfalls to induce a thrilling fear.[2]

Gardens, then, can be seen as reflecting the dominant philosophical theories of their time and place.

In this essay, though, following various lines of thought of the Scottish philosopher David Hume (1711–76), I shall argue that gardens can be a refuge away from metaphysics and philosophical reflection and that they can therefore play a therapeutic role.

Candide

Voltaire, a contemporary of Hume, wrote *Candide* as a parody of religion and of religious apologies for the existence of evil in the world. That there are morally corrupt people and that the world is occasionally beset by natural disasters looks to be incompatible with a morally perfect God, one who is all powerful and who could presumably eradicate such evils. "One could grumble rather at what goes on in our one [world], both physically and morally."[3] Candide's tutor, Doctor Pangloss, teacher of "metaphysico-theologico-cosmo-codology" – a thinly disguised Leibniz (an Enlightenment metaphysician) – argues, however, that we live in "the best of all possible worlds," as a benevolent God would have created. His "theodicies" are explanations designed to account for the existence of evil: "if Columbus, on an island in the Americas, had not caught this disease [syphilis] which poisons the spring of procreation ... and which plainly is the opposite of what nature intended, we would have neither chocolate nor cochineal."[4] The humor is pointed since philosophers and theologians had performed various contortions to explain away the fact that the world does not seem to be the creation of a perfectly benevolent supreme being – and they continue to do so to this day. Candide has many adventures while continuing his philosophical discussions with Pangloss and others; his final optimistic note, though, is not that of his tutor, but the enigmatic claim that "we must cultivate our garden."[5]

This claim has been interpreted in various ways. Voltaire could merely be suggesting that the world is indeed full of evils and that it would be wise to retreat to our own little patch and make the best of it. There is, though, a deeper sense to such a "retreat," one that can be illuminated by looking at the philosophy of another great Enlightenment thinker, David Hume, with whom Voltaire was in occasional correspondence. Writing to Hume, Voltaire says: "The abetters of superstition [religion] clip our wings and hinder us from soaring."[6] Hume claims that we should reject philosophical thinking and return to the concerns of common life – the garden, then, being a metaphor for a life free of metaphysics and theodicy. I shall also argue that gardening itself is exactly the sort of common life activity that could contribute to this therapeutic rejection of philosophy and theology.

Hume and Common Life

Hume is suspicious of metaphysics and particularly hostile towards organized religion. His *Dialogues Concerning Natural Religion* contain seminal criticism of various arguments for the existence of God. In his *Enquiry Concerning Human Understanding* he argues that there has never been any good evidence for the occurrence of a miracle and there is never likely to be any. And in his *Natural History of Religion* he provides a naturalistic account of religious belief, one grounded in fear rather than rational insight or evidence. One aspect of Hume's rejection of religion takes place at the level of common life. His strategy is to remind anyone tempted by religion of their usual everyday ways of thinking. We have to remind ourselves of how we would normally think when not led astray by psychological factors associated with religious belief. In the case of miracles, for example, Hume claims that people are swayed from their usual ways of thinking by several distorting psychological factors. The thought of supernatural intervention fills us with awe, and "the passion of *surprise and wonder*, arising from miracles being an agreeable notion, gives a sensible tendency towards the belief of those events."[7] Our vanity is also massaged if we can report such events: "But what greater temptation than to appear a missionary, a prophet, an ambassador from heaven?"[8] It

DAN O'BRIEN

is such factors that cause us to believe in supernatural occurrences; such factors that promote the mere idea of the occurrence of a miracle to actual belief in such a happening. Hume therefore asks us to imagine what would be believed if these factors were not present; if, say, passion and wonder did not give rise to belief, and if our fellows were not impressed with stories concerning such things. If this were so, then we should explain away such improbable events in the way that Hume describes, and this is just what we do in everyday situations. One believes that somehow a melon seed found its way into the greenhouse if melons start to grow there unplanned (as they have done this year in my greenhouse!); one does not believe that such growth is miraculous. Similarly, one should believe that one has been tricked or one has misunderstood when asked to believe that a man has risen from the dead. Hume does not criticize belief in miracles on philosophical or logical grounds; instead, he offers us reminders as to how we usually think, and how we should therefore think when we are asked to believe in miracles.

Hume's rejection of metaphysics is not limited to religion. Philosophers have an unhealthy attraction to extreme skepticism. Plato sees the world of experience as akin to mere shadows cast on the walls of a cave, shadows of the real things in Platonic Heaven. Descartes meditates on the possibility that our experience of the world could all be a dream or hallucinations planted in our minds by an evil demon. Hume, too, at times adopts such a skeptical perspective and argues that we can only have knowledge of our own sensations; we cannot, as it were, get behind these to take a direct look at the world that we only assume is causing our experience. Further, our experience is regular in various ways: the sun comes up every day and the leaves fall every autumn. We have, however, no philosophical reason to think they will continue to do so. Why think the world (or, rather, our experience) will continue on in the same way? Hume thinks there is no satisfying philosophical answer to this question, and this is worrying: it leads to "philosophical melancholy and delirium."[9] However, in the face of such skeptical arguments, Hume argues that we should rescind to our everyday thinking: act, as everyone in fact does, as if the sun and the seasons will continue to behave as they always have.

Hume does, however, distinguish between the kinds of reasoning we pursue in everyday or common life. There is the vulgar reasoning of the "peasant" and a more sophisticated form of reasoning:

A peasant can give no better reason for the stopping of any clock or watch than to say, that commonly it does not go right: But an artisan easily perceives, that the same force in the spring or pendulum has always the same influence on the wheels; but fails of its usual effect, perhaps by reason of a grain of dust, which puts a stop to the whole movement.[10]

Here, the artisan has a more sophisticated grasp of induction. Regularities are sometimes disturbed because there is a "secret opposition of contrary causes."[11] The artisan explains a broken watch in this way; a kitchen gardener similarly explains his unusually poor harvest as due to cucumber mosaic virus or spider mites. Gardening, then, is the sort of pursuit that aids this immersion in common life and in doing so it inculcates epistemic virtues; it helps us to be good everyday reasoners, developing our appreciation of the regular run of the world. It is an activity especially well suited to this since gardeners must be sensitive to regularities of varying scope – those, for example, manifest by the seasons, the weather, disease, and germination. A garden is in many ways a microcosm of the natural world: we must be aware of long-term and short-term changes and how they embed together. Gardeners are artisans *par excellence*, having a fine-grained appreciation of the causal structure of nature. And the gardener's acquiescence in common life reasoning steers clear of psychologically dangerous metaphysical reasoning and, as we shall see, of the cycle of enthusiasm and melancholia characteristic of religious belief.

For Hume, religious beliefs are akin to an illness; they are disruptive to our mental life and action, and thus they should be rejected; not just for epistemic reasons (that is, because they are false), but also for reasons concerning mental health and the security of our human nature. As seen, such beliefs are not rejected by providing philosophical argument to refute them; rather, they are rejected by embracing everyday cognitive standards, by confining ourselves "to common life, and to such subjects as fall under daily practice and experience."[12] If we are successful in this, then the "contagion" of religion shall not infect us.[13] Hume has a "therapeutic" approach to religious belief. Religion, for Hume, is an "affliction," "a natural frailty," nothing but "sick men's dreams."[14] "As superstition arises … it seizes … the mind, and is often able to disturb us in the conduct of our lives and actions."[15] Belief in miracles, say, may undermine our everyday expectations and, if this is severe enough, it may lead to alienation from the regular, everyday world of sunrises and falling leaves.

As well as disturbing our lives and actions, Hume claims that religion also leads to forms of mental illness. "Terror is the primary principle of religion" and this naturally leads to a melancholic frame of mind, with

DAN O'BRIEN

meditations on Heaven and Hell "apt to make a considerable breach in the temper, and to produce that gloom and melancholy, so remarkable in all devout people."[16] There are occasional pleasures, but these are "fits of excessive enthusiastic joy," and these for Hume are not the steady pleasures that bring us happiness. They "exhaust ... the spirits, always prepar[ing] the way for equal fits of superstitious terror and dejection."[17] Religion takes one on a psychological roller coaster, with such violent mood swings opposed to the "calm and equitable" state of mind that we seek. The extremes of this can be seen in those who pursue the "monkish virtues" and who reject the social life; theirs is a world of wild enthusiasm and dark melancholia. At various places in his *History of England* Hume notes the connection between religion and mental illness. Cromwell, for example, was "transported to a degree of madness by religious extasies."[18] We should thus cultivate ways of thinking that keep us engaged in common life, and in a way that involves "that undisturbed philosophical tranquility, superior to pain, sorrow, anxiety, and each assault of adverse fortune.... And the nearer we can approach in practice to this sublime tranquility and indifference ... the more secure enjoyment shall we attain within ourselves."[19] In an early essay, Hume "laments" those with "delicacy of passion," those that are affected strongly by the ups and downs of life: "men of such lively passions are apt to be transported beyond all bounds of prudence and discretion, and to take false steps in the conduct of life, which is often irretrievable."[20] True philosophy should attempt to "take ... off the edge from all disorderly passions, and tranquillize ... the mind."[21] We must therefore step down from the philosophical perspective and embrace the everyday – we must cultivate our garden. In doing so, we avoid the roller coaster emotional ride associated with religion, and various other psychological and physical symptoms characteristic of one plagued by metaphysical and religious questions.

Those tempted by philosophy should take note that:

> there are ... many honest gentlemen, who being always employ'd in their domestic affairs, or amusing themselves in common recreations, have carried their thoughts very little beyond those objects, which are every day expos'd to their senses ... I wish we cou'd communicate to our founders of systems [to philosophers] a share of this gross earthy mixture, as an ingredient, which they commonly stand much in need of, and which wou'd serve to temper those fiery particles, of which they are compos'd.[22]

Cultivating our garden is thus a metaphor for the therapeutic role that common life reasoning has with respect to metaphysical and theological worries. And actual gardening, I shall argue, can play a role in promoting the kind of tranquility that Hume claims should be our goal. Before we turn to this it is interesting to note that the philosopher Ludwig Wittgenstein took to gardening as a cure for his psychological problems. In a letter to the architect Paul Engelmann, he says:

> I have broken my word. I shall not come your way, at least for the time being.… For in my present dubious state of mind even talking to you – much as I enjoy it – would be no more than a pastime. I was longing for some kind of regulized work which, of all the things I can do in my present condition, is the most nearly bearable, if I am not mistaken. It seems I have found such a job: I have been taken on as an assistant gardener at the Klosterneuberg Monastery for the duration of my holiday.[23]

Gardens and Tranquility

Joseph Addison's (1672–1719) essays in the *Spectator* impressed Hume and influenced him to write extensively in that style:

> I know nothing more advantageous than such *Essays* as these with which I endeavour to entertain the public. In this view, I cannot but consider myself as a kind of resident or ambassador from the dominions of learning to those of conversation; and shall think it my constant duty to promote good correspondence betwixt these two states, which have so great a dependence on each other.[24]

And, in one of these essays, Addison notes the relation between gardens and tranquility:

> A garden … is naturally apt to fill the mind with calmness and tranquillity, and to lay all its turbulent passions at rest. It gives us a great insight into the contrivance and wisdom of providence, and suggests innumerable subjects for meditation. I cannot but think the very complacency and satisfaction which a man takes in these works of nature, to be a laudable, if not a virtuous habit of mind. For all which reasons I hope you will pardon the length of my present letter.[25]

Voltaire also comments on this aspect of gardening. In a letter from his garden paradise of Les Délices on Lake Geneva, a few months before the completion of *Candide*, he writes: "in our little Romantic country … we

DAN O'BRIEN

are doing here what one should be doing in Paris; we are living in tranquility, we are cultivating literature without any cabals."[26] What, then, is the source of the tranquility that Addison and Voltaire describe?

Gardening brings various psychological benefits to the gardener. There are sensory pleasures: the smells, the quiet, the colors. Such pleasures can also lead one to a deeper engagement with the garden: blooms can hold one's attention, as can trees and expanses of grass; certain corners of the garden may not be beautiful in the traditional sense, yet the crushed snail shell or the rotting compost can enrapture. A bloom (or, for that matter, the decaying cabbage) can do so, not because one is focused on the prizes it might win (or on the future benefits that one's compost will bring to the garden); one's appreciation, rather, is for the thing itself – the fritillaria flower, the pumpkin, or the crumbly brown texture of what was once kitchen waste. David Cooper takes our ability to appreciate the garden in this "disinterested" way to be a virtue,[27] and William James talks of the psychological benefits of "involuntary attention," when we find ourselves just looking at the tulip, as opposed to actively looking for the trowel.[28] Such moments of attention are tranquil ones.

Some have also seen gardens as havens, providing psychological protection from the "hostile reminders of human mortality lurking in the terrors of nature."[29] William Adams, commenting on French gardens, says that "[t]o venture into the forest was to run the risk of losing one's soul. To reduce the forest to an ordered, tidy ideal world was salvation here on earth."[30] The tranquility of gardens, then, can be seen to lie in their sensory pleasures, in the way that they can hold our attention, and in their protective role.

Further, the tranquility that gardens and gardening bring should not be seen merely in terms of pleasant feelings or states of consciousness; such tranquility, rather, is rooted in an account of virtue. Gardening is a moral pursuit, but the kind of morality I have in mind here is not that which focuses on the characterization of acts and intentions as right or wrong; but rather morality in the older tradition of virtue theory. Addison, as we have seen, claims that gardens cultivate "a virtuous habit of mind." Virtue theorists focus on character traits and not on actions: a pursuit is moral if it inculcates virtuous character traits. Isis Brook, in this volume, has noted this moral dimension to gardening: good gardeners have patience, humility, and generosity. Hume is a kind of virtue theorist. The virtues, for him, are those aspects of character which bring us pleasure, those of which we approve, those which are advantageous for our own peace of mind and for the good of society. Gardening, then, is a virtuous activity, one that is moral, and one that as a consequence brings the tranquility requisite of a good life.

Gardens, as we all know, take work, and Hume sees industry as a virtue:

> Men are kept in perpetual occupation, and enjoy, as their reward, the occupation itself, as well as those pleasures which are the fruit of their labour. The mind acquires new vigour; enlarges its powers and faculties; and by an assiduity in honest industry, both satisfies its natural appetites, and prevents the growth of unnatural ones.[31]

The clearing of weeds or the eradication of slugs can seem a task akin to that of Sisyphus, condemned by the gods perpetually to push a boulder up a mountain. We know the weeds and slugs will keep coming back. Albert Camus, the French existentialist philosopher, asks whether Sisyphus is happy, and answers "Yes." We, Sisyphean gardeners, can hand on heart also answer "Yes."

The Humean gardener, though, must not be too driven. Virtues have associated vices. One can, for example, be too patient; sometimes there is a need for urgency in the garden: one should water the berberis tonight rather than just wait for it to rain. Conversely, Hume stresses the importance of taking your foot off the pedal: "human happiness ... seems to consist in three ingredients: action, pleasure, and indolence."[32] A balance is required and good gardening keeps this balance. The relentless slug exterminator or the manic composter are not gardening well. One, however, who from time to time leans on his spade, puffing on his pipe, is the virtuous gardener. "I lean and invite my soul, I lean and loafe at my ease ... observing a spear of summer grass."[33] In a recent interview, Monty Don, the TV gardener, talks not of loafing, but of pottering. Pottering in the garden may not be as industrious as one could be, but "pottering and happiness are very likely bedfellows. There is much to be said for it.... To the potterer, the primary benefits of this low level activity are a sense of wellbeing."[34]

In a recent book, Daniel Haybron explores the various dimensions of happiness.[35] There is first attunement. This is manifest in feelings of tranquility or inner surety (what the Epicureans called ataraxia). As one leans against one's shed after a heavy bout of digging one feels "psychically ... at home in one's life" – one's day-to-day anxieties have floated away. Such attunement leads to engagement. One steps inside the shed and becomes engaged in activity – potting on, cleaning one's tools, organizing one's

DAN O'BRIEN

seed trays. One can become lost in such activity, unaware of the passage of time, and even of oneself. The psychologist Mihaly Csikszentmihalyi talks of a state of flow in which one loses oneself in this way – the kind of state experienced by the athlete, the knitter, and the dancer.[36] Before one knows it the sun is setting and one must pack away one's tools. Lethargy or listlessness have melted away in activity. Zeno, the Stoic, talked of happiness as finding a "good flow of life." Engagement then leads to endorsement, and here pleasurable feelings are important. One becomes conscious of one's activity, and perhaps of the productivity of one's plot or the beauty of one's blooms.

To be happy, then, is for one's life to be broadly favorable across these three dimensions of attunement, engagement and endorsement. And Haybron argues that the most important is attunement, the state of tranquility, the state that Hume stresses, and the state that characterizes much of the experience of gardeners. The happiness of gardening is perhaps rarely manifest in feelings of endorsement – blooms and good crops are fleeting; it is more commonly manifest in those foot on the spade, quiet moments. Gardening has its obvious sensory pleasures and rewards, but the therapeutic role of gardens lies not just in these, but in the richer psychological grounds for emotional wellbeing that Haybron explores.

Hume himself was an urbanite: Le Bon David, as he was called in France, was more at home in the salons of Paris than in the garden. Much as he talked of the common life, one cannot really imagine him getting his hands dirty. He also betrays certain negative attitudes to country life. He accuses Cromwell of being engaged in "rustic buffoonery" and calls John Knox a "rustic apostle," although he does praise "agriculture; a profession, which, of all mechanical employments, requires the most reflection and experience."[37] Gardens do appear in the *Treatise*, but only as a source of pride, along with our family, riches, and houses, and to illustrate the workings of the imagination – a poet's description of the Elysian Fields can be enlivened if he has a view of the garden. I am not suggesting, then, that we would find Hume escaping the psychological dangers of his study in his Parisian roof garden. This essay, rather, is a hybrid of my own love of gardening and admiration for the philosophy of Hume. Philosophical problems do not seem important to me when there are slugs with which to deal. Gardening may cultivate wisdom, but not that of the philosopher; rather, that of the common man.

Philosophers and theologians are a strange unearthly breed. They worry about the existence of the external world and about how an all-perfect being can allow evil, and they spend much of their time anxiously attempting to solve such conundrums. Wittgenstein observes:

> I am sitting with a philosopher in the garden; he says again and again "I know that that's a tree," pointing to a tree that is near us. Someone else arrives and hears this, and I tell him: "This fellow isn't insane. We are only doing philosophy."[38]

Well, says the Humean gardener, we shouldn't – we should just get up, prune the tree, perhaps plant some cyclamen around the roots, and then perhaps sit down again.

NOTES

1 C. Jencks, *The Garden of Cosmic Speculation* (London: Frances Lincoln, 2003), pp. 14, 17, 13.
2 E. B. Rogers, *Landscape Design: A Cultural and Architectural History* (New York: Harry N. Abrams, 2001), p. 238.
3 Voltaire, *Candide and other Stories* (Oxford: Oxford University Press, 2006), p. 22.
4 Ibid., p. 11.
5 Ibid., p. 88.
6 *The Complete Works of Voltaire*, ed. T. Besterman (Oxford: Voltaire Foundation, 1968), letter no. 11499R.
7 D. Hume, *Enquiries Concerning Human Understanding and Concerning the Principles of Morals*, ed. L. Selby-Bigge, revd. P. Nidditch (Oxford: Oxford University Press, 1975), p. 117.
8 Ibid., p. 125.
9 D. Hume, *Treatise of Human Nature*, ed. L. Selby-Bigge, revd. P. Nidditch (Oxford: Oxford University Press, 1978), p. 269.
10 Ibid., p. 132.
11 Hume, *Enquiries*, p. 87.
12 Ibid., p. 162.
13 D. Hume, *The History of England*, 6 vols. (Indianapolis: Liberty Fund Press, 1983), vol 1, p. 333; vol. 5, p. 12; vol. 6, p. 491.
14 D. Hume, *Dialogues Concerning Natural Religion*, ed. N. Kemp Smith (Indianapolis: Bobs-Merrill, 1947), p. 86; D. Hume, *Natural History of Religion*, ed. J. Feiser (New York: Macmillan, 1992), pp. 141, 184.
15 Hume, *Treatise*, pp. 271–2.
16 Hume, *Dialogues*, 12.30.
17 Ibid.

18 Hume, *History of England*, vol. 6, p. 5.

19 Hume, *Enquiries*, p. 256.

20 D. Hume, "Of the Delicacy of Taste and Passion," in *Essays: Moral, Political and Literary*, ed. E. F. Miller (Indianapolis: Liberty Fund Press, 1985), p. 4.

21 "The Sceptic," in *Essays*, p. 179n.

22 Hume, *Treatise*, p. 272.

23 L. Wittgenstein and P. Engelmann, *Letters from Ludwig Wittgenstein, with a Memoir* (New York: Horizon Press, 1974), p. 37.

24 D. Hume, "Of Essay Writing," in *Essays*, p. 535.

25 J. Addison, *The Spectator*, No. 477, September 6, 1712.

26 *The Complete Works of Voltaire*, ed. T. Besterman (Oxford: Voltaire Foundation, 1968), p. 6517.

27 D. Cooper, *A Philosophy of Gardens* (Oxford: Oxford University Press, 2006), p. 94.

28 W. James, *Psychology (Briefer Course)* (Indianapolis: University of Notre Dame Press, 1985).

29 W. H. Adams, *Gardens Through History: Nature Perfected* (New York: Abbeville, 1991), p. 52.

30 Ibid., p. 113.

31 D. Hume, "Of Refinement in the Arts," in *Essays*, p. 270.

32 Ibid., p. 269.

33 W. Whitman, *Leaves of Grass* (London: Penguin, 1988), p. 5.

34 "The Joy of Pottering," Giles Wilson, *BBC News Magazine*, June 1, 2008.

35 D. Haybron, *The Pursuit of Unhappiness: The Elusive Psychology of Well-Being* (Oxford: Oxford University Press, 2008).

36 M. Csikszentmihalyi, *Flow: The Psychology of Optimum Experience* (New York: Harper and Row, 1990).

37 Hume, *History of England*, vol. 3, p. 369; vol. 4, p. 41; vol 6, p. 90. Hume is thought to have had the Roman writer Columella's treatise on agriculture, *De Re Rustica*, in his library, as well as two editions of Rev. Adam Dickson's *A Treatise of Agriculture* (1765/1770). See *The David Hume Library*, ed. D. F. Norton and M. J. Norton (Edinburgh: Edinburgh Bibliographical Society, 1996), pp. 83, 87.

38 L. Wittgenstein, *On Certainty*, ed. E. Anscombe and G. H. von Wright (Oxford: Blackwell, 1969), p. 467.

PART V

PHILOSOPHERS' GARDENS

CHAPTER 15

THE GARDEN OF THE AZTEC PHILOSOPHER-KING

Not forever here, but only briefly.
Even jade shatters,
gold breaks,
precious feathers are destroyed.
Not forever here, but only a moment.
Cantares Mexicanos, fol. 17r[1]

The Aztecs of ancient Mexico present a challenge to cross-cultural sympathy because they are best known for their bloody sacrificial rites. In retrospect, these seem not to have been significantly bloodier than the worst excesses of the contemporaneous blood sacrifices ongoing in Europe, also in the name of religious piety. However, "Aztec heart sacrifice" obstructs our view of other, more sympathetic features of this great culture. For example, modern gardens worldwide abound with marigolds, dahlias, cosmos, and many other horticultural wonders native to the Americas and nurtured by the Aztecs. We may not realize it, but when we visit or study botanical gardens, we are appreciating a landscape design format that the Aztecs pioneered.

The botanical gardens laid out by Aztec kings and landscape designers were, like their successors in sixteenth-century Europe, compendia of plants that were meant to represent exhaustively a particular region. Each was, in a sense, a "green encyclopedia,"[2] and a few decades after

Spaniards saw and coveted remarkable Aztec examples of this gardening genre, botanical gardens began to appear in Europe. The intellectual climate of Europe at this time was rife with impulses toward studying and categorizing the natural world and the idea of a botanical garden may have independently arisen in Europe – or possibly been inspired or ripened by the conquistadors' fulsome praise of the Aztec examples.

Today's botanical gardens echo Aztec prototypes in profound homage, but they cannot deliver the spiritual impact of sixteenth-century Mexican examples such as that of Texcotzingo near modern Mexico City. Texcotzingo was the great achievement in the brilliant career in landscape architecture of one of the Aztec empire's most powerful kings, Nezahualcoyotl. Texcotzingo was not just a botanical garden, but it was the family dynasty's own sacred and recreational retreat, their columbarium for ancestral remains and living map of their domain. This imposing hill overlooking the city and imperial capital, Texcoco, was also a triumph of hydrological engineering which brought water from the adjacent lower slopes of Mount Tlaloc, "the holiest mountain of pagan Mexico,"[3] via a massive aqueduct and then sent it downslope, flowing through channels and pools, cascading in waterfalls over the king's extensive gardens and highlighting the sculptures gracing them. Finally, the water fed the terraced farm fields that bordered the lower edge of the royal pleasure park.

We find this to be an admirable display of aesthetic and engineering prowess, one we can appreciate on many levels. But to Nezahualcoyotl – to any Aztec, in fact – it was much more, representing the political realm as defined by its living and topographic components, bathed in water, a most sacred essence in ancient Mesoamerica. The Aztecs were animists, believing there to be no separation between the organic and inorganic worlds – the Aztec cosmos was pulsing with vitality. A mountain was also a mountain deity, and a pyramid, and so on. All of these cognitively connected concepts and representations were thought to be alive and to possess the same vital spirit – and each could share different wavelengths of spiritual power with yet other representations and concepts related to other sacred principles. A mountain bathed in water shared the spiritual energy of the sacred substance. To understand how the garden of Texcotzingo, now in ruins, would have throbbed with life and nuanced meaning in the time of its creator, we must first consider Nezahualcoyotl and the Aztec culture he so splendidly represented.

SUSAN TOBY EVANS

The Aztecs and Their Kings

The history of ancient Mexico saw the rise of several great civilizations. The first, about two thousand years ago, had its peak at the urban site of Teotihuacan which would have a population of over 100,000. About 30 miles northeast of modern Mexico City, Teotihuacan's monumental Pyramid of the Sun and Pyramid of the Moon are so culturally dominant that in Mexico today the site is often referred to as "the pyramids." In a country with so many impressive ancient structures, this is praise indeed.

But all civilizations must fall, and Teotihuacan's fall took place at around 500 CE, a few hundred years before the collapse of Maya civilization in the southern Yucatán peninsula. New cities were already filling the void left by Teotihuacan's decline, and among the most important, by about 1,000 CE, were Chichén Itzá in the northern Yucatán peninsula, and Tula, about 40 miles north of modern Mexico City. Tula's Toltec civilization became legendary for its richness and elegance. Thereafter, fine artisans were known as "tolteca" and the fable arose that Tula was where the streets were paved with gold, where crops like cotton and chocolate not only flourished in this chilly and arid high-altitude environment, but also where cotton grew in colors.

This was a paradise of a kind that contrasts sharply with that of the Judeo-Christian tradition. Unlike the Garden of Eden's fruitful wilderness, the Aztecs' Tollán was a fruitful garden-city, urbanized but highly landscaped to luxuriant productivity. Its denizens were not blank slates like Adam and Eve, but rather were wise people who knew how to enjoy the good things in life; they were master artisans, practicing highly skilled crafts with precious materials, readily supplied by a fertile environment. But while Eden survived human occupation, Tollán became a desert wasteland, its gardens of cacao trees turned to mesquite, a paradise inevitably lost when Tula, like other civilizations before it, fell.

During Tula's period of greatness, however, it was home to many people, some of them migrant workers. Ancient Mexico had always been busy with migrations, as we know from linguistic, stylistic, and DNA studies, but the period around 1,000 CE was particularly active, possibly because of changing climate conditions on the northern boundary of the larger culture area, Mesoamerica. Groups of families related along blood lines and sharing an ethnic identity and spoken language moved across the landscape, stopped for years and sometimes decades where work was available, and then moved on. Among these groups who apparently drifted from northwestern Mexico to the area around modern Mexico City (the Basin of Mexico) around 1,000 years ago were those who hearkened back to a spell of residence at Aztlán (the "place of whiteness" or "place of the white heron"), an island town.

These Aztlán emigrants are known to us today as Aztecs, and the term is loosely applied to many groups known to themselves and each other by more specific terms. The most famous Aztecs were the Mexica, who founded the city of Tenochtitlan, which underlies modern Mexico City, and who gave their name to that city and to the modern nation of Mexico. They vainly tried to defeat a Spanish expeditionary force (and its hundreds of thousands of indigenous allies, who loathed the Mexica for their brutal rapaciousness) and were defeated in 1521.

The Aztec empire, of which the Mexica were the most important rulers, lasted only about ninety years. In about 1430 the Mexica had defeated their local overlords and taken over a small confederation of tribute-paying city states, and then in the mid-fifteenth century had expanded this tribute-gathering operation beyond the Basin of Mexico and eventually, by the early 1500s, it reached from Pacific to Atlantic (the coast of the Gulf of Mexico) and down to the coast of Chiapas, and pulled in revenues from at least five million subjects.

The Mexica Aztecs had not been alone in these efforts. Their staunchest allies were the rulers of Texcoco, across the lake from Tenochtitlan (figure 15.1). And the most important of the Texcocan rulers was Nezahualcoyotl, who shared in shaping the empire and managed to keep his own domain intact in spite of his long and close relationship with the Mexica.

Nezahualcoyotl: Renaissance Man of Aztec Culture

Born in 1401 or 1402 to the son of Texcoco's ruler, Nezahualcoyotl saw his father assume rulership in about 1409 and be assassinated in 1418. His domain having fallen into the hands of his dynasty's enemies, Nezahualcoyotl fled to a friendly city outside the Basin of Mexico. When he returned a few years later, it was to house arrest. The billet wasn't onerous, however – it was the palace of his Mexica cousins in Tenochtitlan.

Among the projects Nezahualcoyotl is reported to have taken on to pass his time was that of designing a royal pleasure park for the Tenochtitlan

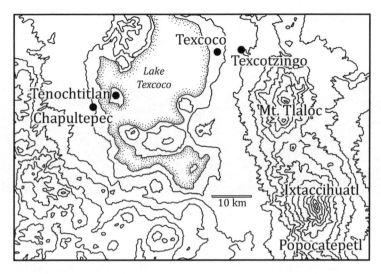

FIGURE 15.1   Location of Texcotzingo.

dynasty. The location was Chapultepec, which had been a refuge for the Mexica in the hardships of their migration, and which was just three miles from the center of Tenochtitlan. Chapultepec was also the source of freshwater springs that the Mexica needed to supply their city. It was perhaps unfortunate that Chapultepec was the property of the Mexica's overlords – or perhaps the conflict over control of Chapultepec was fortunate, because it provided the opportunity for the Mexica to take the reins of their overlords' confederation, control it, and build it into something huge.

Nezahualcoyotl's role during this period of reorganization was complicated. His Mexica cousins were giving him sanctuary, but they had also helped his enemies to vanquish his capital, Texcoco, and received it as a tribute from their overlords. Nezahualcoyotl needed to be very careful to show proper respect while planning on the restoration of his kingdom.

In planning the pleasure park at Chapultepec, Nezahualcoyotl must have been keenly aware of the symmetry between that park and Tenochtitlan, and Texcoco and Texcotzingo (figure 15.2). Duality was one of the great cognitive principles underlying Mesoamerican cosmology, and the balance between the two dynastic capitals and their dynastic retreats is obvious. Nezahualcoyotl's establishment of the Chapultepec park for his cousins would have given them a visual reminder of the bond

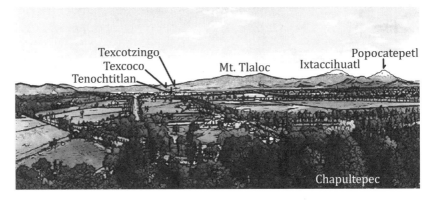

Texcotzingo
Texcoco
Tenochtitlan
Mt. Tlaloc
Ixtaccihuatl
Popocatepetl
Chapultepec

FIGURE 15.2   Mt. Tlaloc and the surrounding province.

between the two capitals and the monumental parks of their dynasties. In a world where features of the landscape were thought to embody active spiritual power, this project of the young exiled prince reveals the philosophical and pragmatic sides of his nature.

Nezahualcoyotl's career as a landscape designer is said by several sixteenth- and seventeenth-century chroniclers to have begun with Chapultepec. Summarizing from these sources, we understand that Nezahualcoyotl while in his twenties "directed the building of major structures there (including a palace and the *bosque* of Chapultepec) in the late 1420s and early 1430s, as well as important engineering projects (an aqueduct, a causeway, and a dike) then and later."[4] While there is no direct evidence that Nezahualcoyotl in fact designed these works and supervised their construction, it is a plausible assertion, given his status as a prince, which would have entailed education in a range of subjects and access to the most skilled and creative members of Aztec society. Aztec civil engineering made clever use of basic forces of gravity and leverage, using wood, stone, and fired clay as materials. Mastering the basic principles and most effective deployment of labor and materials was certainly within the capability of a reasonably intelligent person, and Nezahualcoyotl's later life indicates that his interest in large-scale civic engineering problems was a serious one.

Most discussions of valued qualities in Aztec royals emphasize two things: success in battle and facility with rhetoric. What other pursuits absorbed royal time? Aztec nobles under Spanish colonial rule in the sixteenth century recalled that the pleasures of courtly life involved

SUSAN TOBY EVANS

singing and exchange of proverbs, playing a board game (*patolli*, similar to parcheesi) or a ball game (*tlachtli*, which presaged modern handball and soccer), and gambling on the outcome of such games; royals enjoyed hunting and they established game parks for this purpose, and they also enjoyed the design and establishment of gardens.

Other sources suggest that princes had strong interests in architecture and landscape design. For example, one Aztec king rewarded his brother with a palace that was a copy of a palace in a conquered province, and the king sent an architect, mason, and artist to look at the original in order to plan a copy. We learn several things from a small historical note like this one. First, skilled trained artisans in these fields were part of an Aztec king's retinue. This further suggests that if so inclined, the king could take an active role in these pursuits, learning from his retainers and even formulating his own designs. Furthermore, it would seem that the royal built environment was regarded by kings as an important form of display and source of personal satisfaction, and that status rivalries were played out in this arena.

The Uses of Nezahualcoyotl: Bridging Spanish and Aztec Cultures

Throughout his lifetime Nezahualcoyotl would prove to be adept at the development of his own palace complex in Texcoco, his royal retreat at Texcotzingo, a number of horticultural gardens, and a game reserve. His reputation as a man of many talents was enhanced by the attribution to him of some famous poems, legal judgments, and religious concepts, though these may be retroactive assignments of accomplishment. In the Early Colonial period of Spanish occupation of Mexico, proselytizing Catholic clergy and one of Nezahualcoyotl's descendants, Fernando de Alva Ixtlilxóchitl, seem to have enhanced the image of the fifteenth-century king for their own ends.

Alva Ixtlilxóchitl was born about a century after the death of Nezahualcoyotl, and the glories of his family's past were the subject matter of his books of history. His books are important and valuable works, but must be read using a strong hyperbole filter, given conflicting information from other documentary sources and archeological evidence. Many of his accounts of "conquests" of "cities" and formation of "empires" seem actually to reflect raids on modest towns, and their aggregation into small confederations of tribute-payers. Thus the reader may be predisposed to regard his other claims, such as those touting the achievements of Nezahualcoyotl, with some skepticism.

Scholars stirred by the melancholy tone of poems such as "Even Jades Are Shattered" feel a kinship with Nezahualcoyotl the man, but the Aztec kings commonly employed poets and songwriters to enhance the reputation of their courts. Poems or songs about Nezahualcoyotl's exploits, even those using the locution "I, Nezahualcoyotl ..." may have been written for court entertainments by such courtly poets. Of course, this plausible interpretation cannot be falsified by the available sources; nowhere do we have an eyewitness account of Nezahualcoyotl's undisputed authorship, and nowhere do we know for certain that he never composed verses.

Nezahualcoyotl also developed a strong reputation for able political leadership, and this was used by Catholic clergy with an agenda for the conversion of the Aztecs to Christianity. Alva Ixtlilxóchitl claimed that Nezahualcoyotl developed a new and just code of laws, but other chroniclers find little to distinguish the Texcocan system of proscriptions and punishments from those of other capitals.

Nezahualcoyotl's reputation as a sensitive intellectual also made him a suitable subject for bridging the gap between Aztec paganism and Spanish Christianity. Nezahualcoyotl was touted as having initiated monotheism and peaceful rituals (that is, eschewing blood sacrifices), but little solid evidence can be found to support this claim; he seems to have tolerated a wide range of religious practices and piously supported all the deities important to the Aztec rulers. However, Nezahualcoyotl was a widely respected cultural hero and a convenient foil for posthumous use: he could be cast by the Spanish friars as a man before his time, anticipating the enlightenment toward a belief in one god that conquest by Spain would bring.

Nezahualcoyotl's Place, and the Place of Gardens, in Aztec Political History

The modern scholarly deconstruction of Nezahualcoyotl's reputation as skilled poet, innovative lawgiver, and religious reformer would seem to have stripped the hero of his powers. But many of his most significant achievements persist, attested to by the broad sweep of history and the solid evidence of archeology.

SUSAN TOBY EVANS

It is irrefutable that Nezahualcoyotl served as ruler of Texcoco from the early 1430s to his death in 1472, and in that time regained, consolidated, and expanded his domain while he shared in the empire-building enterprises of his Mexica cousins. He saw the deaths of four Mexica rulers, and – most impressive – during all the upheavals of his times he maintained his rulership without having his kingdom absorbed by the Mexica. Given the overwhelming evidence of Mexica meddling in other polities and their overturning of other dynasties, this alone is powerful testimony to Nezahualcoyotl's skill as a political leader.

Furthermore, he is known to have established horticultural pleasure gardens and nurseries in his realm. The nurseries served diverse purposes. The Aztecs were adept at identifying plants with effective healing properties, and some evidence suggests that rulers kept the rights to the cultivation of some plants for themselves. Flowers and greens were both used to decorate palaces and temples, and royal nurseries could supply these needs, as well as the immature specimens of trees and shrubs that were planted out in gardens and parks.

The establishment of these gardens, with their combined practical and recreational functions, bespeaks a ruler who was both sensible and responsive to beauty. However, the great achievement substantiating Nezahualcoyotl's multiple talents as political manipulator, sensitive intellectual, civil engineer, and designer of monumental gardens is Texcotzingo, offering evidence as solid as the rock into which his pools and reception rooms were built.

Texcotzingo

As the plan of Texcotzingo (figure 15.3) indicates, the hill was the backdrop upon which Nezahualcoyotl the artist expressed his vision. Nezahualcoyotl the civil engineer and landscape architect designed the flow of sacred, life-giving water so that it blessed various shrines, created micro-environments for the cultivation of rare plants, and then irrigated farming terraces that extended down to his capital, Texcoco.

The eastern side of the hill was dominated by two major features: the aqueduct terminus and its receiving pond, and, 130 feet (40 meters) upslope, a set of plazas overlooking the aqueduct and facing Mt. Tlaloc and the rising sun. Mt. Tlaloc's summit, about 13,500 feet (4,000 meters) in elevation, was about 8 miles (14 kilometers) southwest of Texcotzingo,

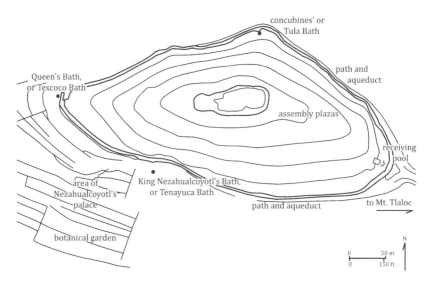

FIGURE 15.3   Plan of Texcotzingo.

and was thought to be the abode of Tlaloc, powerful god of storms and rainwater. It and adjacent mountains were the source of rainfall, runoff, and the regeneration of springs in the eastern Basin of Mexico, Nezahualcoyotl's domain. There was a substantial shrine atop Mt. Tlaloc where Aztec kings made a pilgrimage each year in mid-spring, just before the onset of the rainy season.

The Mt. Tlaloc shrine, with walls about 10 feet (3 meters) high, would have been clearly visible from the east side of Texcotzingo, and the plazas leveled into that side would have been the site of rituals and dances honoring the great storm god. The plazas also would have been excellent for stargazing, one of the responsibilities of Aztec kings. Early chroniclers indicate that there was also a tower near the summit of the hill, but of this no trace remains.

The plazas would have overlooked the feature that made Texcotzingo the wonder of its time: the aqueduct system. The aqueduct brought water from the Tlaloc range and delivered it to Texcotzingo at an elevation of about 180 feet (55 meters) below the summit of the hill. Figure 15.4 shows the western end of the aqueduct, and the small receiving pool from which the waters were redirected to circle the hill. Visiting the site in the mid-nineteenth century, Edward Tylor described:

SUSAN TOBY EVANS

FIGURE 15.4   Tenayuca pool.

an aqueduct of immense size.... The mountains in this part are made of porphyry, and the channel of the aqueduct was made principally of blocks of the same material, on which the smooth stucco that had once covered the whole, inside and out, still remained very perfect. The channel was carried, not on arches, but on a solid embankment, a hundred and fifty or two hundred feet high, and wide enough for a carriage-road.[5]

The western end of the aqueduct has been reconstructed as a set of ascending rectangular platforms built into that end of the hill, the highest being a room fronted with columns looking toward the water as it approached the hill. It is said to have contained an inscribed history of the Acolhua people.

At the same level as the aqueduct, a canal and footpath circled Texcotzingo, and the hill's important monuments are arrayed more or less symmetrically along this feature. There were three main circular rock-cut baths. On the north side is a now-destroyed pool named for Tula; at the west end is one named for Texcoco (also known as the Queen's Bath); and on the southwestern side is the Tenayuca pool (also known as the King's Bath; figure 15.4). Below this southwestern pool lay a series of rectangular and circular rooms that were Nezahualcoyotl's palace.

Near these rooms were special gardens where the spray from water descending from the Tenayuca pool, plus the southwestern aspect of the hill, combined to create a micro-environment where tropical plants were nurtured. This was one means by which Nezahualcoyotl memorialized his domain: he grew the plants that were native to the various areas under his control, and what he and his gardeners could not coax into surviving the chilly high-altitude environment of Texcotzingo, he commemorated with depictions in art. Thus the idea of the botanical garden arose out of a royal imperative to control symbolically the life forms under his political control.

So much of Texcotzingo's complex design has been lost to us. However, we can see clearly that Nezahualcoyotl's great landscape statement not only demonstrated his own technical abilities (or his ability to recognize and use genius in others, another sign of superior intelligence), but also it expressed philosophical statements of several kinds.

First, it was a personal statement of Nezahualcoyotl's own place in the Aztec world: he was a ruler of paramount importance, publicly deferential to the king of Tenochtitlan, but privately taking second place to no one. This is demonstrated by the construction of Texcotzingo, dedicated in 1457, as a statement of conspicuous consumption and elite status rivalry. Having designed Chapultepec Park for his cousins, the Tenochtitlan rulers, he went on to a project that dwarfed that venerable park. While Nezahualcoyotl was completely within his rights to enhance his family's ancient retreat, when Texcotzingo was finished, the Tenochca ruler, Motecuzoma I (r. 1440–69) felt compelled to acquire an extensive property in the tropical climate of the Morelos Valley, just south of Mexico City. There, at Huaxtepec, Motecuzoma had a fabulous garden constructed. For both dynasties, tribute requirements included labor to maintain the gardens and plant material to enhance them, but Huaxtepec was the last great monumental garden to be developed. Nezahualcoyotl died in 1472 and his son, while an able ruler, lacked his interest in expressing a worldview through transforming the landscape.

Second, Texcotzingo expressed Texcoco's place in its own dynastic history. Nezahualcoyotl's ancestors included the kings of Tula, and before Texcoco became their family capital, they had ruled from Tenayuca, across the lake and a little north of Tenochtitlan. King Quinatzin had moved the capital to Texcoco, and was buried at Texcotzingo. Thus the three rock-cut pools represent, respectively, the two ancestral capitals and the present one. The political alliance engineered by Nezahualcoyotl and his Tenochtitlan cousins that was the foundation of the Aztec empire is represented by a set of sculptures set on the edge of the Texcoco pool: three frogs represent Texcoco, Tenochtitlan, and their somewhat less important ally, Tlacopan.

At the cosmic level, Texcotzingo honored the sacred spirits of water and mountains, and here Nezahualcoyotl made his waterfall mountain into a living embodiment of the most important Mesoamerican political principle, that of the *altépetl*, a word which combines the Nahuatl (Aztecan) words for "water" and "hill" into an essential notion of the city state, the most basic unit of political life, conveying the ideas of water and land that provided security to the community. Thus Texcotzingo was another example of a representation linked, metaphorically, to other objects and concepts. In the case of Texcotzingo, the monumental garden is related to a philosophical concept (the *altépetl*) based on geographical reality but standing for a political entity. Nezahualcoyotl had begun his career of landform philosophizing at Chapultepec, another mountain-and-water-source that was essential to the definition of an ambitious community, in this case Tenochtitlan. From the heights of Chapultepec, the young prince in exile could look northeast (see figure 15.2), over Tenochtitlan, over the lake, and discern his capital, then in enemy hands, and beyond it, the hill that was his family's sacred retreat. With huge effort, he would regain his kingdom. And then he would make a water-hill of Texcotzingo that would truly actualize Texcoco as his own vital *altépetl*. Seldom, in human history, has one individual so completely realized in solid form the ideals of his culture as did Nezahualcoyotl at Texcotzingo.

NOTES

1 Translated for this publication by Susan Toby Evans. © 2010 Blackwell Publishing Ltd.
2 S. T. Evans, "Green Evolution: Landscape Design and Culture Change in Ancient Mesoamerica," *Anales de Antropología* 39 (2005): 99–110.
3 F. Diego, *Book of the Gods and Rites and The Ancient Calendar*, trans. and ed. F. Horcasitas and D. Heyden (Norman: University of Oklahoma Press, 1971), pp. 3–47.
4 E. Umberger, "Appendix 3: Material Remains in the Central Provinces," in F. F. Berdan, R. E. Blanton et al., *Aztec Imperial Strategies* (Washington, DC: Dumbarton Oaks, 1996), p. 251.
5 E. B. Tylor, *Anahuac: Mexico and the Mexicans* (New York: Bergman, 1970).

CHAPTER 16

EPICURUS, THE GARDEN, AND THE GOLDEN AGE

The School in the Garden

Epicurus was a citizen of Athens, but he was always something of an outsider. He was born to Athenian parents, not actually at Athens but on the island of Samos in 341 BCE, and first founded his school of philosophy on the island of Lesbos at Mytilene before moving to Lampsacus in Asia Minor, and finally to Athens in either 306 or 307 BCE. Athens was the center of the philosophical world at the time and any serious philosopher who wished to make their mark would want to live and teach there. However, Epicurus' insular and liminal origins seem to have shaped his outlook on life since when he moved to Athens he bought a house with a garden on the outskirts of the city, near the Dipylon gate and on the road to the Academy, rather than in the center. It was in this garden that he set up his school. The unusual setting for a Greek philosophical school in a secluded private garden gave rise to the use of the name "the Garden" as a name for the school.

It is worthwhile to compare the name of the rivals of the Epicureans, the Stoics ("Men of the Stoa"), which derived from their practice of teaching in the *Stoa Poikile* ("Painted Colonnade") in the agora of Athens, the bustling civic and commercial heart of the city. The choice of the locations of the two schools provides a useful geographical illustration of their fundamental attitudes towards the city that they both inhabited. As Long and Sedley have put it: "Philosophy at Athens was always a supremely public affair, and in concentrating their activities on the agora the Stoics were never likely to be far from the public eye."[1] In contrast the attitude of Epicurus is neatly expressed by his injunction: "Live unnoticed." The paradox of a philosopher moving to Athens, founding a school, attracting students, giving lectures and writing and publishing books, but also advising his followers to live unnoticed attracted critical comment in antiquity. It was Epicurus' decision to found his school in a garden and this essay concerns what the garden means for his philosophy and that of his followers.

Epicurus' school was not simply a school of philosophy in the sense of a regular gathering of like-minded thinkers; it was also a community of friends that lived within the walls of the garden and worked there together, studying under Epicurus, writing philosophical works, and also working in the garden and growing their own food. Their ideal was to be as self-sufficient as possible, and this stood them in good stead during a siege of Athens when Epicurus kept them alive by sharing out among them the beans they had grown in the garden. The school was organized more like a religious cult than a philosophical school, and the members swore an oath of allegiance to Epicurus: "We will be obedient to Epicurus, according to whom we have made it our choice to live." Rank within the school was determined not by wealth or birth but by advancement towards wisdom, and the members of the school included slaves and women. The latter fact caused much salacious gossip and speculation about what the Epicureans got up to in their garden since men and unmarried women lived there together in close proximity: a thing unheard of in normal Greek society. Epicurus himself was considered wise but was not given the title of "master," unlike in more hierarchically organized schools. The "better" person was one farther advanced in wisdom, and the close friends of Epicurus such as Metrodorus and Hermarchus were "guides" or "leaders" of the students. Epicurus' system of philosophy was considered by the Epicureans to be the only true philosophy, but what was even more important was the community of friends that gathered around Epicurus. The Epicurean school was a community based on friendship and in which friendship was considered the most important thing of all. According to Epicurus, "friendship goes dancing around the world proclaiming to us all to awake to the praises of a happy life," and "of all the means which are procured by wisdom to ensure happiness throughout the whole of life, by far the most important is the acquisition of friends."

Moreover the main function of the philosophy was therapeutic and Epicurus considered that philosophy was not worthy of the name if it had no therapeutic value, saying, "empty are the words of that philosopher who offers no therapy for human suffering. For just as there is no use in medical expertise if it does not give therapy for bodily diseases, so too there is no use in philosophy if it does not expel the suffering of the soul." The members of the school were actively engaged in self-improvement and the improvement of others by mutual admonition and correction. The aim was to inculcate goodwill, mutual love, gratitude, respect for wisdom, self-control, frankness, openness, and moderation in all things. Arrogance, greed, jealousy, boastfulness, and anger were faults to be removed by gentle correction rather than by coercion or punishment. Similarly, in ethics, moderation was the key. Notoriously, Epicurus had a hedonistic theory of ethics and argued that pleasure was the goal of human action and that one cannot live a virtuous life without living a pleasurable life. Pleasure, however, was defined very narrowly. The types of pleasures to be sought were "natural and necessary pleasures," such as eating bread when hungry and drinking water when thirsty. "Natural but unnecessary pleasures" such as drinking wine when not thirsty, or eating rich foods, were to be avoided if possible, and "unnatural and unnecessary pleasures" such as amassing wealth, or seeking fame, political power, or honor, were to be avoided completely. The Roman philosopher Seneca records the inscription upon the entrance to the garden:

> Stranger, here you will do well to tarry; here our highest good is pleasure. The caretaker of this abode, a kindly host, will be ready for you; he will welcome you with bread, and serve you water also in abundance, with these words: "Have you not been well entertained? This garden does not whet your appetite; but quenches it. Nor does it make you more thirsty with every drink; it slakes the thirst by a natural cure, a cure that demands no fee. This is the pleasure in which I have grown old.[2]

Epicurus' garden, then, had an important ethical function: it was the source of the pleasure that heals both body and soul – the simple natural pleasures that quench our desires rather than inflame them. Protected within the walls of the garden the philosopher could preserve the peace of mind essential for true happiness.

This peace of mind or *ataraxia* ("freedom from disturbance") was the ideal Epicurean mental state, and to achieve it and preserve it the philosopher had to withdraw from the disturbances of everyday life as much as possible. Epicurus recommended that his followers should avoid being involved in public affairs since this was a particular cause of mental disturbance and disquiet. In contrast the Stoics encouraged their followers to engage in public affairs as much as they were able. Epicureanism was an apolitical or even anti-political philosophy, and the Epicureans were criticized in antiquity for their seemingly hypocritical attitude toward the city, enjoying its amenities and protection while refusing to help in its organization and governance. The location of the garden on the outskirts of the city again provides a useful illustration of this attitude.

Prehistory and the Rise of Cities

To find an explanation for the negative Epicurean attitude toward the city and for their seclusion in the garden it is necessary to examine their ideas concerning the origins of cities and civilization. Lucretius, the Roman Epicurean poet of the first century BCE, has provided us with a detailed account of prehistory in the fifth book of his *On the Nature of Things*. According to him, the first humans had been born into a harsh, unfriendly world and had lived without the aid of any technology, lacking even fire and clothing. They had lived a wandering life like wild beasts in forests and caves, lashed by wind and rain, wrapping themselves in leaves at night to keep warm. They were frequently attacked by wild animals and, if they were not killed immediately, often died in agony from their wounds without the aid of medicine. However, despite this dark picture, Lucretius depicts other aspects of their lives in very attractive terms. Here he describes their diet:

> And for many rolling cycles of the sun through the heavens they led a life in the wide-wandering manner of wild beasts. No one was a tough guider of the curved plough, nor did anyone know how to work the fields with iron, nor to plant new shoots in the ground, nor to prune old branches from high trees with sickles. What the sun and showers had given, what the earth had created of her own accord, this was a pleasing enough gift for their hearts. Among the acorn-bearing oaks they cared for their bodies for the most part; and the arbute berries you now see ripening in winter time with crimson Punic colour, at that time the earth bore most abundantly and larger than now. And the flowery newness of the world then bore much tough fodder besides, ample for poor mortals.

But to quench their thirst the rivers and springs called them, just as now the waters rushing down from the high mountains call afar loud and clear the thirsting races of wild animals. And then they stayed in the woodland temples of the nymphs known to them from their wanderings, from where they knew gliding waters flowed and washed the wet rocks with a great gush, washed the wet rocks dripping above with green moss, and sometimes burst out and gushed onto the level plain.[3]

So, although the first humans had no technologies and no agriculture, they were able to feed themselves from the spontaneous bounty of nature, wandering in an attractive flowery landscape grazing upon berries and acorns. Their simple wild diet is "ample" for them as "poor mortals," and is "a pleasing enough gift for their hearts." As yet they are happy with what the earth has provided "of her own accord." Lucretius has already described how mother earth nurtured them as children. They have not yet developed unlimited desires, and they have no ambition and no greed for more. Their desires are simple and easily met from nature's bounty. Their drink is simply water from streams, but Lucretius paints a gorgeous pastoral picture of "the woodland temples of the nymphs" for us, worthy of the landscapes of Claude Lorraine. In this way they live, in fact, an ideal Epicurean life in accordance with nature: a virtual golden age. The archaic Greek poet Hesiod, writing around 750 BCE, was the first to establish in his *Works and Days* what became the dominant idea of the golden age. The first humans were a golden race who lived in harmony with one another in perfect peace and leisure in an eternal spring, and were beloved of the gods. The gods granted them all good things and the earth spontaneously gave up her crops for them. There was no need for farming or for work of any kind, and the people never knew sickness or weariness. Lucretius does not entirely agree with the traditional Hesiodic vision of the first age of humanity as a golden age of peace, leisure, and harmony, but, on the other hand, some aspects of the lives of the first humans were utopian. Early people's lives may have been harsh in some ways but in others they lived better than we do. Many people then may have been eaten by wild beasts, but they were free of many of the evils that beset modern life:

But, a single day did not bring destruction to many thousands of men led under the standards, nor did the turbulent waves of the sea smash ships and men on the rocks. Then, at random, pointlessly, frustrated, the sea would often rise and rage and lightly lay its empty threats, nor could the seductive deceptions of the placid sea with its laughing waters entice anyone to their ruin. Then the wicked art of sailing lay hidden. Then scarcity of food gave their languishing limbs to death; now abundance drowns us. They themselves unwitting often poured poison for themselves; now more cunningly they poison others.[4]

So, the advantages of civilization begin to be called into question. We may have learned to protect ourselves from wild animals, but now we see many thousands of people destroyed in warfare, or drowned at sea, voyaging for luxuries. In the past people often starved, but now we drown ourselves in abundance. And finally, we need not think we are morally superior: whatever their faults, they were not murderers as some people are in the modern world.

Then Lucretius describes a second stage, in which the first societies formed. People developed the basic technologies of fire, animal skins for clothing, and huts to live in and began to settle down. They softened physically under the influence of fire and psychologically under the influence of marriage and childcare. This softening allowed them to evolve an ability to cooperate and even to formulate the advanced concept that "it is right for all to pity the weak." Care for women and children and friendship pacts made between eager neighbors formed the basis of these first societies. They were indeed proto-Epicurean societies. Lucretius describes the friendship pacts as agreements "neither to harm nor to be harmed." There is no need for restrictive legislation in these first societies, nor for any kings or rulers to keep order and make people behave well. The friendship pacts are enough by themselves to ensure that society works. Perhaps not everyone kept the pacts, but it was necessary only for the majority to do so. This is a very Epicurean notion: the world is not perfect, but it works.

According to Lucretius, then, the first societies were proto-Epicurean gatherings of neighbors who became friends and cooperated in order to survive. If they had not cooperated, Lucretius says, the whole human race would have died out. This stage is as near to an Epicurean ideal as it was possible to achieve for primitive people. They have just enough technology to survive and to thrive, but they have not yet developed luxuries or excessive desires. There is no trade mentioned and so no need for seafaring in search of luxuries and profit, and, we can reasonably assume, no warfare. Politics and political strife have clearly not yet arisen to threaten the peace of mind of the first villagers. We are not told the details of their economy, but we may assume they have exchanged the wandering, hunting and gathering lifestyle of the first stage of humanity for a settled agricultural life. Gold has not yet been discovered and so there is no money to corrupt people. The land and flocks have not yet been divided up and so there is no property and therefore no greed for more. There are no kings or politicians struggling to gain power, wealth, and reputation, and there is no warfare between city states since they do not yet exist. No laws had yet been introduced since most people kept the friendship pacts faithfully and so there was no coercive justice to be afraid of and to spoil people's enjoyment of life. All of these horrors developed in the next stage when Lucretius describes the rise of cities,[5] where those best able to control the new technologies became kings. They built citadels to defend themselves, and parceled out the land and flocks and gave them to their favorites. Gold was discovered and money invented. People began struggling to amass wealth and gain power. Then the kings were overthrown in a revolution and there followed a period of anarchy in which each man sought domination. Finally, exhausted by strife and conflict, people agreed to be bound by restrictive laws and coercive justice, and magistrates were appointed to administer the cities. This is hardly an ideal state of affairs, as Lucretius says, "hence fear of punishments taint the prizes of life."[6] Cities, then, for the Epicureans, are not the pinnacle of human achievement; they are, rather, a decadent decline from a previously existing near-paradise of friendship, simplicity, and harmony in the first village societies. We can therefore begin to understand the decision to live secluded from the city in Epicurus' garden: ideally, the Epicurean community would establish itself in the countryside far away from the evils and disturbances of the city but, given the modern state of things with city states and empires warring against one another, it is prudent to take advantage of the protection offered by the city while still enjoying the secluded peace of the garden.

The *Locus Amoenus* and the Origins of Agriculture

The end of the first village societies is not explained by Lucretius, but the reason is not far to seek. The Epicureans attribute all of the evils of society – greed, conflict, competition, lust, ambition, politics, and warfare – to the fear of the gods and of death.[7] For the Epicureans, the gods exist, but are perfectly happy beings who do not intervene in human affairs and do not either punish or reward us. The soul exists, but dies with the body and so cannot be punished or rewarded in an afterlife.

GORDON CAMPBELL

Whether people know it or not they suffer from a psychological disturbance caused by their irrational fear of death. Seeking to remedy this disturbance they seek wealth and power in order to give themselves some feeling of security in their lives. This very seeking for wealth and power, however, causes even more insecurity and disturbance as people compete with one another. The first humans, Lucretius tells us, had a naturally occurring true form of piety.[8] They knew the gods existed, but it was only when they started speculating about the motions of the heavens and other natural phenomena that they were unable to explain rationally, that they made a fundamental mistake and assumed that the gods must control all these things. This has left a terrible legacy of fear for us, their descendants, Lucretius says.[9] It was, then, the rise of such religious beliefs and the fears associated with them that led to the insecurity that we see driving the kings to found the first cities and to the competition for wealth and position which led to their downfall.

Despite this disaster, however, it is still possible to regain something of the former state of rural bliss: Epicurus recreated a version of it in his city garden, and, in this way, to walk through the gates of the garden beneath the inscription offering the visitor the simple delights of Epicurean pleasure was to go back in time to a simpler, purer age in which friendship had been the basis of society, and where a simple life lived in accordance with nature had been shared by everyone. Lucretius similarly pictures the Epicurean ideal in the *locus amoenus*, the Edenic "pleasant place" of Roman pastoral poetry. Not all progress had been bad, either. Here is Lucretius on the origins of agriculture:

> Then they tried one way after another to cultivate the sweet little field, and they saw that wild fruits became tame in the earth with indulgent and kindly cultivation. And every day they forced the woods to retreat further into the mountains and to give up the lower lands for farming, so they had fields, lakes, rivers, corn crops and rich vineyards, and the green strip of olives to run between them, pouring over hills, valleys and plains; just so, now you see the whole countryside laid out with varied charms, interplanted with sweet apples and hedged around with fertile plantations.[10]

The clearing of the land for agriculture and the development of cultivated plants from wild varieties is presented as both a moral and an aesthetic project. The first horticulturalists "love" their "little plot." The "wild fruits" are "tamed" as if they were sentient creatures, and they are treated kindly and with "friendly tillage." They are softened and improved just as the early humans were in the first societies, and just as the

Epicureans soften and improve themselves by their studies in the garden. This is a process of "civilization," but one that produces a paradise rather than the hell of the city – or in Hesiodic terms, a return to the golden age from the harsh iron age of the city. The project drives wild nature back into the hills but results in an improvement in nature, one that is as much for the delight of the senses and the soul as for the mundane production of food. Lucretius describes a paradise achievable in this world, outside the city in the beautiful Italian countryside of his own day.

There is slippage between the present and prehistory in Epicurean thinking and the possibility of regaining a state of rural bliss is nicely illustrated by Lucretius' description of two picnics. The first comes from book two of his poem in a passage arguing that the simple life is far preferable to a life of luxury and riches:

> So we see that very few things are necessary for our bodily nature: things that take away pain, and also those that can supply many pleasures. Nor does nature itself ever need anything more pleasing, if there aren't golden statues of youths all through the halls holding blazing lamps in their hands to supply light for night time feasts, or if the house does not gleam with silver and beam with gold, or no panelled gilded ceilings echo to the lyre, when, however, lying stretched out together on the soft grass beside a stream of water under the branches of a tall tree, people refresh their bodies delightfully at no great expense, especially when the season smiles and the time of year strews the green grass with flowers.[11]

The simple *déjeuner sur l'herbe* is more pleasurable than banquets in gilded halls and is near at hand, available at little cost: a happy gathering of friends in a pastoral *locus amoenus*. This Epicurean picnic is set in the present, but Lucretius shows that it is a return to an earlier state of bliss by repeating several of these lines in book five when describing the setting for the origins of music:

> Then gradually they learnt the sweet laments that the pipe pours forth, tapped by the player's fingers, the pipe invented amid the trackless groves, woods and glades, among the empty haunts of shepherds and their open-air leisure. These tunes would soothe their hearts and please them when sated with food, for then everything is delightful. Often, therefore, lying stretched out together on the soft grass beside a stream of water under the branches of a tall tree, people refreshed their bodies delightfully at no great expense, especially when the season smiled and the time of year painted the green grass with flowers. Then there were jokes, conversation, and laughter, for then the country muse was vibrant.[12]

GORDON CAMPBELL

This idyllic scene takes place in prehistory, when people first learned the art of music, and we can see music playing an important role in soothing the minds of the simple rustic folk, and aiding their pleasure in this social gathering. All these are key Epicurean ethical ideals – the gaining of peace of mind and of pleasure in a group of friends. These are properly Epicurean picnics, then, with an important ethical and therapeutic function. The people may be playing music and laughing rather than discussing philosophy, but they are achieving the ideals that the Epicurean philosophy was created to achieve. The repetition of the lines in these two passages is not accidental or an oversight on Lucretius' part. He intends to show us how the practice of Epicurean philosophy can enable us to regain something of the former state of Edenic rustic bliss.

Diogenes of Oinoanda and the Future Epicurean Golden Age

If Lucretius shows us that a temporary return to a state of rustic bliss is possible in gatherings of friends picnicking in the countryside, a fragment of a later Epicurean philosopher indicates that the Epicureans also had a grander possibility in mind and that a permanent return to the golden age could be achieved.

In the third century CE, a certain Diogenes, a wealthy citizen of the Greek city of Oinoanda in Lycia (now in modern Turkey), provided the city with a fine new agora. On the walls of this agora he had his own account of the Epicurean philosophy inscribed for the benefit of his fellow citizens. Over the centuries since Diogenes' time the agora and its inscription fell into ruins, and many of its stone blocks were buried or were recycled for other buildings. One of these fragments, recently rediscovered by Martin Ferguson Smith, provides a tantalizing glimpse of a future utopia. (Reconstructions of damaged text are in square brackets; lost text is denoted by ellipses.)

[So we shall not achieve wisdom universally] since not all are capable of it. But if we assume it to be possible, then truly the life of the gods will pass to man. For everything will be full of justice and mutual love, and there will come to be no need of fortifications or laws and all the things which we contrive on account of one another. As for the necessaries derived from agriculture, since we shall have no [slaves at that time] (for indeed [we ourselves shall plough] and dig and tend [the plants] and [divert] rivers and watch over [the crops), we shall] ... such things as ... not ... time ..., and such activities, [in accordance with what is] needful, will interrupt the continuity of the [shared] study of philosophy; for [the] farming operations [will provide what our] nature wants.[13]

Diogenes doubts whether all people can achieve wisdom, but if it were possible (and the grammar he uses suggests that it may well be possible) then we could achieve a utopian state of being in which the Epicurean ideals would be realized, a new golden age in which the world "will be full of justice and mutual love." Remarkably in this future utopia there will be no need of fortifications or laws. There will be no warfare and so fortifications will be unnecessary, and similarly, laws will be redundant since all people will naturally cultivate justice. It seems that it will be a return to a pre-civilized state, such as existed before the rise of cities, and, as we have already seen in Lucretius, it was the fear of death and of the gods that led to the founding of cities and the imposition of restrictive laws. Early people, lacking the wisdom of Epicurus, were unable to account for the motions of the heavens and so wrongly attributed control of the world to the gods, thus leading to fear that they would punish us either in this life or in the afterlife. In response to these fears people struggled to amass wealth and gain power. Cities were a product of fear. In the future, when all have gained wisdom, cities themselves will become unnecessary and it will be safe for us to return to the countryside, without fortifications, free from fear of attack from outside, just as in the original golden age. So, the entire world will come to be an ideal Epicurean community of friends. There will, naturally, be no slavery in such an ideal world and so we shall work the land and grow our own food. It will be an agricultural golden age. According to Epicurus, the needs of the body are simple and are easily provided for, and so we shall be self-sufficient farmers and gardeners, just as Epicurus and his original community aimed to be within their garden. But without any need for protection from the outside world Epicurus' garden will have no need of walls and will encompass the whole world, and all people will become gardening philosophers.

Epicurus' garden and the community of friends within it withdrew from the city, recreating a walled and protected golden age of peace and harmony, living in harmony with nature and tending the plants, waiting for the day when the walls of the garden no longer have any purpose and all people will become gardeners. However, just as swords may be forged into plowshares, the opposite can also happen, and I must end this essay by reporting the final irony that the block of Diogenes' inscription that predicts the day when city walls will become redundant was found by Martin Smith after it had been recycled as part of the new city walls of Oinoanda.

NOTES

1 A. A. Long and D. N. Sedley, *The Hellenistic Philosophers*, Vol. 1 (Cambridge: Cambridge University Press, 1987), pp. 2–3.
2 Seneca, "Epistle 21" in *Moral Epistles*, 3 vols., trans. R. M. Gummere (Cambridge, MA: Harvard University Press, 1917–25).
3 Lucretius, *De Rerum Natura* (*On the Nature of Things*) (Cambridge, MA: Harvard University Press, 1982), 5.931–942. Translated for this publication by Gordon Campbell. © 2010 Blackwell Publishing Ltd.
4 Ibid., 5.999–1010. Translated by Gordon Campbell. © 2010 Blackwell Publishing Ltd.
5 Ibid., 5.1105–1160.
6 Ibid., 5.1151. Translated by Gordon Campbell. © 2010 Blackwell Publishing Ltd.
7 Ibid., 3.59–86.
8 Ibid., 5.1161–1193.
9 Ibid., 5.1194–1203.
10 Ibid., 5.1371–1378. Translated by Gordon Campbell. © 2010 Blackwell Publishing Ltd.
11 Ibid., 2.20–33. Translated by Gordon Campbell. © 2010 Blackwell Publishing Ltd.
12 Ibid., 5.1384–1398. Translated by Gordon Campbell. © 2010 Blackwell Publishing Ltd.
13 M. F. Smith, *Diogenes of Oinoanda: The Epicurean Inscription* (Naples, 1993), fragment 56.

CHAPTER 17

GARDENER OF SOULS

Philosophical Education in Plato's *Phaedrus*

Would a sensible grower, who cared about his seeds and wanted them to yield fruit, plant them with serious purpose in the gardens of Adonis in summer and delight in watching them become beautiful within eight days? Or would he do this as an amusement and in honour of the holiday, when he did it at all? Wouldn't he use the science of growing and plant the seeds he cared for in proper soil, and be content if what he sowed reached their perfection in the eighth month?... And the man who has knowledge of what is just, noble, and good – are we to say that he is less sensible with his seeds than the grower?

Plato, *Phaedrus* 276b1–c5

So begins one of the most intriguing discussions of philosophical education in Plato's dialogues. Socrates is engaged in conversation with a young man called Phaedrus (from whom the dialogue takes its name), and he wishes to explain how written words can contribute to philosophical education. To do so, he likens philosophical development to the growth of plants in a garden. A wise grower, Socrates says, will not plant his seeds in pots at the height of summer and watch them reach their peak within eight days, as people did during the festival of Adonis. Such seeds have only shallow roots, and in the summer heat they wither as fast as they have grown, offering no more than passing pleasure.[1] Instead, he will plant his seeds in appropriate soil, using his knowledge of growing, so that they develop gradually and bear properly formed fruit. Just so, the wise educator will choose a "proper soul," and plant in it λόγοι – words or discourse – together with knowledge. Once the words have had time to mature fully, they will produce an abundant harvest. They will be capable of generating philosophical development in other people, by themselves producing "a seed from which more discourse grows in the character of others." And they will make the person who possesses them "as happy as any human can be." This is what we can hope to attain if the seed of discourse grows in our soul, like seeds in a well-tended garden.

This passage has long held a special place in the interpretation of Plato's dialogues. It draws together many ideas about philosophical education that emerge elsewhere in Plato's works, and it forms part of a discussion of philosophical writing that must have implications for his own texts. In what follows, I explore in more detail what the image of the grower has to tell us about Plato's distinctive approach to education and his own activity as an educator. For, as I hope to show, viewing education from the perspective of gardening can help us appreciate why Plato may have chosen to write philosophy using the distinctive dialogue form, and how his works can help sow the seeds of discourse in the souls of those who read them.

Education as Gardening: An Image of Natural Growth

Striking and engaging, the passage I have quoted contrasts the frivolity of a foolish grower in the hot lazy days of summer with the patient graft of the careful husbandman. Like many of Plato's images, it cuts across the texture of the dialogue, offering an accessible approach to its subject matter and an inspiring invitation to philosophize. At the same time, it invites closer study: its carefully crafted details challenging us to consider what we can learn about Plato's approach to philosophical education.

At the very heart of the image is a connection between education and natural growth. The wise grower outdoes the foolish one by choosing conditions suitable for growth (the time of year, the soil, the growing period): his role is to help his seeds achieve their full potential as natural organisms. The wise educator does the same, by choosing a soul that provides suitable "soil" for the seed of discourse to flourish. The analogy suggests that it is simply in the natural order of things for philosophical development to occur within us. The only thing that may be lacking is the seed of discourse; once this is provided, growth can occur in the innate fertility of our souls.

This growth, moreover, is part of a cycle of development. Once the seed of discourse has matured, Socrates tells us, it "produces a seed from which more discourse grows in the character of others." A person will, in other words, in time be able to help others develop by planting the seed of discourse in them. In this process, the learner's own personal growth is crucial. The planting of the seed in her soul is what enables it to grow; and the new seed that she produces – the discourse – achieves life through her. Socrates' imagery here suggests that participating in philosophical discourse involves a kind of philosophical reproduction – an idea that emerges even more obviously in *Symposium*'s image of psychic pregnancy and *Theaetetus*' depiction of Socrates as a midwife (*Symposium* and *Theaetetus* are other dialogues written by Plato).

A seed, then, enables a person to fulfill her natural potential both by providing the opportunity for discourse to grow in her own soul and by allowing her to give birth to new seed. This connection between philosophical discourse and natural fulfillment is crucial, I think, to the happiness or wellbeing that Socrates says education can bring. A plot of rich land left untended and unsown fails to reach the full flourishing it could achieve when filled with flowering plants. So too, a soul fails to reach its best possible state when thought, dialogue, and ideas do not develop within it.

Our modern familiarity with the idea that education promotes the development of the individual may make it easy to overlook just how striking Socrates' claim is. He is not merely asserting that education involves individual engagement, personal growth, and the fulfillment of one's own potential. We may grant this, while still insisting that the ultimate goal of education is something external, like the success and monetary reward that the Sophists offered their clients and our schools promise their pupils. For Socrates, human flourishing is bound up with the process of education; engaging in philosophical dialogue and reflection is simply what enables us to achieve our best possible state as humans.

Do We All Possess Fertile Souls?

Socrates' image appears to promise happiness and fulfillment to all those who engage in the philosophical process. And if this process is about fulfilling our natural function, then it should be one in which we can all participate.

But what happens if the gardener finds himself with sterile seed or with barren soil? Surely, in that case, a plant will not grow – whatever his skill. Can all people, then, be educated – or are there some of us who simply cannot change, cannot progress? This question haunts the dialogues, peopled as they are with characters apparently impervious to Socrates' attempts to open their eyes to their own ignorance and self-delusion. A Euthyphro may be too lazy to change; a Cephalus too complacent; a Callicles or a Thrasymachus too aggressively committed to his own ideals of power and advancement. What are the prospects for such men, the ordinary characters of the dialogues?

Socrates addresses the problem of sterile seed – seed that does not generate philosophical activity in the soul receiving it – by telling us that the wise educator sows seed that is "not barren" but capable of producing new seed. It seems to be inherent in the character of the good grower that he has – or chooses – fertile seed. The very nature of his discourse is such, Socrates suggests, that it cannot fail to encourage further philosophizing in the souls of those who receive it.

Barren soil presents more of a problem, however. In telling us that the wise educator must choose a "proper soul," Socrates appears to acknowledge that only in certain souls can the seeds of discourse take root. The phrase suggests that it is part of a wise educator's job to select productive souls and concentrate on them; just as we would expect a knowledgeable grower to test the fertility of his soil before cultivating it. If this is so, the potential for philosophical development – as well as true fulfillment and happiness – is open, according to Socrates' image, only to a restricted group. We might view this as a practical assessment of the limitations of human character, or an elitist assertion of the superiority of a selected few – but either way, it would leave us with a pessimistic picture of human potential.

Socrates' choice of words is interesting, however. He does not say that the wise educator must choose a "good" soul, but a "proper" one. The word here translated "proper" (προσήκουσαν) is often used of things that are proper or fitting for their purpose or circumstances. And this resonates with what Socrates says shortly after our passage, when summarizing the circumstances in which a speech can be philosophically valuable:

> [A person] must understand the nature of the soul ... he must determine the kind of speech appropriate to each nature, and prepare and arrange his speech accordingly, offering complex and elaborate discourse to a complex soul and simple discourse to a simple one.[2]

In saying this, Socrates appears to be referring back to an earlier point in the dialogue,[3] where he discusses the composition of the soul. There, he compares the soul to a team of two winged horses, one good and one bad, driven by a charioteer. The three parts of the soul each have a different character, and it is easy to see how – on this conception of the soul – souls might differ in type. In the passage just quoted, Socrates returns to this idea, indicating that each different type of soul needs a different kind of speech – or, in the language of our garden image, a different seed. He does not suggest that there are some souls to which no speech is suited; he rather stresses the role of the speaker in selecting the type of speech required by each. If this is the case, then it leaves open the possibility that we all have fertile souls. To be sure, some may need more care and attention: they may need weeds removing, stones dug out, fertilizer applied; they may have lain fallow, or been over-cultivated. But with the correct nurturing, all will be able to support some growth – or so at least seems to be the promise that Socrates' image holds out to us, if we seek a gardener who can provide us with a suitable seed.

The Gardener: What is His Contribution to the Growth of the Seeds?

The wise grower, then, is crucial for the development of the seeds. But what exactly is his role? To put this question into focus, let us turn to a passage from the *Republic* in which the orator Thrasymachus, frustrated at his inability to persuade Socrates, asks: "Shall I pour my argument into your mind?"[4] – like liquid into a vessel. The vessel, it seems, plays no active part in the process; it simply contains the

ANNE COTTON

knowledge poured into it. Just so, the learner in Thrasymachus' image has little or no role in generating the ideas and views she takes on, simply accepting those offered to her. For Thrasymachus, the educator is the key player.

Now it is clear that, in our gardening image, the gardener puts something into the learner's soul: the λόγοι or discourse. But here, any resemblance with the vessel model ends. The value – even the possibility – of obtaining knowledge from another is something Socrates constantly inveighs against in the dialogues. He insists that inquiry should start from what his discussion partners believe; he asks them to say only what they themselves think; and he questions the validity of ideas adopted from authorities, whether famous Sophists or religious figures. The gardening image, through its emphasis on the interaction between soil and seed, soul and discourse, draws to our attention the contribution made by the learner. Without the fertile environment of his soul, the seed cannot develop; it is an interaction between the two that produces growth. If this is so, then philosophical progress is not in any simple sense about ideas put forward by a teacher, however wise; it is about the development they undergo in the mind of the learner.

That said, we must be wary of stressing the importance of a person's inner resources to the extent that we ignore the role of the educator. He must nurture the seed till it reaches fruition, guiding the process to success. He must also provide the seed, choosing the one best able to fertilize each type of soul. As Plato suggests elsewhere, too, without him – the person who plants the seed – most souls will not grow at all. The lazy horse, which in the *Apology* represents the Athenian populace, needs the sting of the gadfly to spur it on its way; and in the *Republic*'s famous cave image it is the unnamed educator who turns the prisoners towards the light and drags them up the painful path to the outer world. As these images show, there are different ways of thinking about the educator's role. He may provide the discomfort that punctures a person's complacency and spurs her into questioning her way of life. Or as the more positive image of the grower implies, he may provide nutrients (ideas, questions, or stimulating dialogue, perhaps) that nourish the plant. Either way, though, the process is a collaborative one – and the educator is in some ways the leading partner. His contribution makes the education of the soul analogous to the controlled and purposeful growth of the garden, rather than to the haphazard development of plants in the wild.

Gardening: Labor and Reward

Every gardener knows that behind the healthy plants that give him such pleasure lie hours of painstaking, tiring labor – the weeding, feeding, staking, and watering without which his garden would not have flourished so successfully. The same understanding emerges from Socrates' contrast between the fleeting delight of the bad grower and the more sensible – even tedious – practice of the wise grower who waits eight months. Though Plato does not here highlight the discomfort and pain of the educational process, as he does in the steep ascent of the prisoners from the cave or the gadfly's stinging of the horse, the image of gardening must, for readers ancient and modern alike, evoke the hard work which goes into growing things for oneself. Like gardening, Plato emphasizes, education is not easy, quick, or painless – something that will offer the trivial entertainment experienced by the bad grower. Instead, it requires resilience in the face of slow progress, and the self-motivation to keep ourselves on the right path.

Yet it does bring its own sort of satisfaction. The wise grower is "content" when his seeds bear fruit and his seed makes a man "as happy as any human can be." This is the contentment that comes from the true flourishing of the soul – and it extends a powerful invitation to philosophize. By highlighting the two sides of the process, Plato combines inspiration with something of a warning of what, should we embark upon it, philosophical education will be like. He invites us to participate, yet also asks us to prepare ourselves for the task ahead.

Plato as Gardener

Phaedrus, from which our image is taken, is unusual among Plato's dialogues in being set in the countryside outside Athens. Socrates is more usually to be found frequenting the haunts of the city, which throng with people he can talk to, so it is striking to find him, here, strolling peacefully along the river Ilissus with just one companion. Far from fading into the background, references to the landscape repeatedly punctuate the discussion: tall shady trees, warm sun, clear waters, light breezes, and humming cicadas. And though unusual, the country setting complements the theme of natural growth that is central to the dialogue's treatment of

ANNE COTTON

discourse and education. As we read, it reminds us of the beauty of growth and regeneration, in nature as in education, just as the trees in the grove where Plato's Academy was located may have acted as a tangible reminder to those who met there for debate.

Through his activity in the Academy, Plato would have acted as planter and grower to the soil of his students' souls. The foundation gathered together people keen to learn, whose souls, one trusts, would have been receptive and fertile. Face-to-face dialogue would have allowed the grower to tailor his care to the needs of each individual. Ongoing participation in the community would have ensured that students' souls received the sustained care of the gardener, as well as fostering the dedication, commitment, and self-motivation required by the learner. Furthermore, its members might develop into "gardeners" themselves, by participating in debate on equal terms with their peers and eventually leading discussion with their juniors. The conversations of Plato's mature dialogues show learners who are required to follow increasingly complex arguments, interrogate more advanced thinkers' views, and offer ideas of their own. These works may illustrate the potential for students to grow into increasingly independent thinkers, capable of fostering the growth of discourse for themselves.

The dialogues themselves, however, when approached as the products of a "grower," are a much more difficult case. Most commentators would agree, I think, that they are concerned with the education of their receivers. This was an intention attributed to a range of ancient genres; but the dialogues, by choosing to represent serious philosophical activity, proclaim themselves as concerned with education in a much stronger sense. They were produced by someone who, as a disciple of Socrates and founder of the Academy, existed in an educational context. And from their earliest receivers onwards, they have been treated as possessing educational intent. On some level, then, they invite their readers to engage in philosophical dialogue with them, just as the interlocutors within the text engage with each other. Yet in the world of the dialogues, it is conversational dialogue – face-to-face discussion between individuals, rather than dialogue with a written text – that is presented as the ideal type of philosophical engagement. Indeed, in the very passage from which our gardening image comes, Socrates seems to question the value of written discourse within the philosophical project.

A written work, Socrates says, can never contain knowledge, yet it appears to do so, potentially persuading us that we have no need for further philosophizing. It cannot choose its audience, nor offer encouragement, admonition, or advice suitable to our particular case. It cannot explain itself, answer questions, or support its points with other arguments. And as readers, we can put it away at any moment. If all this is so, it is hard to see how a written text can play the role of face-to-face dialogue. It may sow ideas, questions, puzzles, in the reader's mind, but it cannot foster a long-lasting relationship with her, as the wise grower does in tending his plants. Nor, more fundamentally, can it guarantee that it has provided the type of writing that can effectively stimulate discourse in her particular soul. How then can Plato's dialogues, without the aid of a "live" philosopher, fulfill the role of a wise grower?

Dialogue Between Text and Reader: Cultivating the Seeds

In addressing this question, we need to take a closer look at the distinctive character and construction of the dialogues. For this is at the heart of their ability to foster a relationship with us that is akin to the one between the wise grower and his plants.

To begin with, the dialogues encourage a certain type of engagement in the reader. It is a commonplace among interpreters of Plato that the dialogues use a range of techniques to pose questions and put forward ideas, without telling us what to think. They present fictionalized conversations between complex characters of whom none – not even Socrates – can straightforwardly be identified with Plato. A great many of the dialogues, even "later" works traditionally regarded as more didactic in approach, are aporetic, in that they end without a clear conclusion. The works are full of contradictions and puzzles, as well as passages whose meaning appears intentionally opaque. In short, they are challenging to read. It is difficult to progress through a dialogue from start to finish without stopping or breaking off in confusion. The dialogues ask us to work backwards and forwards through the text, as we bring together different passages on similar themes, or puzzle over contradictions. And at the close, we are often left without a feeling of resolution, facing questions to which we have no definite answer. The responses that the dialogues evoke in us are, in consequence, particularly strong: ranging from awe and inspiration to frustration and annoyance; they ensure that we do not remain uninvolved.

Though not peculiar to the dialogues, this is central to the way that Plato can act as a wise grower in relation to his readers. The dialogues

ANNE COTTON

sow the seed of further thought in our minds, by challenging us to think about their questions and puzzles, and by making those questions matter to us. Yet knowledge has certainly not been transplanted into our minds fully grown, as a young man buying education from a Sophist might hope that it would be, and the seedling must instead be nourished in the soil of our own souls. For the texts refuse us answers or resolutions, instead inviting us to engage in a process of ongoing reflection, both while we are reading, moving backwards and forwards through the work as we are encouraged to, and in the reflection we move onto afterwards – a process, of course, that involves our ongoing commitment and hard work. In consequence, any conclusions that we do reach are very much our own. The seed of discourse, nourished by our own reflection, has grown into a plant that is as much our own as it is the grower's.

Teaching Us to Become Gardeners of Our Souls

Equally crucial for cultivating a productive relationship with the reader are the dialogues' techniques for increasing the reader's awareness and understanding of the learning process.

Firstly, the dialogues contain a great deal of explicit reflection on philosophical development. Our gardening image is just one instance; the dialogues are in fact peppered with passages of this sort. Besides the prisoners' ascent from the cave in the *Republic*, "psychic pregnancy" in the *Symposium*, and midwifery in the *Theaetetus*, one could point to the image of philosophical love earlier in the *Phaedrus*, learning as recollection in the *Meno*, the ascent to the "real" world in the *Phaedo*, and, again in the *Republic*, education as the turning of the soul towards the true, the good, and the beautiful – to name but a few. Such passages increase our understanding of what the learning process involves, and they heighten our awareness of our own role as a learner within it. The gardening image asks us to think of our mind as fertile soil, which must welcome the seed of discourse and the guidance offered by the grower, and also to face the reality that productive growth is slow and sometimes difficult. In doing so, it highlights our contribution to the success of the process: for the seed to grow, we need to demonstrate sustained commitment in the face of hard work, and the ability to develop into independent agents who can support our own progress. Asking us to reflect on our own role in this way increases our self-consciousness about how we are actually engaging with Plato's texts (are we inclined to skim read? to skip over difficult passages? to put the work down in confusion or annoyance?) and how we might ideally do so. Potentially, it also increases our motivation, as we aspire to become better learners who engage with the texts in a more productive way.

A similar effect is created by Plato's portrayal of his characters in conversation, in as much as they illustrate various possible responses to the learning process. In fact, only rarely does Socrates encounter someone who responds to him in a truly productive way; much more often, his discussion partner will walk away hostile or oblivious. We observe the anger, frustration, and aggression of interlocutors who find Socrates' questioning difficult to accept. We see characters who are eager to avoid the rigors of philosophizing, and those who are unable to perceive the need for it. In this way, Plato is showing us the willfulness of some learners and the wastefulness of their response to the opportunities offered them, and he is leaving it to us to consider what a more productive response might have looked like. In doing so, he is giving us an occasion – one that the characters within the conversations do not themselves have – to increase our understanding of our own progression as learners. We begin to develop the ability to analyze ourselves and to guide our own learning, and in consequence we have a better chance of ensuring that we remain productively engaged in the process of philosophizing that will enable our seeds to grow into flourishing plants. We start, that is, to become gardeners of our own souls.

Plato's Literary Garden: A Corpus of Works

Each of Plato's dialogues may, as I have suggested, encourage us to take responsibility for our own learning, as well as stimulating a process of ongoing reflection that takes us beyond the confines of the text. But there is also a further way that the works can offer us the sustained care that is so central to the grower's role. One of the advantages of the Academy, I suggested, was that it allowed students to engage with their educators over an extended period, in a self-contained community akin to a garden. While reading a single dialogue cannot provide this, we need not approach Plato's works as isolated, self-contained units. For each dialogue also fits into a wider whole, the entire corpus of Plato's philosophical works, and this provides us with a kind of literary garden to inhabit as the seed of discourse grows in our soul.

The notion of a corpus was central to ancient thinking about Plato's works; and for some ancient commentators, the texts offered a kind of program for the reader. On one interpretation of this, the dialogues target us at different points in our philosophical progress. To put it simply, some dialogues address the complacency of those who think they have no need to improve, offering dazzling invitations to philosophize combined with sometimes brutal assaults on our perception of our own wisdom. Others address learners at an intermediate stage of development, those who need the stimulation to develop their ideas further. Yet others address learners at an advanced stage, those who are ready to take more responsibility for their learning, and can cope with the austere challenges of demanding and superficially uninviting texts. Together, the works help guide us through the different phases of learning; and at each point on the way, Plato offers us a different type of nurture. In some dialogues he may be pruning dead wood, removing our old ideas, in a sharp and shocking way, or removing the stones in our soil by tackling the mistaken self-perceptions that make us think we have no need to engage in learning. In others, he may be bringing us into the warmth of the shining sun, which inspires us to further philosophizing, or sowing the seed by providing themes and ideas for us to reflect on. It remains the case, of course, that we, as readers, are responsible for participating in this ongoing program of learning: we need to take responsibility for placing – and keeping – ourselves in the garden where Plato's philosophical seeds and his care as a grower can benefit us. But if we do so, we are already showing that our soil is fertile, taking the first steps on the path to developing the seeds within ourselves, acting as gardeners to our souls, and becoming, as Socrates says, "as happy as any human can be."

Gardeners of Souls

Plato's image of the wise and foolish gardeners presents us with a memorable and striking image of education. But it does much more than that. As a tantalizing and difficult passage, it requires our careful thought. As an explicit reflection on the nature of learning, it raises our awareness of what learning involves and what our own contribution must be. In doing so, it helps us develop the ability to be self-conscious and self-critical commentators on our own progress as learners. To do this is not to reject the value of external advice, guidance, and stimulation, or the role of discussion and collaboration. It is simply to recognize our potential, as individuals, to become independent and self-sufficient learners; plants that can take responsibility for their own development even without the routine care of a gardener. In reality, of course, we live not in the protected groves of the Academy or in Plato's ideal state, but in the wilderness of the ordinary world. Plato's portrait of Socrates offers us the vision of a man who strove, in hostile conditions, to realize his potential for individual development and achievement. By suggesting, in this image, that we can become gardeners of our souls, Plato is affirming our potential to do the same.

NOTES

1 During the midsummer festival of Adonis at Athens, women planted seeds in pottery vessels called Gardens of Adonis. These sprouted quickly, then withered just as fast, in the harsh heat of the summer sun. Gardens of Adonis came to be a by-word for insubstantial and transient pleasures. The image calls to mind the biblical parable of the sowing of seed (Matthew 13, Luke 8, Mark 4), in which the seed sown in the shallow soil of the pathway springs up swiftly but soon perishes.

2 Plato, *Phaedrus*, 277b8–c3.

3 Ibid., 246a ff.

4 Plato, *Republic*, 345b.

NOTES ON CONTRIBUTORS

LAURA AURICCHIO, PhD, is an assistant professor of art history at Parsons the New School for Design in New York. Her first book, *Adélaïde Labille-Guiard: Artist in the Age of Revolution*, was published by the J. Paul Getty Museum in 2009. She is currently working on a visually informed biography of Lafayette. Laura, who is allergic to most varieties of pollen, prefers to admire gardens from a distance of two hundred years.

ISMAY BARWELL, PhD, has degrees from Otago, Oxford, and Victoria universities. She is a senior lecturer in philosophy at Victoria University of Wellington. Apart from aesthetics, her major philosophical interests are in narrative theory and feminist philosophy. Her garden is an edible forest with flowers.

ISIS BROOK, PhD, is a senior lecturer in philosophy at the University of Central Lancashire where she teaches on the MA in values and environment, and manages the journal *Environmental Values*. She has published a number of papers bringing a philosophical perspective to bear on gardens and gardening, and would like to think that her gardening activity also informs her philosophy. Although her gardening is currently constrained to a small yard, that does not stop her from planning a magnum opus.

GORDON CAMPBELL, DPhil, is a lecturer in ancient classics at the National University of Ireland, Maynooth. He specializes in Hellenistic philosophy and especially the Roman Epicurean poet Lucretius. Gordon went to university as a mature student, already keen on gardening, and was drawn to Lucretius particularly because of the poet's celebration of nature and love of the pastoral world. He has planted a garden of old roses and wild flowers in County Kildare in Ireland, and, as Lucretius would approve, communes there with nature to cure his weary soul.

DAVID E. COOPER is Professor of Philosophy (Emeritus) and Associate Director of Project Sri Lanka at Durham University. Among his recent books are *World Philosophies: An Historical Introduction*, *The Measure of Things: Humanism, Humility and Mystery*, and *A Philosophy of Gardens*. His interest in gardens was sparked by a visit to Kyoto, reignited by encounters with modern garden design in South Asia, and confirmed by a growing appreciation of gardening as a virtuous relationship to the natural world. His own garden, in rural Northumberland, is eclectic in inspiration and borrows liberally from the Cheviot Hills in the distance.

ANNE COTTON, DPhil, studied at Christ Church, Oxford, where she received her BA and MSt in classics and later completed a DPhil on Plato. She now teaches classics at Magdalen College School in Oxford and continues to pursue her research interests. When she is not occupied with either teaching or Plato, she is often to be found tending her own small garden or planning the ideal garden she aspires one day to create.

JO DAY, PhD, is a teaching and research fellow in classical archeology at the National University of Ireland, Galway. She received her PhD from Trinity College Dublin, and has also lectured in Greek archeology there. Her interest in gardening emerged at a young age, when she discovered that planting one potato could yield numerous potatoes a few months later. Her research includes the floral iconography of the Minoans and gardens of the ancient Mediterranean. Recent digging exploits have been based at the excavation at Priniatikos Pyrgos in east Crete.

SUSAN TOBY EVANS, PhD, is a professor of anthropology at Pennsylvania State University. Her major research interest is Aztec culture, and she has surveyed Aztec settlement systems and excavated the site of Cihuatecpan (Teotihuacan Valley, Mexico). Author of *Ancient Mexico and Central America: Archaeology and Culture History* (2008) and winner of the Society for American Archaeology's Book Award, she is also editor of *Ancient Mexican Art at Dumbarton Oaks* (2010). With Joanne Pillsbury she edited *Palaces of the Ancient New World* (2004), and with David Webster she edited *Archaeology of Ancient Mexico and Central America: An Encyclopedia* (2001).

HELENE GAMMACK is the gardens research assistant for the National Trust and has worked on a variety of subjects, including eighteenth-century shrubberies, American gardens in Britain, and early twentieth-century gardens. Most recently she has been researching the history of the self-sufficient estate. Helene has several years practical experience as a gardener and designer, as well as a Master's degree in garden history which sparked an interest in the history of food production in the orna-mental garden. She is attempting to create her own edible garden at home with varying degrees of success.

MATTHEW HALL, PhD, is a postdoctoral researcher at the Royal Botanic Garden, Edinburgh, and a founding member of the Ecological Humanities research group (www.ecologicalhumanities.org). Combining botanical training with environmental philosophy, his research is directed towards attempting to understand the perspective of those green beings that cover our Earth. This work includes conservation theory and prac-tice, as well as philosophical ramblings on the ethics of human-plant interaction, most recently in his book *Plants as Persons: A Philosophical Botany* (2010).

ERIC MACDONALD, PhD, is an assistant professor in the College of Environment and Design at the University of Georgia. His research interests include American landscape architectural history, and the ways in which landscape history can promote bonds of community and advance environmental stewardship. During 2008–2009 he was a Fellow in Garden and Landscape Studies at Dumbarton Oaks Research Library and Collection. He's still not sure exactly what a garden is, though he's amazed by what a garden can do; give him a couple of hours in a garden, and he'll be smiling for days.

MARA MILLER, PhD, is a gardener, philosopher, Asian art specialist, artist, and author of *The Garden as an Art* (1993) and *The Philosopher's Garden* (forthcoming). Dr. Miller publishes and lectures internationally on gardens, philosophy of art, selfhood, East Asian art history, women's studies, and environmental aesthetics. She lived in Japan and travels extensively in China and Korea. Her paintings (maramillerart.com), exhibited in New York City and Philadelphia, are in collections in twelve cities. A former Master Gardener in Colorado, she won a number of blue ribbons for gardening at the Boulder County Fair – where she was also a chili judge.

MICHAEL MOSS, PhD, is by training an archivist – he is a research professor in archival studies at the University of Glasgow – but his passion is growing vegetables, particularly Brussels sprouts, which his wife adores since she did not attend an English public school. Her Scottish education put her off cabbage. Gardening on a windy hilltop in sight of Arran provides ample opportunity for reflection, buffeted by the elements and soaked to the skin. Michael has written widely on archival and historical topics; but his pride and joy is being self-sufficient in vegetables the year round without recourse to the freezer.

ROBERT NEUMAN, PhD, is a professor of art history at Florida State University, where he lectures on Baroque art and modern popular culture. He has published on the subject of French and Italian art and architecture, as well as the American theme park. When he is not pulling weeds in his back yard, his greatest joy is to visit historic houses and gardens in the US and abroad.

DAN O'BRIEN, PhD, is a research fellow in philosophy at Oxford Brookes University, honorary research fellow at the University of Birmingham, and associate lecturer with the Open University. His books include *Introduction to the Theory of Knowledge* (2006), *Hume's "Enquiry Concerning Human Understanding": A Reader's Guide* (with A. Bailey, 2006), and *Hume's Dialogues Concerning Natural Religion* (ed., 2011). His research interests include discovering new ways to cook the yearly harvest of courgettes, the necessary connection between footballs and broken greenhouse glass, and the ethics of slugicide.

JOHN POWELL has postgraduate qualifications in landscape architecture and music and is currently writing a thesis for an MA in philosophy. When not playing the piano or working as a landscape architect he gardens on a pocket handkerchief in Wellington, New Zealand, and on a coastal property on the west coast of the North Island. He has a special interest in Moorish gardens and the Western "classical" music associated with them.

MEGHAN T. RAY is a museum scientist at the University of California Botanical Garden at Berkeley. She has a BA in classical languages from

Queens College/CUNY and an MA in garden history and landscape studies from the Bard Graduate Center in New York. She has written on horticultural subjects for the Brooklyn Botanic Garden, *Fine Gardening*, and *Garden Design*. She has logged thousands of hours in the garden and spent many of them wondering what it all means.

ELIZABETH A. SCOTT is a PhD candidate in the Department of History at the University of Saskatchewan, Canada. Her research interests include grassroots political activism, community gardening and food security, and perceptions of empire and colonialism at home in Victorian Britain, particularly in East London. Her current research is generously funded by a Joseph-Armand Bombardier Canada Doctoral Scholarship.

GARY SHAPIRO, PhD, is Tucker-Boatwright Professor of the Humanities-Philosophy at the University of Richmond, Virginia. He credits part of his interest in gardens to the university's campus, designed by Warren Manning, who followed F. L. Olmsted's aesthetic. Shapiro laid out his small, urban, enclosed garden by framing it with vines and applying picturesque principles. When not struggling with Virginia creeper and other intruders, he teaches and writes about aesthetics and European philosophy, and has published a number of books and articles, including *Earthwards: Robert Smithson and Art After Babel* (1995) and *Archaeologies of Vision: Foucault and Nietzsche on Seeing and Saying* (2003).